*when you grow up*

# when you grow up

Connie Nungulla McDonald
*with Jill Finnane*

MAGABALA BOOKs

First published by Magabala Books Aboriginal Corporation
Broome, Western Australia, 1996

Magabala Books receives financial assistance from the State Government
of Western Australia through the Department for the Arts; the Aboriginal
and Torres Strait Islander Commission; and the Aboriginal and Torres
Strait Islander Arts Board of the Australia Council, the Federal Government's arts funding and advisory body.

Designed by Samantha Cook
Printed by McPherson's Print Group
Typeset in Sabon 10/12

National Library of Australia
Cataloguing-in-Publication data

McDonald, Connie, 1933-
When you grow up
ISBN    1 875641 26 2
1. McDonald, Connie, 1933- . 2. Aborigines, Australian - Women -
Biography. 3. Aborigines, Australian - Social life and customs. I. Finnane,
Jill, 1946- . II. Title.

305.89915

Department for
theArts

Government of Western Australia

Australia Council
for the Arts

*Dedicated to my parents*

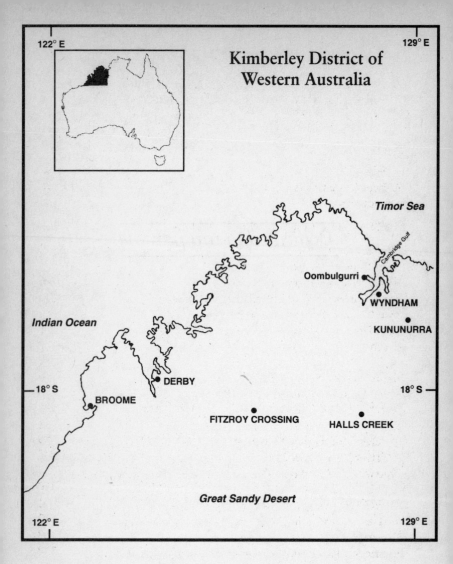

# Kimberley District of Western Australia

122° E

129° E

*Timor Sea*

*Cambridge Gulf*

Oombulgurri

**WYNDHAM**

*Indian Ocean*

**KUNUNURRA**

— 18° S

**DERBY**

18° S —

**BROOME**

**FITZROY CROSSING**

**HALLS CREEK**

*Great Sandy Desert*

122° E

129° E

## NOTE

At the back of this book is a background note, which might be useful for readers unfamiliar with Kimberley and mission history.

The words from Aboriginal languages used in the book and listed at the back of the book are not intended to be linguistically accurate, but reflect the author's usage and memory.

Some names have been changed to protect privacy.

# ∽ Contents ∽

## PART THREE: *GOING HOME*

# *Foreword*

Constance Nungulla McDonald brings to the readers of her book a very demanding story of her life. Its pages take us on a journey that has humour, sadness and challenge, as well as courage, determination and victory.

Connie opens her heart, revealing deep cries, questions and hopes in her struggle to be the human being that she believes she has the right to be. The victory comes in her turning to God, who is her refuge and strength.

Much of what Constance shares is similar to the cry of so many Aboriginal people still living and struggling today. Her story will leave the reader with many challenges to think about.

I commend this book,

*The Right Reverend Arthur Malcolm, C.A.*

# Acknowledgements

I would especially like to thank three people who encouraged me to write a book about my life; 1954: King Peter Warriu, Forrest River W.A.; 1958: Lorna Schrieber, Yarrabah, Nth Qld and 1959: Muriel Callope, Cairns, Nth Qld. I would like to thank Mr Harry Taylor of the Department of Community Services, W.A. for sending me the information I asked for about my parents and myself from the government records; the Australian Board of Missions for letting us browse through their library for some information on my early childhood, which we found; Mr Neville Green, author of *The Oombulgurri Story*, who told me a few stories that some of the mission people told about what a stubborn child I was and a real rebel; Mrs Margaret Smith (nee Gerrard) who told me that she didn't know I was a relative of her mother until her mother told her, and also about what she heard about me from other people; Mrs Freda Chulung, Mr Frank Chulung and Mr Alan McDonald, close relatives of mine for their part in supplying me with vital information about my father and mother; I would especially like to thank cousin Freda Chulung for telling me the true nature of my mother's death, thanks cousin; Mr Peter Bibby for his advice and the points on how and what to write in the book, his advice was much appreciated; the staff and committee at Magabala Books for their work in publishing this book; Mrs Cherine Savage (nee Schrieber) for giving up her time by typing out the corrections of the mistakes that were in the book, thank you, Cherine; last of all I must say thank you to Jill Finnane and her family. Special thanks to Jill who gave up her time to help and encourage me to write this book, because without her this book would not have been written; it would still only be a dream of mine; thank you, Jill.

# Introduction

For as long as I can remember, I have had two ambitions: to be a teacher and to be a writer.

One of my dreams became a reality when I was young and that was teaching. I was given the task of helping to teach in our little mission school. Even though I was only a teacher's aide, I was happy because I was helping to do the one thing I always wanted to do. I knew I couldn't go away to a white teachers' training college because in those days Aborigines were not allowed to leave the missions and reserves.

The second dream became a reality in 1987. I met Jill Finnane and she would often take me to her place and we would chatter about things in general. I would tell Jill about my life on the Forrest River Mission and all the things that happened to me and my people. I often talked about writing a book of my life. Jill saw the chance and asked if I would like to write the book. She said she would help me to do it and I readily agreed. We have been writing the book on and off ever since.

It has been a long, tiring journey with lots of tears being shed over the sad things that have happened and are still happening to me and my people. But there have also been lots of laughs as I told Jill all the funny things and much joy at my achievements. I would like to thank Jill for her patient and consistent help.

We hope this book will encourage all people who read it to realise that no matter who we are or what we are, we are all human beings and we should all treat each other as equals. In doing so you will be giving back to me and to my people the self-respect, pride, self esteem and dignity which our ancestors had long before we became dispossessed when the white men came to this land.

*Connie McDonald*

When I first heard Connie telling some of her stories, I was surprised at the extent of the differences between her life and mine. Connie's accounts of a childhood totally controlled by church and state and her amusing descriptions of the bold and inventive ways she overcame racism struck me profoundly. Her stories had a way of bringing to life the facts, figures, issues and campaigns of the Aboriginal struggle for a fair go. As I listened to her, and watched the enthusiasm and understanding that she evoked from local school students, I came to believe that her stories could touch all Australians. Fortunately, Connie agreed and we started writing.

First, we worked on stories that Connie had retold many times. Our task then developed a new depth and purpose as we explored the meaning of Connie's stories and relationships, the patterns of her life and the implications of her experiences of living between two cultures. This required long hours of reflective listening and a thoughtful, unhurried approach that allowed Connie's deeper memories to become part of the book.

Throughout the process we were careful to ensure that the final decision about what to be put in, how to express it and how to arrange it was always Connie's.

I want to thank my family for their encouragement and practical help during the many years we have been working on this book – Michael, my husband, and our children Rowena, Eddie, Jamie and Brendan have all performed numerous errands and tasks connected with the book. In particular I want to thank Rowena for discussing with us the themes in the book, reading the manuscript along the way and proofreading.

The members of Action for World Development have, for over twenty years, raised my awareness of justice issues and challenged me to work in solidarity with Aboriginal people. I want to specially to thank the members of Revesby Social Justice Group, whose loving support throughout the writing of the book has been an inspiration to me.

My thanks are also due to Tranby Aboriginal College in Sydney, for providing courses that gave me an appreciation of the wider Aboriginal struggle of which this book is a small part.

*Jill Finnane*

# PART ONE

## FORREST RIVER MISSION

# One

## *"The death of a young native girl"*

As I sit in my little flat in Revesby, NSW, I often wonder to myself, "Who am I? What am I doing here? Am I an Aborigine? Or am I a gudiyar (white person) with an Aboriginal skin? Should I be back in the Kimberleys where I was born? Do I still belong there? Who are my people now?"

When I made my entrance into the world, little did I know that all my life I would be fighting for equality and the right to be treated as a human being. Little did I know of the struggle I would have uncovering some of the secrets of my birth, a struggle that continues to this day. And little did I know of the conflicts that awaited me as I tried to find out where I belong.

I am a human being, and not an animal. I often wonder to myself for how many more years I, and the rest of the Aboriginal race, will have to prove to white society that we are ordinary human beings like them.

Every person needs to belong and I am no exception. Not knowing very much about my family has weighed heavily on my mind all my life. It was government policy that Aboriginal mission children were not told where we came from or who our parents were. Not even tribal people living outside the mission dared to break this regulation. Thus I grew up knowing almost nothing about my background or my early childhood.

Tribal people told me a few stories about my early years. They explained to me that I didn't belong to the tribe and that I had been brought to the mission with my mother by the Wyndham police. "We bin proper yirrbarra (ashamed) to see her with a baby," they said to me. When I was fifty-six years old, I began the long journey of searching through some sketchy government records. According to this information, I was born on the twenty-first of January, 1933 at or near the Four Mile, an Aboriginal 'selection', four miles from town.

My mother, Biddy, was an Aboriginal girl whose country was recorded in government files as 'Kurungi to the Key'. Her parents were said to be from the King River tribe and she was the tribal promised wife of a young man called Sendy who died in 1932 after being assaulted by a gudiyar man and a brengen (tribal man). My mother was fifteen years old when I was born.

My father, Duncan McDonald, was born in 1910 at Inverway or Kirk Kimbie, Northern Territory. His father was James McDonald, a Scotsman who owned the station Kirk Kimbie. His mother was an Aboriginal woman from the Ord River area of the Kimberleys. For years I understood that my father's mother came from Samoa or Fiji because my tribal people told me she came from another country. The government records indicated that 'another country' was simply the Ord River area, which is an area beyond the boundaries of the local tribes.

My father was never a resident of a mission. He spent his early years at Inverway Station and then worked for several years at Kurungi Station. I was always told that at the time of my birth he was away droving. Indeed, it was not until the end of 1935 that my father signed a form declaring, "I am the father of the child of Enid, otherwise known as Biddy" and agreed to pay regular maintenance for my upkeep.

When I was four months old, my mother and I were taken to the Forrest River Mission. Documents show that the protector for Aborigines at Wyndham, Sergeant J.F. Flinders had consulted with his fellow protector, Dr Webster, and they decided that it was in my mother's "best interests" for us to be taken to the mission. They feared that left in Wyndham, "she would become a victim to the lust of degenerates – whites and Afghans."

I can only imagine how my mother must have felt as the launch wended its way up the ancient river and pulled into the jetty – coming to live with people who were not of her tribe, to be in the care of others who were not of her faith or culture and bringing

3

with her a baby whose father had few tribal contacts and who was not to be found.

Three weeks after my arrival three other babies were given their personal Aboriginal names. These names were decided by the men and women of the tribe, according to a significant happening around the time of conception. In the tribal custom, a child is 'found', having come from the Dreamtime in the form of something from nature such as an animal, plant, landform, or the like. For example, during a drought, an Aboriginal relative of mine went in search of water. After walking some miles, she heard a noise which sounded like water. She followed it and to her amazement found not just water but a running stream. Around that time she became pregnant. When the baby, a girl, was three weeks old the tribe decided to call her Mindigmurra, meaning flowing stream.

I was not given a personal Aboriginal name and always wondered why this was so as I believed my mother was a member of the Oombulgurri tribe. However, I was given the tribal ancestral skin name of nungulla. This name determined my role in my own tribe and gave me relationships with all the neighbouring tribes. Because of tribal law, this meant that if ever I chose to travel anywhere in Western Australia or the Northern Territory or any of the other states in Australia where Aborigines still used the skin names, I would be cared for.

Later, on the twentieth of September, 1933, the four of us were baptised by the Bishop and given our Christian names. Although I had had a name when I arrived at the mission, I now became Constance. No one ever told me what my original name was. My mother was also baptised and given the name Enid, though everyone still called her Biddy. My mother and I lived in the mission dormitory in the section for unmarried Aboriginal mothers. Mostly these young mothers came from cattle stations where they had been sexually exploited by white station owners or workers.

On the twenty-first of October, 1933, my mother would have participated in an important event, a celebration to farewell the Reverend James Noble, an Aboriginal deacon, highly respected by all on the mission. He and his family left Forrest River after eight years and returned to Yarrabah in Queensland. Just one year into

4

his mission, he helped lead trackers who found evidence of the tragic massacres by police of tribal men, women and children in the Forrest River region.

In January, 1934, my mother took sick and on the twentieth of February the following letter was received by the police in Wyndham from the Forrest River Mission.

*Dear Sir,*

*I have to report the death of a young native girl. 'Enid' (Biddy) died on Friday January 12th at 2.50pm. She had been sick for a few days and had been carefully tended. We were unable to receive medical aid as the launch, our only means of conveyance, was away on a visit to Wyndham.*

*Enid showed signs of recovery but on January 12th she fainted and the end came quickly. She had been in the habit of chewing tobacco but the real nature of her sickness I am not qualified to judge.*

*Enid arrived here from Wyndham on Monday, May 22nd, 1933. She brought with her a young baby which is well and being cared for by a young woman, resident on the mission. If any further details are required will you please instruct me.*

*I am*

*Yours Sincerely*

*Fr Bush (Supt)*

For a time the senior dormitory girls cared for me, then one day my arm was broken and I was placed in the care of the missionary nursing sister. I kept her awake at night and her health suffered, so the superintendent called a meeting of all the mission staff to discuss what to do with me. They decided that it would be best for me to be fostered by an Aboriginal family so that I would grow up with brothers and sisters and a mother and father. The following Sunday morning when the people were gathered at church the superintendent, who was also the chaplain, announced that he wanted them to stay behind. He then asked if any married couple would be willing to foster the baby Constance.

A spokesperson for the people said that as my father's father was a gudiyar and they did not know which tribe his mother came from, they believed that my father and his family should take the responsibility of caring for me. So here I was, sixteen months old and paying the price for being a child of mixed parentage. The superintendent pointed out to them that there were only two practical choices for me, either foster parents on the mission or Parkerville Children's Home, Perth. Eventually tribal kinship law determined that I was placed in the care of my mother's tribal relative, Nora Albert (nee Nolan), who had six children of her own, a girl and five boys, the youngest of whom was still a baby. They were known as village people because they lived in a house on the mission and were one of the Christian families.

It seems I became very much a favourite in my new family and the other children were told to take good care of their little sister. I began to grow strong and healthy. While I had been living with the nursing sister, I hadn't been drinking very much and she had been very worried about me but when I was taken in by my Aboriginal family things started to improve. I have been told that I grew fat, eating just about anything I was given, bush tucker as well as gudiyar food. Apparently I was a happy child, always smiling and laughing when I had a full tummy and a dry nappy, but letting everyone in the house know in no uncertain manner when I was wet, hungry or bored.

My new mother used to breastfeed her youngest boy and me at the same time. This caused quite a bit of commotion on the mission as some of the women felt that she was taking on more than she could handle. Mummy Nora once told me that when the women used to make remarks about her looking after me, she would say to them, "What about some of you women come and help me?" Then they would all walk away and she would say to them, "If you don't want to help me look after this little baby, don't make those silly remarks."

I can remember the day I took my first step. I only remember because I broke both legs. Apparently they just crumbled under my weight. I was lucky the Flying Doctor's plane had just landed at the mission. According to Mummy Nora, as soon as he saw me he realised that I was suffering from osteogenesis imperfecta, commonly known as chalky bones and sometimes confused with rickets.

The Flying Doctor told the nursing sister to get me ready for a plane trip to Wyndham where I was to have an operation and my legs put in plaster casts. He said that my bone condition required special food and medicine. When I returned from my first trip to the hospital at Wyndham, my recovery had to continue in the Forrest River hospital as my Aboriginal family were being kept awake with my crying in pain. It seems I cried and cried when Mummy Nora left me and continued for two days, cheering up only when visiting time came. The whole family would come and stay with me until I had my supper and went to sleep.

Acccording to the tribal people, at about this time my father returned to Wyndham. He was met by his brother, Uncle Sandy, who told him that my mother had died. My father was devastated by the news and hired a boat and two crew members to undertake the treacherous journey up the Forrest River. On arriving, he was asked by the superintendent what the purpose of his trip was. My father told him that he had come to get his daughter as his brother had told him that his wife had died.

The superintendent told my father that the Native Welfare Department in Perth had stated that as my father was now a widower and a drover without a permanent job, the child was to become a ward of the state until such time as he marry again and be in employment. My father was allowed to see me though. Years later, tribal people told me that the only time they felt sad for him was when they saw him crying while he was nursing me. He stayed for about four hours, and then he left the mission. He did not see me again until I was thirteen years old.

When the family came to collect me along with my special medicine and my special food, the doctor told them that because of the danger of my bones breaking, they would have to carry me everywhere, even around the house. Despite these precautions, my legs and arms were nearly always in plaster. Life became very hard for my Aboriginal family and the strain was telling, especially on Mummy Nora.

The other women on the mission told her that she would have to give me back to the missionaries because she was neglecting her own baby and family in order to give me the care I needed. So the superintendent asked the senior girls in the dormitory to take it in

7

turns to care for me until the mission and the Native Welfare decided what to do. I found out later that quite a few of them looked after me including Susan Clark, Lily Johnson and Ivy Mills.

I was then placed with various gudiyar families. Until I was three, I was cared for by the Reverend Victor Johnson and his wife Edith. Years later, Mrs Johnson told me that they applied to adopt me but the Native Welfare Department wouldn't allow it. I can remember another gudiyar family that I stayed with for a time. The father of this family came from Queensland with his wife and eight children to take up the position of head stockman on the mission. I fitted in quite well with them and although I was young, I can recall sharing a room with two of the girls. We got on very happily and we used often sneak into each other's beds. I was treated just like the other children, when I was good I would be praised. On the other hand, if I was naughty I was punished – only the punishment was verbal because of my bone condition.

My broken bones were not only a trial to me but to all those responsible for me. Indeed the health of the mission children must have caused constant frustration to the superintendent and the staff of the inadequately-equipped hospital. In the *Australian Board of Missions Review* of February 1936 p.19, the superintendent told the following story:

> Some of the smaller girls had pushed seeds into their ears with a view to having a trip to Wyndham to see the doctor. Their little trick proved futile, for the doctor came to the mission. In the meantime the girls went swimming and the seeds began to swell to the size of haricot beans. The doctor had to give a general anaesthetic and it was a very wearisome operation for him, performed under the exceptionally hot conditions of the mission ward, the roof of which is iron and only a few feet above the head.
>
> He was able to spend a couple of days with us and make a final clean up of all the bad teeth and perform several minor operations. Joyce, a little orphan girl he pronounced blind in one eye and nearly blind in the other. She, with the girl, Eileen, who has boomerang shins and Constance, another orphan child whose

*bones break at the slightest touch...nothing can be done for them in the way of treatment, but they are improved if their general strength is maintained. I shall be glad to receive gifts of malt extract, Fellows or Eastons syrups or hypophosphates from any one who would like to help these unfortunate children.*

It seems the superintendent's request was granted as I was well supplied with foul-tasting medicine for the rest of my childhood. But the ongoing pain in my left leg did not disappear even when my broken bones were fixed. I heard the Flying Doctor say to the nursing sister, "I think Curly Pet has not only got chalky bones but polio as well."

I was mad with him for calling me Curly Pet so I broke in and said, "If you call me Curly Pet again, I won't be your friend."

"If you won't be my friend any more, I won't fix your broken bones."

"You have to fix my bones. You're a doctor," I said, feeling very pleased with myself. But several doctors since have suggested that that the calliper on my left leg is probably the result of polio rather than all the broken bones.

I remember clearly a time I broke both legs. I was so excited when I found out that I was going to Wyndham with the Flying Doctor that I forgot all about the broken legs. It was quite an adventure, although a short one, as the trip took only forty-five minutes. On arriving at Wyndham aerodrome, a car was waiting to take us about three miles out to the Native Hospital.

I was scared because I didn't know what they were going to do to me. The theatre light was frightening so I asked the doctor what the big light was for. He said it was to help him see better while he was working and that it would not hurt me. As the matron moved closer with the ether mask, he told me to count to ten but I only managed to get to five.

I didn't like having both my legs in traction as it restricted me from moving freely in bed so I asked where the doctor was. The nurse told me that the doctor had left to attend a white patient in the town. This man had been rushed to hospital with a broken leg and facial injuries when he fell from a building he was painting. The next morning, I asked again where the doctor was. This time he was on a mercy flight to a cattle station where the station owner was critically injured when he was thrown from his horse and knocked unconscious.

I found out that all the staff in the hospital were Aboriginal except for the hospital matron, and her husband, who was the manager of the place. Even though I enjoyed learning all about the workings of the hospital, I was delighted when I was eventually told by the doctor that I could go back to the mission. I was even more glad when I found that I would not have to stay in the mission hospital but could go back to my Aboriginal family as they wanted me to come straight home.

Despite all the love and care I received from so many people, my early childhood was full of upheaval. My stays in hospital seemed to last forever and I was no sooner out of hospital than I was back in again with another broken arm or leg. I was unhappy and cried a lot – not only because of the continual pain from my broken bones but also because I didn't feel secure. I would just be settled in to Mummy Nora's home and then I would be in hospital. When I came out I would expect to be returning to her family but sometimes I would be placed somewhere else instead. I felt as though I belonged to Mummy Nora's family and I couldn't understand why I had to go to gudiyar families. This continual shunting around caused me to come to believe at a very early age that no one really wanted me and that feeling of insecurity is something that has stayed with me all my life.

# Two

## *"You was a proper cheeky one"*
### ∾ *School* ∾

Not far from the dormitory was the school. It was one room, enclosed by verandahs. The walls of the room were about waist-high and built from thatched grass and wire for coolness. It had an iron roof like all the main mission buildings.

I started school at the age of six and my first day was very exciting. All the new boys and girls were overawed by this new adventure; a couple of them were bawling their eyes out and the few of us who braved the fray were getting up to all sorts of mischief, me being the ringleader of course – throwing chalk across the room, making faces at each other and scribbling all over the desk with chalk. After the mothers left the school the teacher, Miss Gillespie, addressed the class, welcoming the new girls and boys to this great place of learning, and telling the older ones to look after each new child.

Having paid allegiance to some gudiyar King who lived on the other side of the world, we were shown to our places. Each child had a seat except me, because the school seats were too high; if I fell off I would injure myself. Instead, I was placed on a small mattress on the floor next to the teacher's table. For the first three months the kindy children attended school only in the mornings. Some of us tired easily, especially me, if I happened to be in plaster.

School fascinated me because I enjoyed learning all the new things, like the alphabet, counting to ten, then to twenty and on to a hundred, putting letters together to make words and drawing pretty pictures on our slates with our slate pencils and chalk. Was I happy! Imagine my joy when one day I managed to write the word

11

cat and drew a cat all by myself. I was so excited that I got off my mattress and was about to jump up and down when I lost my balance and fell and broke my right arm. Miss Gillespie laid me down on my mattress and sent one of the older boys to get the nurse. I was not worried about the arm because I was so proud of my drawing and the word 'cat'. We had never seen a live cat or a picture of one until the teacher showed us. The other children thought I was very silly getting excited over spelling a gudiyar word.

At the time I was living once again with a gudiyar family, where English was spoken all the time. While I had been living with my Aboriginal family, we spoke our tribal language with a mixture of the English language thrown in every now and then. For the other children this was still the case and the word 'cat' was a foreign word to them. Government policy forbade the speaking of the tribal language on the mission. The missionaries enforced this policy ruthlessly but kindergarten children were only just starting to be exposed to it. Gradually we were to learn that every time we spoke in our own language at school, we would be belted – everybody except me because of my bones.

Two weeks after I broke my arm, I went back to school and one morning Miss Gillespie said that she was going to teach us a nursery rhyme about a cat that was in a well. We knew what a well was because we had quite a few around the mission for water. The teacher started to sing the nursery rhyme which went like this "Ding dong bell, pussy in the well." Imagine our surprise when we heard the word 'pussy'! She explained that the word 'pussy' was another word for cat. So every time we sang "Ding dong bell, pussy in the well," I sang, "Ding dong bell, cat in the well." Was I mixed up! Not only me, but the other little boys and girls in my class.

One day Miss Gillespie asked me to spell 'pussycat'. I spelled 'pussycat' but it came out 'catpussy'. Then she asked me to spell 'cat' so I spelt 'cat' which was right and the other children cheered. Then she said, "Spell 'pussycat' again Connie." Once again I spelled it 'catpussy'. She said, "No, no Connie, that's not the way to spell 'pussycat'. The word is spelled the way you say it – pussycat." Not to be beaten, I replied,"Why didn't you teach us to spell 'pussycat' the right way in the first place instead of teaching us to spell it backwards, 'cat' first and then 'pussy' afterwards. It is your fault, not mine." I thought, "This teacher's proper walla-marrah-ni-barndie (mad in the head)!" Miss Gillespie was dumbfounded to hear such a statement coming from a six-and-a-half-year-old child. She then said to me, "Connie, why is it that you are so intelligent?"

I said to her,"I don't know, maybe God gave me this 'intelligent'. What does 'intelligent' mean?" So she told me it meant clever and I felt very pleased with myself.

I was always questioning things. For example, we had never seen a mat and we laughed and asked a lot of questions when the teacher wrote on the board,"The cat sat on the mat." I wanted to know if a mat was alive and if it was an animal like the cat.

One morning I had a bright idea, I said to one of the girls, "Let's stay away from school." We told the other girls to tell Miss Gillespie that we were in the dormitory, sick. It was just after the first rains and the cane grass had grown tall so when they had gone to school, we crept through the grass behind the dormitory and made our way to Dadaway, one of our favourite spots half a mile from the mission.

Unfortunately, Miss Gillespie didn't believe the other girls and sent a note to matron. It wasn't long before the girl's father came towards us on his horse.

"Oh, we're in trouble now," she said. "We'll get a belting."

Her father rode up, put me on his horse and said to her. "You walk home. Fancy bringing this poor little girl out here."

"It wasn't me. It was Connie's idea." But she was the one who got into trouble.

Miss Gillespie had a large desk covered by a cloth that came right down to the floor. One afternoon Doreen and I were being rather rowdy in class. Miss Gillespie said to us, "You girls. Get under my table and stay there until you quieten down."

I thought this was the funniest thing going. Doreen wasn't a rebel like me and didn't find it funny at all. Sitting under the desk, I whispered to her, "What about we tie her shoe laces together?"

"You do it, but not me," she said angrily.

I went ahead and gingerly did the deed. Doreen would have none of it and moved to the corner of the desk, knowing that when the bell rang, Miss Gillespie would stand up.

I was grinning like a cheshire cat. Suddenly the bell rang. Miss Gillespie went to stand up and I came out from under the table saying, "Please Miss Gillespie, don't stand."

"Why?" she asked.

I stood there.

"Doreen, come out from under the table and tell me why Connie doesn't want me to stand up."

Doreen crawled out looked up at her and said, "Lift up the cover and look at your feet."

There were so many knots tied in her shoes it was hard to believe they had been done in such a short time. Miss Gillespie glared at me and said, "I don't have to ask who did it. Doreen, when the rest of the class go, you can go home. Connie, you can stay and undo the knots."

After that, whenever I misbehaved I was put in the corner in full view of Miss Gillespie and the rest of the school. Doreen told me later, "If you hadn't had chalky bones I would have bashed you up right there."

As Mummy Nora told me years later, "Connie, you was a proper cheeky one."

For the Aboriginal child living on the mission, life was one big task of learning. For the girls, it was going to school to learn the 3Rs; going to church to learn about God and learning to cook at home, learning to sew, learning to set a table, learning to run a household so that when a girl got married she would know how to run and look after her home and family.

And for the boys, it was going to school to learn the 3Rs; going to church to learn about God; learning to become good stockmen, by droving cattle or working; learning to become good husbands in readiness for when they would marry and also to become good carpenters so that they would be able to build their own homes. The boys and men did most of the garden work, like ploughing the land and sowing crops. But it was the women and girls who did the harvesting.

It seems that there was no time for play or recreation as we were doing things all day long except when we stopped for two hours after lunch to have a siesta. In the Kimberleys, it gets very very hot in the summertime and everyone needs to rest. The only time we had for recreation and fun was on the weekends.

We were served the same meals every day. The only time our meals were varied was when we went walkabout. Bush food was delicious! The meat would be kangaroo, goanna, fish, turtle and eel. For fruit and vegetables there would be yams, wild tomatoes, wild cucumber and lily roots. For sweets, we enjoyed wild figs, honey (called sugar bag), various berries and wild potatoes. The potatoes looked like ordinary potatoes but they were very sweet and were eaten raw as they disintegrated when cooked.

The whole tribe, whether living in the camp or the mission, went walkabout for two weeks, usually around July. A walkabout is an integral part of Aboriginal spirituality and culture and a time of learning about humanity. The Law of Wandjina was very strong and it was on walkabout that we had an opportunity to learn it. We feared Wandjina more than we feared this whitefella God. I learnt that I could not eat echidna because it is my totem animal and it would be like eating my own brother or sister. Laws like this were for the preservation of the animal and of the tribe.

Walkabout was a time to be with family, loved ones and friends. It was also a time for renewal of our tribal spiritual life. Our people went bush to communicate mentally and spiritually with our ancestors who had left this mortal life. At this time we always felt closer to mother earth and to nature. Everything seemed to come together for the Aboriginal people on the walkabout. I know as I have experienced it several times in my life. You have to be an Aboriginal person to experience such peace of mind, tranquility and harmony with the land and nature.

School may have been a place of learning but for me, walkabout was a source of wisdom.

# Three

*"When you grow up"*
◦ *Parents* ◦

Mummy Nora cared for me on and off from the day my mother died and I always believed that she was my real mother. I was proud of what I thought was my family. However, when I was seven, Mummy Nora was told that the Native Welfare Department had instructed the superintendent of the mission that I was to be taken to the matron's house. She was told that this was because of my physical disabilities and because I was on medication.

This didn't make sense to me as Mummy Nora and her family were caring for me very well, but obediently she delivered me into the care of the matron. On the way she said, "Ngumballa (child), I've got something to tell you." I thought she was going to say, "I'm going to be taking you out every weekend." Imagine my confusion when she said, "I am not your mother. You can't call me 'Mummy' any more. I just grew you up. I took care of you when your real mother died." Mummy Nora kissed me and left in tears.

I was dazed. I couldn't cry. I couldn't believe what I had heard and from that day I decided that I would love and trust no one again. I still called her Mummy Nora and she visited me from time to time but it was never the same. Gradually I realised that maybe this rearing business was over and that Mummy Nora had to devote herself to her own large family.

In 1990, while researching for this book I was told a little more about this big change in my life by a former teacher from Oombulguri. When he was there some of the elders had talked about me and some of my antics. "I heard tell that none of the missionaries would take you on even when you were a child," he

16

said. Apparently the old people told him about me with great relish and pride. They said to him, "That ngumballa – she was a proper cheeky one. She didn't worry about them gudiyars." And so he told me one of their stories.

"When you were seven, the government and the mission wanted to send you to Parkerville Children's Home. You were told that the boat was ready and matron had packed your case. Everybody went down to the jetty to see you off and there was much weeping and wailing. The superintendent got on board and called out to the passengers, 'All aboard'. Everyone got on board except for you.

"'Why aren't you getting on board, Connie?' the superintendent asked.

"Apparently, you folded your arms across your chest, pouted your lips and said, 'I am not going to Parkerville,' and immediately sat down on the ground, dug your toes into the ground and stayed there. Nobody came to pick you up and you sat there defiantly – amused because you knew that the tide was on the turn.

"Then Uncle Robert Unjumurra stepped in and said, 'This ngumballa not going to Parkerville. She stay here. We are her people,' and to the superintendent he said, 'You force this little girl on the boat – I make a hole in the boat.' So they gave your case to the matron and she took you back. Matron, it seems, was not pleased about this but she did as the superintendent said and the boat left without you."

The matron of the girls' dormitory was in charge of seventy girls whose ages ranged from six to twenty. All of these girls lived in the dormitory, while I lived at matron's house because of my chalky bones. The two years I lived with her were meant to prepare me for life in the dormitory. She was a very big lady, quite strict and domineering, and I was always very frightened of her. I thought she was cruel because of her punishments. Every time she called me I would hide under the bed, in the cupboard, behind the door or outside in the toilet because I was afraid she might hit me.

Every Saturday, after breakfast, I would sit on the verandah of matron's house and watch the parents coming to the dormitory to pick up their daughters for the weekend. At times, when their parents couldn't come, their grandparents or their aunties, uncles or even their elderly relatives were given permission by the parents to collect their girls for them.

One particular day, when the girls had all gone for the weekend, I said to matron, "Matron, why can't I go out for a weekend with a foster family?" Shaking her finger at me her stern reply was, "Connie, you know you have chalky bones and you have difficulty walking, and besides, your legs are so weak you can hardly stand on them."

"What's that got to do with it?" I demanded.

"Everything!" was her reply. "The Flying Doctor's order is that you must not do too much walking as you get tired very quickly. Furthermore, you are an orphan and no one will take the responsibility of caring for you." Stunned, to be told that no one wanted me, I blurted out, "What does the word orphan mean?"

Standing to her fullest height she defined for me, "An orphan is a child who has lost both its parents."

"Oh, a gnarnie?" I said. "I know that my mother is dead but many times I have heard the girls talking about my father. Do you know anything about my father, matron?"

"I've heard," she replied, "that your father is a drover and is often away droving cattle all over the Kimberleys, Northern Territory and Queensland."

Triumphantly, I informed her, "If my father is still alive, then I am not an orphan, and that is that."

Not to be outdone, matron replied coldly, "The Native Welfare Department has classed you as an orphan."

Changing tack, I asked her if she knew anything about my mother, and she said, "I only know what I've been told by the Native Welfare Department." So I asked her if she was on the mission when my mother died. She wasn't.

"Well, do you know what caused my mother's death?"

"Connie, I have not met your mother. Therefore I do not know what caused her death," was her final reply.

I was sad about my mother's death and even at this early age, I would ply any person I met with questions.

I asked Mummy Nora, "Gaga (mother), why did my mother die? Could you please tell me where she came from? What tribe did

18

she belong to and who were her parents? And how old was she when she died?"

She replied, "Ngumballa, you are too young to know about your mother and what happened to her. When you grow up, I'll tell you." I was angry but knew better than to press the issue.

One day, I was sitting on a log at the front of matron's house with my head in my hands, deep in thought. Daphne, one of the senior girls, came up and asked what I was thinking about?

"I'm thinking about my mother."

Sitting down beside me, she asked, "Why do you keep on thinking about your mother? She's dead and gone."

"Well," I insisted, "It hurts every time I think about my mother?" and after a pause I added, "How old are you Daphne?"

"Nineteen years old."

"Well, you'd be old enough to have known my mother. Maybe you can remember your parents and relations talking about her."

Pointing her finger at me and with a stern voice she said, "Connie, I do not know anything about your mother, so don't ask any more questions about her, please."

But my thoughts were always for my mother. I kept thinking about who she was, where she came from, what tribe she belonged to, where she was born, who her parents were. Was she tall, short, fat or thin? Did she have long, straight, black hair? Or was it short and curly like mine?

One day, I went to the hospital to see the nursing sister because I had a splinter in my right index finger. I sat next to an old tribal man when I suddenly thought of my mother. So I said to him, "Uncle," (all the boys and girls always called the older men "uncle" because that's the tribal law), "Uncle, could you tell me anything about my mother?" He looked at me and said, "Ngumballa, you are too young to know about your mother yet. But when you grow up, we will tell you."

Here was this phrase 'grow up' again. I was beginning to think there must be something remarkably important about being grown up and I looked forward to the day when I would be known as a grown-up person.

Even though I lived at the matron's house, I had all my meals with the dormitory girls. One morning at breakfast one of the senior girls who was sitting at my table said to me, "Connie, you've got a father."

Pretending to be surprised, I said, "A father! Who is my father?"

And the girl confided, "Your father's name is Duncan McDonald. He is half gudiyar – his father was a Scotsman."

"Oh, that's news to me," I said. "Who told you?"

The girl answered, "We all know about him. Our parents told us about him."

Trying to hide my excitement and curiosity, I said in my most matter-of-fact voice, "As you know about my father, perhaps your parents may have told you about my mother – which tribe she belonged to, who she was, where she came from and what caused her death." The girl's cousin, who was sitting next to her, chipped in stating that they did not know anything about my mother.

Disappointed, I told them that I found it hard to believe, and they said, "You can believe what you like but we don't know anything about your mother and why she died. We only know that you were a very young child when it happened."

Some time later I found out some more about my father. We had a word we used for people of mixed race, many of whom had white fathers or grandfathers. The word was ubergarge. Some of the children used to call me ubergarge. I was puzzled at this. I thought it must have meant 'chalky bones'. It seemed to me to be a derogatory word so I asked the other children what it meant. "Because you got a gudiyar grandfather. And your father is ubergarge too."

I thought to myself. "Gee, I must be ubergarge." Then, one of the girls said to me, "Take your top off and look at your skin and then look at mine."

I did as she said and when I saw the different shades of our skin, I was surprised. I realised for the first time that I was different.

One day I asked Miss Gillespie about my mother. But like the rest of them she said she did not know very much. "But," I insisted, "somebody must know who my mother was as everyone knows all about my father." So I said to her, "Could you please see the superintendent and ask him if he can write away to the Native Welfare Department in Perth to ask for information for me about my parents."

Looking down at me, she gave the by now standard reply, "But Connie, you are too young at the age of eight, going on nine, to know about your parents."

"But miss," I pleaded, "I am not too young. I would like to know what happened to my mother and how she died." "All right," she sighed, "I will see the superintendent and pass on your request." Later on that day, she instructed me to stay in after school telling me that she had spoken to the superintendent and that he said he would honour my request. Some months later one of the teenage boys who worked in the fields brought a message for me to go immediately to see the superintendent, who started off, "Miss Gillespie, your teacher, has told me about your request concerning your mother and your father."

I broke in, "Yes, that's right I want to know who my mother was and who my father is."

And then he said, "Aren't you a bit too young to know what happened to your mother?" I thought to myself "Here we go again!".

He continued, "I did get in touch with the Welfare and they said to tell you that as you are too young to know about your parents, they would rather wait until you are grown up."

I thought, "This word 'grown up' is beginning to get on my goat." So I asked the superintendent, "Why do I have to be grown up before anybody can give me any information on my parents?"

He replied, "When you have reached the age of eighteen, you can apply to the department yourself for information."

Upset, disappointed and feeling very alone, I thanked the superintendent and went back to school. The girls rushed around me asking what the superintendent had wanted. They said, "You know they won't tell you anything until you are old enough to understand and are properly grown up." I cried out, "If anybody ever mentions that phrase 'grown up' again, I'll scream!"

Of course, the girls all thought it was funny and burst out

21

laughing. I said, "You can all laugh. You've got your parents, you've got your grandparents, you've got brothers and sisters. I have nobody. It is important to me that I find out all about them."

So they said, "We have already told you about your father."

I said, "Yes, thank you very much but it is mainly my mother that I want to know about." As soon as I said my mother, there was a wall of silence and I began to think that something drastic must have caused my mother's death and that perhaps somebody had had a hand in it. I knew that they were trying to protect me from the trauma of my mother's death, but I couldn't help it. My thoughts kept going back to her, and the continual lack of answers convinced me that there was something sinister about how she died. It seemed that no one was willing to talk about it, let alone tell her daughter.

One day during the war, I went with Aunty Dudgulla to the camp for a day. Feeling that this was an opportune time I asked her boldly, "How come I have no blackfella's name?"

Her reply was, "Even though your father's mother was a narlie (woman from the East Kimberley), him father was a gudiyar and he not a tribal Aborigine. That means you cannot have blackfella name. We don't belong to this tribe." I was shocked by this reply and didn't ask any more questions. I started to realise that Aunt Dudgulla was not only a tribal aunty but that she might be a blood relative. Every night when I went to bed I would say my prayers and I would say to God, "Please God, help me to grow up quick because then when I'm grown up all the people will tell me about my mother."

And the years of my childhood passed with me not knowing about my parents except for the little bits and pieces that I would hear about my father such as where he was, what he was doing and why he was wanted by the police in Western Australia and the Northern Territory. But I was not interested in what my father was up to; I was totally engrossed in finding out the answers to my mother's ancestry and what caused her death.

# Four

## *"The wearing of hessian clothes"*
### ❦ **The dormitory** ❦

We were often told that all missionaries were servants of God and that they were sent to remote areas of the Kimberleys to "educate and make Christians of heathens". They told us that they set up Aboriginal missions and reserves to bring us God's word through the Holy Bible and to prepare us to live in the white society.

Before colonisation, Aboriginal people cared for their families successfully for over 40,000 years, long before there were missions, reserves and Native Welfare Departments. At the time I was growing up, very few Aboriginal parents were allowed to keep their children, because of the policies of both church and state. It was the church that decided how Christianity should be taught and the church's policy was to spread its teachings without so-called tribal interference. The Western Australian government through its Native Welfare Department had the overall authority over the lives of Aboriginal people and did not believe that Aboriginal parents were able to care for their children. By the age of six, most boys and girls had been taken from their parents and put into separate dormitories on the mission.

The girls' dormitory was a huge building of corrugated iron and fencing wire. It consisted of one large room with two windows at the front of the building and one on the east side. All the walls went from the floor up to the roof, the only ventilation being from the windows which were covered with wire. The roof was also corrugated iron, and in summer it was so hot we could not sleep at night. There was a wide verandah on three sides of the building that was completely closed in with fencing wire. The main door was made of such solid iron that a prisoner from Long Bay would not have been able to open it by himself. Then there was the outside verandah door, and another one on the south of the building. All of these doors were locked from the outside with big heavy padlocks to form an elaborate fortification to protect the girls from 'danger' and 'temptation'.

As well as children from the mission, the dormitories housed children from outlying cattle stations, most of whom were fathered by white station owners. These children were brought to the dormitories by the police. Once a year the police also did a 'round up' to take the Aboriginal children from their tribal families in the bush.

Girls were kept in the dormitory until they married. At the age of twenty-one, they were considered to be adult and were allowed to go and live in the village with their families. The only women who stayed in the dormitory after the age of twenty-one were those who were orphans and those who were unmarried. They looked after the younger ones.

I was sent to live in the girl's dormitory when I was nine. My dormitory experiences left me very confused about this God of theirs and as I grow older I can see more clearly that the dormitory system was part of the colonisation of Australia

After we sang a vesper and said the Lord's Prayer, the matron would blow out the light, lock the doors from the outside and go to her own residence using a torch to find her way, leaving us in complete darkness. We were locked in at six after the evening church service and then let out at six the next morning. There was no lighting except for one hurricane lamp that was used only when we were making our beds. Beds consisted of two blankets spread out on the floor, one to lie on and one for cover. Inside the dormitory there were two one-gallon drums filled with water in case we needed a drink during the night. We also had a couple of two-gallon drums which we used as toilets.

During the winter we would be taken down to the river for an early morning swim (being tidal, the water was very warm). Back at the dormitory, we would wash in fresh water to get rid of the salt from our bodies, get dressed and go to church. Morning and evening, we were marched to church like soldiers. In fact, wherever we went, we marched in military style with the matron 'bringing up the rear'. The boys on the mission were in the same situation as the girls, except that their dormitory was built of wood, iron and grass and was much smaller and much cooler in the summer than the girls, and they were under the supervision of the superintendent.

I was restricted even more than the other children. I wanted to go out at weekends and I found it very hard to accept that I couldn't. There were some exceptions, like the time I was allowed to go out with the Macale family for a day. Dick Macale and his wife Nancy lived with their two children at the west side of the village. Nancy was a tall, slim woman with a lovely smile. To me she personified beauty. She was kindness itself and would feed anyone. I was elated when Nancy and the children came to pick me up. When Nancy told Ruth and Arthur that they would have to take it in turns to carry me home, I thought, "Poor little me. Someone does care for me." Nevertheless, there was still a doubt in the back of my mind that the Macales were just taking me out because they felt they had to. I found it hard to believe that they would do it because they wanted to. Looking back now, I realise that these people did care for me and that they did want to give me a day away from the dormitory.

The village mothers were allowed to send food to their children in the dormitories. My father's cousin, Freda Chulung (nee Ryan) had daughters in the dormitory with me. When she sent food up for them she would put in extra saying, "Tell them to share the food with Connie." The older daughter, Isobel, was willing to share with me but Doreen was more reluctant. Fortunately for me she did what her older sister told her and I was able to enjoy some home-cooked food. For many years I thought Freda was just having pity on me as mission regulations meant that I was not told she was my cousin. One Christmas, I was ready as usual to go to the superintendent's house with the other children who had no family. Matron said, "You are all coming except Connie."

"Why? What have I done?"

"No, Connie. You have been invited to have Christmas dinner with the Chulung family."

I was excited. Here was I allowed to go to have dinner with a family. I started to wonder what good thing I had done to deserve such an honour. "Me, Connie McDonald?"

During dinner, Freda's sister Rosie announced that she had something to say to me. I thought, "What me again? What have I done now?" and I started to feel scared.

She said, "Connie, you are part of our family. Freda and I are first cousins to your father." I couldn't comprehend that this was family or what it would mean. I thought to myself, "I had better not get too excited. Maybe if I wake up tomorrow, I will find it has just been a dream."

I said, "Why are you telling me now?"

Rosie said, "Well, you know what government regulations are. We invited you for Christmas to tell you when you were away from the missionaries and in the presence of our children and husbands. We wanted to tell you because you seem to feel that you have no one." And then she added, "The government and the missionaries have a lot to answer for not telling dormitory children about who their relatives are."

I enjoyed my day with my cousins' families and I began to hope that maybe someday someone would say to me, "I am a relative of your mother."

One of the aims of the mission was to teach us modesty. For the missionaries, this meant clothing. They told us it was unseemly not to cover up. Being children of nature, we thought this was funny but we went along with it as we had no real choice. For the children who came in from the camp and outstations this education in modesty was a gradual process (unlike myself who was brought up on the mission and clothed from the very beginning). When they first came in, they were introduced to a western-style bath, that had hot water, soap and towels instead of a fresh running stream, dried acacia blossoms and a warm sunny rock.

Clothes for the girls, began with Australian Board of Missions supplies of panties and skirts. For the boys, a piece of cloth called a naga was wrapped twice around their loins and tucked in at the waist. Four times a year everyone on the mission and the camp were issued with two sets of clothes. The women and girls were issued with dresses and singlets and we made our own petticoats and underwear. The men and boys were issued with trousers and shirts. The women and girls, were also issued with two sewing needles, two reels of cotton, one white and the other the colour of one's choice, a pair of scissors, some elastic, hooks and eyes, press studs and buttons. These items were to last us at least a year.

Most of our everyday clothes were made from materials from government stores, mainly flour bags, dungaree, calico and khaki material. To our great embarrassment dresses made out of flour bags always had the brand stamp right in the middle of our sit-me-downs. As I grew older I began to suspect that this might have been another form of punishment for us heathens.

I could see that for the tribal people in the camp, nudity was a way of life. One day I asked one of the missionaries, "Did God say we have to wear clothes? When God made Adam and Eve they were naked so whose rule is it that we wear clothes?"

I was told, "Everybody wears clothes. It is society's rule."

All clothes were made from master patterns drawn up by the government department. The village women were allowed to alter their patterns if they wanted to. They used to embroider flowers and pretty pictures on their dresses to make them look nice but the dormitory girls had to wear the dresses made to the government regulations and so we all looked the same.

Freda Chulung was chosen to be seamstress for the mission. She was very good at her work and was called upon to make special party clothes for birthdays. Freda used to come to work every day, without fail. At nine o'clock, she would arrive at the matron's house to work at her treadle sewing machine. I remember her coming even when she was pregnant. She would even bring her babies with her to work.

All the children admired her, even me, her cousin. We girls were impressed with the way Freda presented herself. Freda was short with brown curly hair. She was always properly dressed, her hair in place and she carried herself 'real proud'. We also marvelled at the lovely clothes she made for her daughters. When I made my confirmation, at the age of twelve, there was no white material in store so cousin Freda was instructed to make confirmation dresses from any material that was available. She found a big roll of pink material so she made up fourteen pink confirmation dresses with white collars and white binding around the sleeves. We wore the traditional white veils as these were special and were kept in store. They were safely locked in boxes with moth balls scattered in them to protect them, as they had to be used over and over again. I must say we looked pretty smart on confirmation day in our beautifully-made pink dresses and white veils. As Aboriginal people love colour, it didn't matter to us girls that we weren't dressed in white for our big day as long as we were confirmed.

When we had important visitors from the south, we were issued with colourful dresses and ribbons, and special pants and petticoats. Cousin Freda made most of these but some were sent up by the Australian Board of Missions. These special clothes were kept in a storeroom in matron's house and most of the girls hoped for visitors so they could put them on and look nice for them.

There was one exception. Me!

I would say to the matron. "Why all this dressing up?" Her reply would be, "We have to make a good impression on the visitors." It riled me that it was not good enough for the gudiyars to see us in our dungarees. Moreover I could see that it gave the visitors the impression that life on the mission was in some way idyllic. It seemed to me that the visitors were deliberately being shown that it was the right thing for the Aborigines to be brought into the missions to be changed from our own way of life into the ways of the gudiyars. It made me feel that the gudiyars had us under their control and that they could do with us what they wanted. Even though I couldn't fully understand what was happening I resented this whole charade and I still do.

In the dormitories, we were subjected to all kinds of bad treatment. A common punishment was the wearing of hessian clothes. This punishment was for trivial things such as lying, swearing, stealing, fighting, talking in church or for not doing our chores properly. The girls would be made to wear hessian dresses and the boys hessian shorts or trousers.

The punishment we feared the most was to be locked up in the dormitory for a month or more. The length of time depended upon the severity of the offence. The offences that were punished in this way were swearing at or back-chatting any of the missionaries, fornication, failing to attend church when told to do so or absconding from the mission.

The offender would be locked up in the dormitory day and night, was not allowed to go anywhere including church, school, concerts, corroboree and walkabouts. Friends and relatives were refused permission to visit and the offender was not allowed to talk to anyone. Meals consisted of dry bread and water. Girls and boys who went through this punishment were literally treated like prisoners. I had some friends who experienced the 'lock up' punishment and it was quite a traumatic experience for them. Fortunately, I did not have to endure this particular punishment.

If a boy or girl stole food, vegetables, watermelons or someone else's clothes they were made to wear front and back a placard which had the words 'I am a Thief' printed on it in big bold letters. Occasionally if someone told a big lie, the same applied with the words, 'I am a liar'. The offender was made to wear the placard in church, standing in front of everyone in the chancel. This punishment would usually last for a month – luckily I never had that one either.

One of the mission rules was that talking was not allowed at night after we were locked up. During the reign of one of the matrons, to be caught talking meant that we were taken out of the dormitory and made to stand in front of her while she sat in a chair with a stick which had a pointed end. This matron would make us stand for about one or two hours and if we looked like falling asleep she would prod us in the stomach with the sharpened end of the stick If this was not effective, she would hit us on the legs with the stick.

I was excluded from any physical punishment because of my bone condition, but I remember one night while that same matron was in charge, I was made to stand up and I kept falling down because my legs couldn't keep me up. In anger, she got off her chair, went over to the fire, put the stick in the fire and let it burn until it was red hot. Then she came over to me and put the burnt end of the stick on my left leg. I screamed and when I looked at my leg all I saw was two burnt patches. I couldn't believe that someone could do such a thing to another human being. She warned me that I was not to tell anyone what had happened.

The next morning when the matron came to open the doors she was confronted by one of the older girls whose turn it was to look after me. She asked the matron, "Did you burn Connie's leg?"

The matron said to the girl, "You dare to accuse me of burning this little girl's leg, I will report you to the superintendent."

She did so and the girl and I were called up before the superintendent. The girl told him what she knew of the accident then I told him exactly what had happened the night before. He asked me to show him my left leg and there were the burn marks which by this time had started to fester. Two weeks later, that matron's job was terminated and she left the mission. To this day, I still have the two small scars on my leg.

Another form of punishment was beating. The senior girls and boys were beaten with axe handles. The axe heads were removed and the handles were used for beating. The younger boys and girls were whipped with green hide (untreated hide of cattle) or leather.

One day all the girls, both big and small, were summoned to the dormitory. We were made to form a line with the senior girls on one side and the junior girls on the other. I was still a junior girl. At the head of the line was one of the older girls who was led in by a new matron. Present was the superintendent, the nursing sister and two Aboriginal men from the village. The superintendent announced that the girl had done something very bad and therefore she was to be punished. I think the older girls knew why she was punished but even to this day I don't know why.

The two Aboriginal men from the village were told to hold the girl's wrists so that her hands were stretched out in front of her. The superintendent then moved forward and meted out the punishment of twenty cuts on the hands with axe handles. As an axe handle broke it was replaced with a new one. In all, four axe handles were used.

She did not whimper or cry while being beaten, but collapsed at the end of her ordeal. All the girls thought that she had died. Later, she was examined by the Flying Doctor. He then told the same two Aboriginal men to carry her to the hospital. They did so on a stretcher which was brought to the dormitory by two brengen before the beating.

That day none of the girls ate any meals; we went on a hunger strike. In fact, the whole mission went on a strike; the place was silent except for the crying. It was as if we were mourning the death of a loved one. The girl's parents, brother, sisters and grandparents were at her bedside. When I saw that proud Aboriginal couple sitting beside their granddaughter's bed I couldn't help but wonder what it was she had done that was so terribly wrong.

After she regained consciousness, the Flying Doctor left, giving instructions to the nursing sister for the treatment and medication she was to receive. It was not until several days after the girl regained consciousness that the people decided to go back to work and to attend church services again, and we felt the pain and agony this girl was going through for several months. During that time school and church were poorly attended especially by the village children and the children who lived in the camp, though of course the dormitory girls and boys were made to attend church and school as usual.

The girl's grandfather (her mother's father) was the King of the Oombulgurri tribe. He decreed that there would be no singing or dancing until his granddaughter had fully recovered. No corroboree or singing took place up at the camp for about three months as the beating of this girl was deeply felt by the tribal people.

The girl could not use her hands at all for nearly three months and it took twelve months before she could use them fully. She had to be fed, bathed and clothed by her family as they insisted that they be allowed to do these things for her, and they demanded that she was not to be handled by any white person. Her hands were dressed daily by the Aboriginal assistant nurse, and her medication was administered by the Aboriginal nurse under the supervision of the white nursing sister. That girl's hatred for all white people was so intense that she said to her parents one day, "If any gudiyar come anywhere near me, I will kill them." I believe that this was no idle threat.

When I was eighteen years old, I asked this girl who was by

31

now a married woman with two daughters, the younger girl being a godchild of mine, why she was punished so brutally so many years before. Her reply was, "Connie, you wouldn't want to know; it's over and I don't want to talk about it." I never got an answer so I just let it be. But I haven't forgotten the incident. There were other punishments but they still haunt me so much that I don't want to write about them. I could not comprehend how one human could do such things to other humans. It was a shock to me to find out later on in my life that Aboriginal people from all over Australia were treated just like we were. We were told that these punishments were necessary to help us become civilised people and to help beat the savagery out of us. It made me wonder who the real savages were.

Some of the missionaries didn't believe that we could think for ourselves. They would tell us that animals had more brains than us. I believe the people to blame for our so called lack of intelligence were the government and the Native Welfare Department by putting us on reserves and missions and treating us like convicts, by ruling over us with an iron rod, and by insisting that they do the thinking for us.

For me, growing up under the dormitory regime was one big confusion. I didn't realise it but when I raised questions about clothes, it wasn't just the clothes I was objecting to. On my mind was, "Who am I? Am I an Aborigine who doesn't need clothes or am I a gudiyar that I have to wear clothes?" Once my relatives had been revealed to me, my life in the dormitory became much happier.

# Five

## *"You are a better nurse than I am"*
### ⤳ War ⤳

One Monday morning, in March of 1942, after we had saluted the Union Jack and sung *God Save the King*, Miss Gillespie told us all to sit down. "There will be no school today or any other day." One of the senior girls asked her why? She told us that she had read in the paper that Australia was helping to fight a war against the Japanese, and that she had a dream that night that the Japanese had dropped a bomb on Wyndham.

Seeing that we were not far from Wyndham, she was frightened that we could be the next target. She told us that the Japanese were a race of yellow-skinned people who lived in a country called Japan and that they were fighting against the Americans, a white race of people who lived in a place called America. This all sounded strange to us.

Miss Gillespie had no sooner finished telling us about the war than we heard the droning of engines and, before we knew what was happening, there were six small planes coming over the horizon heading for the mission. The teacher yelled to the children to run for their lives. There was pandemonium in the classroom, with slates, slate pencils, chalk, plasticine and picture books flying everywhere, thrown by the boys and girls as they ran for the door. Those who couldn't get through to the door jumped the waist-high walls which surrounded the schoolhouse.

I stayed where I was, in a corner, where I felt safe from the stampeding children. When they had all gone, Miss Gillespie and I looked out to see what was happening. We saw the people all waving to the pilots in the planes. The teacher told me they were Japanese planes, as she recognised the markings of the red sun on the white background and she showed me a picture of them.

As the children ran for cover, they shouted to their parents and the other people. In about ten minutes, the mission was completely deserted apart from Miss Gillespie and I. The planes circled the mission and then flew off in the direction of Wyndham. Some of the school children came back. Miss Gillespie asked them why they had returned and they said it was because they didn't want to leave us alone. The children started picking up the chalk, books and slates, some of which had broken, and started to clean out the room and yard. Once everything was put back in the cupboard, the teacher said we could do what we liked, so most of the children, especially the big ones read or drew pictures or we just sat around and talked. It is very strange how people become one in a crisis. We looked on Miss Gillespie with admiration because we saw her as one of us. We were going to protect her at any cost, maybe with our lives, and she realised this.

We asked her to tell us where she came from, and so she explained that she came from England, a country far away, the same place where the white King lived, the one we paid allegiance to every morning. She also told us that England was called Great Britain and that people who came from there were known as British or English, just like we were called Australians because we lived in Australia.

While the teacher was talking to us one of the older boys (actually the fourth son of my Aboriginal foster mum) asked the teacher if he could leave the room. He went straight up the hill and became our unofficial lookout. A few minutes later, we heard this great yell, "Miss, your dream has come true! The Japs have bombed Wyndham! I can see the big smoke." This time no one needed to be told what to do. People ran for their lives, down to the river, into the thick bushes, between the long grass or even climbed the trees.

Doreen Chulung grabbed me by the arm and dragged me out of the schoolyard towards the hill known as the jump-up. As we were running through long elephant grass, we heard the engines of the planes returning from Wyndham and before we knew it they were circling the mission. We both fell to the ground and in doing so we parted the long grass which made it easy for the Japanese pilots to see us.

Doreen and I were terrified. We dared not breathe nor stir. If a poisonous snake had come by we still wouldn't have moved a muscle. Quietly Doreen whispered, "Goodbye Connie." Even more quietly I replied, "Yeah, you too. Goodbye Doreen." At that precise moment we heard a loud crack like a gunshot. This made us even more frightened. We thought someone had been killed. We were convinced that we would be next. As we were preparing for the end, the planes suddenly disappeared. They had frightened the whole community. Later we heard that the loud crack was a stockwhip being wielded by a gudiyar man bringing in some cattle. He must have been oblivious to the drama going on around him. We all said, "He's a proper silly fella."

Three weeks later, we heard the drone of the engines as the Japanese approached us again. This time a senior girl picked me up and ran towards a large cave on the mission side of the hill. She told the teacher to follow us. Two other senior girls and three senior boys also came to help her carry me. It was quite a long way to the cave and I wasn't exactly a light weight. On the way, the girls and boys broke branches off some of the trees to make a comfortable place for the teacher and myself to sit . They also camouflaged the entrance to the cave with branches, leaves and grass. When they had finished, you couldn't even notice that under the camouflage there was a cave.

While we were waiting to see what would happen, we sat outside talking about the Japanese and the War. When I had to go to bungle, the girl who was looking after me said, "Just squat down behind that tree over there". It was a stone's throw away from the cave, so I went over and squatted down behind it. The three boys went inside to talk to the teacher. Would you believe it, halfway through this important task, we heard the droning of the Japanese planes, as they were returning from Wyndham. Luckily for me it was bungle I passed and not the other, warie, or I would have been in strife.

As I was making my way back to the cave the planes came into view, and before I knew it they were flying right over me. Suddenly the three girls disappeared leaving me behind to fend for myself. I couldn't run or walk properly so I just stood there. Something caught my eye. It was a kangaroo that had been sheltering in a hollow in the ground. The noise frightened it so it hopped away. Immediately, I sat down and rolled into this hollow. As I rolled on my right arm I heard a snap and I knew I had broken it. With my left hand I managed to pull some grass, leaves and twigs over myself.

The planes were circling very low over the mission so I was sure the pilots had seen me, and I thought to myself, "This is it, they are going to drop bombs on the mission, and probably shoot me too." I lay quite still not daring to move. The other boys and girls and the teacher were watching what was going on through the holes in the camouflage but were worried when they couldn't see me. I was in dreadful pain, and after what seemed a lifetime the planes finally left making their way home to who knows where.

The others crawled out of the cave and I heard them calling my name but because of the pain I kept passing out. Eventually, they found me lying on my stomach in the hollow. One of them rolled me over and realised I had broken my arm. The boys came back with the stretcher and so did Sister Drage, who gave me two tablets that she told me would stop the pain and make me sleep. All the people were worried because they thought I must have been shot by the Japanese. My procession to the hospital was a dramatic one with lots of onlookers, concerned about their first war victim.

Our lives changed dramatically after that first encounter with the Japanese. The missionaries were told by the church that they were to be evacuated to their home states. Only the Aboriginal people were left on Forrest River Mission with the exception of our old storekeeper, Mr Tenny Thompson, (we called him Ubla – brother) and every so often a priest or a matron stayed with us for a while during the war.

After the missionaries left, the tribal elders took it upon themselves to become caretakers, peacemakers and law enforcers of their own community. So we took back some of the responsibilities for the running of our lives. Dormitories were no longer locked up and we even slept under the stars some nights. The changed dormitory system meant more freedom and a much more relaxed lifestyle for all. The constant ringing of bells almost ceased during the absence of the missionaries.

During the war, the dormitory girls and boys were given a special privilege. We were allowed to visit our people both in the village and the camp and we were taken on walkabouts where we were told about tribal law. It was an opportunity we greatly appreciated.

One Monday morning, the tribal elders held a meeting for the village people who lived on the mission and also for the tribal people who lived in the camp on the periphery of the mission. The bell was rung and we all gathered in front of the church. People who were regarded as educated and who knew the ways of the gudiyar were given the tasks of taking the daily services in the church, teaching in the schools, running the hospital, overseeing of the sawmill, the stockwork, and the running of the mission in general, while the roles of caretakers, peacemakers and law enforcers were left to the tribal elders.

As I recall, the allotments of jobs went like this:
An older man, Daniel Evans, who had been assisting the chaplain for some years, led the church services with the help of a younger man, Stanley Roberts, who could also play the organ by ear. Daniel was a quiet man who went about his duties very efficiently.

The job of overseer of the sawmill was given to a young man who had been the apprentice to the gudiyar sawmiller. He took great pride in his work explaining carefully to the younger men under his supervision what the different shapes and lengths of timber would be used for. We were all very proud of the calibre and comfort of the houses built during that time. They consisted of one large room with mud brick walls and thatched rooves. There was a small room out the back that served as a kitchen. The floors were made of compressed ant-bed.

The job of head stockman was given to Dick Macale, originally from an outlying cattle station. He was a no-nonsense fellow, mission-educated, proud of who he was and of his family. He demanded the very best from the young men he chose to work as stockmen.

Ubla Thompson, the only gudiyar to stay on at Forrest River, kept his job as storekeeper and was quite happy. Ubla Thompson wouldn't leave us because he said we were his people and if we were to die at the hands of the Japanese he would die with us too. He loved us and we loved him and respected him as he was the only missionary at that time who really understood us. We could communicate with him in our mother tongue because he could understand and speak our tribal language.

Ubla Thompson was from Queensland. Before coming to Forrest River Mission, he had worked on the Yarrabah Mission in North Queensland and had married a Yarrabah girl. When their first child was born his wife died and he married again. His second wife grew up in Yarrabah. Many years later I was to meet the families of both these women when I went to Yarrabah to teach.

A group of men and women were given the task of providing food for the mission. For a while we were self-sufficient growing our own vegetables, corn, peanuts, the biggest watermelons and pumpkins you ever saw, and sweet potatoes. A couple of men and women were also selected to gather and catch sufficient fish to supply the whole mission, fish being a very important part of our diet.

Other basic foods were usually kept in store after coming by boat from Perth. The state ship, the *Koolama* had been sunk during the second raid on Wyndham and merchant ships were banned from going beyond Broome. This meant that our food supply ran out and it was necessary for the people to go bush to hunt and gather bush food so that we would have an adequate diet. This gave the village people who had been brought up on mission food an opportunity to relearn traditional hunting and gathering skills.

Some men had to go out and gather and chop the wood then bring it back to the mission in bundles which were distributed to each household. Wood was also supplied to the main kitchen. Here, food, including bread was prepared and cooked for the girls and boys who lived in the dormitories and also for the camp people.

The children were also given jobs. They were to keep the crows, cockatoos, pigs, donkeys and other animals away from the crops. The younger children were delighted with their job because it meant they didn't have to spend all day at school.

The mission hospital was a small building with three tiny rooms which were used as wards. The running of the hospital was allotted to an Aboriginal woman who had been trained by the nursing sister (a triple-certificated nurse). This Aboriginal woman ran the hospital efficiently, expecting a high standard from the two young girls she was training as nurses. When the missionaries were being evacuated I recall the gudiyar sister saying to the Aboriginal woman, "I don't have any qualms about leaving the sick in your hands as you have learned thoroughly all there is to know about nursing. In fact I'm ashamed to say that you are a better nurse than I am."

We all clapped and were very proud to think that one of our own women had become a nurse. When I was in my teens, I often wondered why this Aboriginal nurse didn't go away to do a training course in one of the big cities. Later, I was to find out why! In those days, Aboriginal people were not allowed to leave a mission or government reserve without first going through the extremely difficult task of obtaining citizenship rights. She was unable to do this. The bureaucracy was very selective about who were fit recipients of citizenship.

No one was allocated the job of dentist. Dental problems did not cease because there was a war on and the only place where proper treatment was available was at Wynhdam. One day, eleven other children and myself were sent to Wyndham for dental treatment and extractions. We went in our mission launch, the *Hovenden*, an old passenger boat. Once we reached the junction where the Forrest River flows into the Cambridge Gulf, we had to wait until night so we could sail in under the cover of darkness on the evening tide. The crew members were all Aboriginal except for Ubla Thompson. The township of Wyndham had been taken over by the Australian army and somehow communications had failed and Wyndham had not been told that the *Hovenden* was arriving. As the boat turned into the Gulf, we were met by a barrage of bullets.

In total confusion, the captain yelled to us, "Get the bloody hell down below!" We scrambled into the hold and sat with our arms around each other screaming, crying and shaking with fear, listening to the whistle of bullets as they whizzed past the boat. Fortunately for us, the army did not defend Wyndham with a cannon or we would have met our 'Waterloo' in the middle of the Gulf. Disregarding the onslaught of bullets, our captain continued on through the wartime darkness and as we were nearing the jetty we heard a voice calling out , "Ahoy! Identify your bloody boat."

The captain yelled back, "The bloody motor vessel *Hovenden* from Forrest River." There was instant silence. The guns stopped, the screaming stopped, the shouting stopped and the engine stopped. Out of the pitch dark, an army launch approached our vessel and the voice continued, "What is the reason for this trip?"

Speaking more softly, the captain replied "I have twelve children on board who need dental care." By this time we also needed a lot of comforting.

The army launch escorted the *Hovenden* to the Wyndham jetty where we children were carried off by the soldiers and taken to our emergency accommodation, the exercise yard in the Wyndham gaol. This was the first and last time I have spent a night in gaol. The gaol was guarded by soldiers with guns that had frightening-looking bayonets on the end. We were so afraid of our protectors that we could not sleep.

In the morning, the army dental nurses came to collect us from the gaol to take us to the Wyndham hospital. Again we were accompanied by an escort of khaki-clad, armed men. We were all very frightened and some of the children started to cry.

On examination, the dentists, found that extractions were needed in all cases. I was the first one to go in. Before I sat in the chair, I saw the dentist wielding a needle so I asked him, "What are you going to do with that needle?"

"See this here. It is filled with medicine which I will inject into your gum and you won't feel any pain."

We had never had injections before as the Flying Doctor would just pull our teeth out. We preferred it that way we decided, especially when the injection took effect. The injections made our faces feel larger than they were and fearing that our heads would explode we all wept even more and sobbed goodbye to each other.

When the dentist attempted to pull my teeth out they simply crumbled because of my bone condition. But I didn't feel any pain and I walked out smiling. My happy survival gave the other children courage and there was no more weeping.

The teaching duties at the mission were given to a senior girl, Coralie Roberts, who lived in the girls' dormitory and had been working as a teacher's aide with Miss Gillespie since 1930. During those years she had watched Miss Gillespie teaching and had learnt much from her. Since I had been at school I had often seen her taking notes and I had wondered what she was doing. Coralie was willing to look and learn – me, on the other hand, I thought I knew everything.

So when the raids by the Japanese meant we had no gudiyar teacher, the tribal elders said to her, "You learnim all them wongalongs (children) – you and that ngumballa there." Though I was only very young, they chose me to help Coralie as her assistant teacher. Because I had lived with both gudiyar and Aboriginal families, they thought that I should know more about the white way of teaching than anyone else.

It is true that I excelled in reading and writing and spelling and was able to communicate with young and old, black and white. And, even though I was only a youngster, I was striving hard to learn all I could about practically everything. Even so, it was quite a responsibility for one so young and I was overawed by their honour and trust. At the same time, I felt very pleased with myself. Humility was not developing as one of my chief characteristics.

Looking back, I often wonder how I was able to help the boys and girls with their lessons when I was still a student myself. Perhaps the need for me to be properly prepared to teach them meant that I actually learnt more. Before school I had to prepare my lessons for the day and get the classroom ready. The older children attended school from nine to twelve and the younger ones from two to four. I would do my own lessons from one to two. After school each day, I continued my own study using the text books that belonged to the school.

Coralie payed a lot of attention to me. She would say, "Just because you are helping to teach, you needn't think you are going to get out of lessons," and she would help me, especially with my

41

arithmetic. I owe much to her because of her persistence in educating such a rebellious and unorthodox child. I became aware of her as someone I wanted to be like.

Coralie was a tall, strongly-built person and a leader like her mother, Aunty Louisa Unjamurra, but she was of a much quieter nature than I was. Every now and then I can see her in my mind's eye as I saw her in my first years at school, with her beautiful and kind face. She was not only intelligent, she was also compassionate and good natured, what I would call a 'real Christian', always there to help when there was sickness. Coralie was also the one called on to sort out problems in the dormitory. She had often told the matrons how to handle difficult situations, tactfully saying, "I think we should do it this way..."

Coralie had the wonderful gift of music. Both she and her brother Stanley took it in turns to play the organ at the church services and considering neither of them could read music both played the organ beautifully. It was listening to their playing that inspired me to start to learn to play the organ under Coralie's supervision and I learnt that I had the same talent for music.

Some people were jealous of her and there were murmurings among them, and yet she went all out to help their children. If she kept the children in after school to do some extra work, some of the parents would be saying, "Why this?" "Why that?", not realising that she did it to help the children and that she always demanded the best of all of us. Coralie did not allow such things to worry her. She told me, "Connie, lead your own life. Be your own person. Don't stop at anything," and she added, "and don't back down if our people anywhere are being ill treated."

I started to grow up during the war. The coming of World War Two could have meant the end of my gudiyar education just as it was about to begin but because of the dedication of Coralie Roberts it continued. Moreover working with Coralie, as her assistant, taught me other things about life and growing up and enabled her to nurture the responsibility and leadership that she saw in me. It also meant that she was able to instil in me the belief that if you have gifts then you should use them.

# Six

## *"They been killing our people all the time"*
### ᔐ *The army* ᔐ

Our Patronal Festival of St Michael and All Angels was on the twenty-ninth of September. It was on this day in 1913 that the mission had been founded by the late Canon Ernest Bulmer Gribble, an Anglican priest from North Queensland. War or no war, missionaries or no missionaries, our 1942 Festival was celebrated as usual with our sports day.

On the edge of the sports ground was a big bough-shed, a kind of marquee made of grass, spinifex and leaves the back of which was closed in. The elders stored the prizes, food, soft drinks and medicine in the rear of the bough-shed and organised the races from the front.

As usual, because of my bone condition, I watched the events from the bough-shed. Sadly, I sat on the ground wishing that I too could take part in the sack race, the egg-and-spoon race or the relays. I even longed to do battle in the greasy pole race. I imagined myself as one of the contestants scaling a greasy pole to retrieve the prize which was hanging on strips of rope suspended from a wheel.

I decided that come what may I would take part in Catch the Greasy Pig. The person who caught it would take it home as their prize. Needless to say, in all the noisy confusion of the pig squealing and people falling over each other, I ended up sprawled on the ground, exhausted. Fortunately, I recovered in time to watch my favourite event, the spear and boomerang throwing competition for the men and boys. Later I was able to join in the fun of tracking and retrieving a supposedly lost child with the women and girls.

To confuse the women, the men took out several other children and encouraged them to wander through the area mixing up the tracks. Before setting out, the trackers were told the age and a few other details of the child. Though lots of fun, this game was a real test of tracking skills, bushcraft and resourcefulness. I was proud of my skills at recognising footprints, by studying the impressions and their direction. I liked the challenge of studying the disturbance left on rocky ground.

Later, while the obstacle race was on, we heard a tribal man shouting to us from the camp, "Plenty gudiyar men coming". There was a pause and then, with a raucous belly laugh he announced, "They all walking in a row like emus." We joined in his laughter at the thought of marching emu men.

Suddenly we heard a loud, rasping voice saying, "Left, right, left, right". All our activities were abandoned, and everyone stared in the direction of the voice. In horror, we ran to the bough-shed as we feared that these men were Japanese, coming to kill us.

Eventually, the khaki-clad men appeared on the horizon and we nervously watched them march across the dry creek bed and come towards us. As they came near, we were relieved to see that their features were not Japanese. What we did not know was that they were part of a secret commando force known as Curtin's Cowboys.

The 'emu-men' marched on to the sports ground, came to a halt and stood to attention. Before dismissing them, the leader of the 'flock' told us that they were soldiers assigned to our area by the Australian army. He then introduced himself as Sergeant Shannon and asked the elders if he and his men could take part in the activities. The king of the tribe granted his permission, and the soldiers mingled freely with the people.

At tea time, we sat in a large circle with each soldier taken in by a family for the duration of the meal and festivities. The sergeant and four of his men sat with the elders. We were looking forward to enjoying the culinary delights of bush tucker prepared by the women and girls. There was kangaroo, wild turkey, wild duck, goanna, fish, crocodile, turtle – cooked in a large ground oven and accompanied by wild honey, berries, wild tomatoes, yams, wild potatoes, wild watermelon and gooseberries.

The soldiers had never tasted these foods before and they quite enjoyed their first meal with us. One of the soldiers asked if we had any tomato sauce and salt. We all laughed because tribal people did not use salt or sugar in their food. As we watched the soldiers pouring on the sauce and salt, we all whispered that it would spoil the taste for them.

The tribal elders then invited the soldiers to give out the prizes. The people, especially the young women and girls, were shy at first to receive their prizes from these gudiyars. The elders told us that the soldiers were not going to do any harm. After being assured by the elders of our safety, the young people received their presents from the soldiers without fear.

While we remained sitting in a circle waiting for the customary vespers and benediction, Sergeant Shannon rose and stood in the centre. He asked us if we had heard that Darwin had been bombed by the Japanese and the elders explained that we were well aware of the situation. He wanted to know how we found out about it as no one was allowed to use the wireless. One of the village men translated this message to an elder, who told the man to tell the sergeant that blacks didn't need to have a wireless because the message was relayed to the Aborigines living in the different areas of the Kimberleys by means of smoke signals. The sergeant and his men were amazed to learn that smoke signals were a frequent means of communication between the tribal Aborigines.

The sergeant told the elders that they had come up in small boats and that they had to return to the mouth of the river where their supply ship was anchored. He asked King David if he and his corporal could come back next day as they wanted to find a suitable place to set up their army base. The king indicated that they could come back, but the elders would have to be present at all times while the sergeant and his men were looking for a place.

The next day, the sergeant and his men arrived in an army 'duck', which being able to travel on land and water, came up Forrest River and straight into the mission. We had never seen anything like it. The driver of this weird-looking vehicle was ordered by the sergeant to stop and all the little girls and boys were invited to have a ride on it. I didn't come forward because I was scared and shy so Corporal Aldridge jumped off the duck, picked me up and tried to persuade me to sit on his lap.

The sergeant and his men found a spot on the mission where they wanted to put their base but they were met by the elders who had already decided on another site. It was five miles across the other side of the river at a place called Bremlah, meaning eternal spring. The elders wanted to make it quite clear that they did not want them near the mission, saying, "You stay Bremlah. We look after women and girls." The sergeant agreed and the army set up camp at the designated site.

The children were disappointed as we thought that would be the end of our new-found lolly supply. As it turned out they continued to give us lollies, chocolates and soft drinks and some of them even chose us to be their little girl or boy and would buy things for us and no one else. Of course, being Aboriginal children, we shared everything with each other as sharing is one of the most important laws in the Aboriginal culture.

When the army base was completed the elders called a public meeting (we were always having meetings!), as they had heard murmurings in the village about the army being placed at Bremlah. The leader of the elders, a tall man with white hair, who always carried a nulla nulla, addressed the people saying, "It is for your own good, especially the young girls and women, that we decided that the army should be camped well away from the mission." He warned that if any girls or women were involved in sneaking off to the army camp they would be punished by tribal law.

Because of the risk from the enemy, the Flying Doctor service was curtailed. I had access to the medical books in the hospital and, when anyone was sick, we would try to work out what the symptoms meant. In the army contingent were a doctor, a dentist and a chaplain who was an Anglican priest. Whenever the symptoms were too difficult for us to work out, the army doctor would be called in. Anyone needing emergency treatment or hospitalisation was taken into Wyndham by the army.

After the army settled at Bremlah their first task was to have a meeting with the elders, advising them that air-raid shelters were to be dug in and around the mission. The sergeant explained to the elders what air-raid shelters were for and the elders in turn told the people.

The men in the village were given the measurements. As I remember it, the trenches were dug in L-shapes ten feet long, eight feet wide and three feet deep. Planks were dug lengthwise into the top of the shelters with a space wide enough for us to jump into quickly when the enemy was approaching. The shelters were camouflaged with branches and leaves. They looked like rabbit burrows. We also grew pumpkin, watermelon and wild gooseberry bushes near the shelters so that as the vines and branches grew they would spread over the shelters giving us more protection from being seen by the enemy. Steps were dug into the shelters to enable the pregnant women, the elderly and the sick to get into the shelters with ease. To me the steps were a blessing as I was able to get into the shelter by myself if I was near one with no help.

The shelters were built close to main building areas such as the school, church, hospital, the girls' and boys' dormitories and near each home in the village. The army would let off a cannon to warn us of the approaching enemy. When we heard this signal we would race into the air-raid shelters long before the enemy appeared on the horizon.

The people thought the shelters were a great idea until we heard about a terrible tragedy that happened at the Kalumburu Catholic mission, about halfway between Derby and Wyndham. We were told that a number of people were killed by the Japanese, most of these were children and there was also a priest, all of them were in two trenches that were near their school. Apparently some of the little ones were still running to the trenches with their teachers when the enemy planes came into view. As they approached the mission, the pilots saw the people jumping into the trenches.

The planes flew around the mission and then came in low towards the trenches and strafed the lot. Not satisfied at doing it once, the Japanese flew over the mission a second time and firing again into the trenches made sure that everyone was dead. Apparently the adults, parents and elderly people witnessed this terrible tragedy. After hearing this, the people of Forrest River did not use the trenches again. We preferred to go bush, as we had done before the trenches were built, just hiding in thick scrub, in the caves, the river and in trees.

Throughout the rest of the war missionary priests, nursing sisters and one or two other women were allowed to visit the mission for short periods of time to help, especially at times of sickness and to give us the sacraments. They would always arrive escorted by the army who seemed reluctant to let them in.

Towards the end of the war, around midnight one night, at a time when we had both a gudiyar matron and superintendent working at the mission, we heard a noise at the back of the dormitory. We wondered what it was until suddenly we saw a light shining in a hole in the wall and the senior girls sneaking out. They told us junior girls to go back to sleep.

Next morning, matron opened the doors to find only us junior girls. She asked us where the senior girls were and we said we did not know. It really was the truth as we had been told nothing. While we were saying the Lord's Prayer, matron noticed the gaping hole in the back wall. After prayers she took the whole fourteen of us around the back of the dormitory and asked us to look for footprints.

There were quite a few footprints. We could tell by the shape and depths of the impressions in the sand that most of them were the tracks of the girls. There were also the heavy footprints of an Aboriginal man. Three others were boot marks and these belonged to the soldiers. Then matron asked us to tell her whose were the tracks without shoes. We thought she was being funny and I immediately said, "Matron, there are about fourteen pairs of big footprints not wearing shoes."

Not seeing the funny side she continued, "Connie come over here and tell me whose footprints these are."

The footprints she showed me were a man's and I knew straight away whose they were, but I said, "I don't know." I was telling proper gammon.

She asked the other girls and they said they didn't know either. Matron was angry as she knew that we recognised the footprints. "Don't lie to me," she said. "You know who the tracks belong to. Aboriginal people are the best trackers in the world. Fancy me trying to go bush with you lot after me! You'd track me down in no time." Then matron asked me again who the tracks belonged to. The other girls gave me a look that said, "If you tell

48

matron we will bash you up," so I said, "I don't know."

Looking at me with as much determination as she could muster in the circumstances, matron said, "You know what the punishment is for lying." For dormitory girls, it meant being forced to wear a dress made from a coarse hessian bag. Matron again asked the other girls, and again they told her they didn't know. As there were only two hessian-bag dresses available we were then told that we would all be grounded for a month and I was sent off to fetch the superintendent.

Breakfast was held up until we identified the footprints. After a while we talked among ourselves as to whether we should keep silent. Eventually hunger won and I was chosen to be the one to tell matron.

After breakfast, the superintendent rang the work bell which summoned everybody in the village and the camp people to assemble in front of the store where they were usually given their jobs for the day. When everybody had gathered, the superintendent called the elders and told them what had happened during the night. They were all shocked and upset and when the rest of the people were told, they too were most concerned. The fathers, brothers, grandfathers and uncles of the senior girls volunteered to go to Bremlah and bring the girls back to the mission.

The elders then instructed everyone to go down to the river and wait for the arrival of the girls and their escorts. We junior girls and boys were excited and curious trying to work out what the punishment would be for such daring behaviour. Two hours later, the senior girls and their escorts appeared on the opposite bank of the river. With them was the Aboriginal man who had taken the girls over to Bremlah. We could see that the brengen had a proper yirrbarra look on his face. Bringing up the rear marched the sergeant, the corporal and some of the soldiers who were involved in this clandestine affair.

When the party reached the river bank, the full tide was on the turn and the girls were ordered to get ready to swim the river. The girls became very agitated and sat down nervously on the bank. The rest of us were shocked at these instructions and understood the reluctance of the girls to obey the command. It is extremely dangerous to swim the Forrest River at full tide as that is the time when crocodiles and other sea creatures are around. The elders moved behind them urging them towards the river while we waited tensely on the other side. Just as the girls were edging into the water, the assembled crowd saw a large crocodile surface in midstream. Shouting, screaming and vigorous displays of sign language followed as we tried to get the attention of the elders and tell them of the impending danger. After what seemed like an eternity, they also saw the crocodile which was just swimming lazily. The terrified girls skidded up the bank so quickly it seemed they hadn't been in the water at all. And on our side of the river there was a collective sigh of relief.

We waited for the tide to recede. Eventually the whole party crossed the river. The senior girls were told to form a line and were marched back to the mission. The tribal leader, two of his men and the army contingent went ahead of the girls while the rest of the elders and the other men walked behind them. Bringing up the rear were the rest of the village people including us dormitory boys and girls excitedly discussing what might happen next. After reaching the mission compound, we were all told to assemble in front of the church. Then the meeting began in earnest. The superintendent stood out the front facing the very downcast group of young women and demanded, "How did you girls come to go over to Bremlah?"

One of the girls replied, "We were woken up by someone banging on the walls, so we went to see what it was. We saw a brengen standing beside a hole in the wall with pliers and cutting shears in his hand. We asked him why he had come. He explained that some of the soldiers from Bremlah had asked him to come and get some girls for them and they would pay him when he delivered them. We were frightened and told him that we weren't going. Then he said, 'I have brought three soldiers with me.' By this time we were really scared but we didn't know what to do so the brengen said, 'If you don't come with me the soldiers won't pay me.'"

One of the other girls then took up the story, "All of a sudden, three soldiers came out of the dark and told us to make up our minds as the time was slipping away. So the girls who were with me all agreed to go, so I went and woke the rest of the senior girls and asked if they would like to come too. They agreed to come so we all went one by one through the gap in the wall. When we got to the river, we were happy to see that the tide had not come in and so were able to walk safely across."

The girls continued their explanation until eventually the superintendent told them to stand up in front of the whole assembly. The people, especially the parents of the girls, were terribly upset to think that their daughters were involved in such a risky exploit. On the other hand, all of us younger children from the village and the dormitory were getting morbidly excited as the time for punishment was approaching. Our vivid imaginations were generating some highly creative possibilities. We could see them being speared through the foot, being stripped naked and made to walk in front of the whole assembly or being caned by the superintendent.

To our great disappointment, none of these punishments happened. The superintendent announced that the senior girls were to be grounded for three months and the sergeant said that the soldiers involved would be transferred immediately.

This caused great sorrow for the younger dormitory children as some of these soldiers had been very kind to us. It meant the end of lollies, chocolates, biscuits and soft drinks. The grounding of the girls on the other hand did not change life very much as it was an ongoing punishment for all dormitory offenders.

For me, twelve years old and approaching puberty, observing this incident led me to decide that as I had my whole life in front of me, I would never be caught in such an unpleasant situation.

Soon after this there was a rumour that word had been sent to the army that if the Japanese took the Kimberleys every Aboriginal man, woman and child would be rounded up and shot. After hearing this rumour, King David assured us that if this thing should happen we would all go together. "No parents will be left without children and no children without parents." He also reminded us that this was "nothing new", and that "since the gudiyars came to this country they been killing our people all the time."

A couple of weeks after hearing this, we heard another rumour. The army, we were told, had said that they would refuse to carry out any such order. Despite the second rumour, we children, from that time on, were afraid of the army.

Though the rendezvous incident had not affected our feelings towards the soldiers, these rumours did change the way we felt about them. After the initial shock of learning that we could have all been annihilated by our friends, on the orders of the powers-that-be, fear took over and the whole community's trust in the army was no more. Before this happened, we were all happy to have the soldiers in our midst and we felt confident that they would keep us safe from the Japanese. The little children on the mission and the camp had trusted these men because they gave us sweets. We, the children, were now sad and afraid, to think that although these men cared for us, they had the power to end our lives. Even today I still puzzle about why such a command could be considered.

# Seven

*"It is not for us to say who is to live and who is to die"*
~ *Epidemic* ~

As the war was coming to a close, a terrible flu epidemic broke out. All the people went down with it, with the exception of three of us: Ubla Thompson, the Aboriginal nurse and myself. This crisis convinced the Anglican church to send some missionaries to assist us. The Reverend Wheatley, the Reverend Best and his wife Betty and two army nursing sisters came from Perth to Forrest River to help during the epidemic. My role was to help carry around the medicines and to wipe the fevered brows of the very ill.

The army doctor and his orderlies were kept very busy. They came over from Bremlah and stayed at the mission. Most of the people were nursed at home with only the very ill people being hospitalised. Those who were really sick were taken by the Australian air force to either Darwin or Perth depending on the severity of the illness. During the epidemic, we lost three babies, two toddlers and five old people. We worked tirelessly and often wondered how we ever managed to keep going. Occasionally the Flying Doctor would visit us, in a private plane, and we would be happy and relieved to see him.

Mummy Nora and Lydia (King Peter's wife) were responsible for laying out the dead and when the three babies died, she said to me, "Ngumballa, you are now old enough to learn how to do this task. You are proper sensible and clever and you learn quickly." She thought that I was ready to take on such a task at twelve years old.

At first I was afraid to touch a dead body, but when my foster mother told me that it would not harm me, I began to take notice and watched as Mummy Nora laid out the first baby. She told me to observe carefully because I was to lay out the other two little ones.

When my turn came to do the task, I started to cry and said to her, "Gaga, why do these wongalongs have to die? They haven't even started to live." She did not answer but let me blurt out my sorrow. Then she said to me, "You finished walla walla? Ngumballa, you listen to me. Everything must darar-bru, even the young. It is not for us to say who is to live and who is to die."

Being young, this profound statement did not mean anything to me. I was so angry that these little babies should die, but as I grew older I began to realise that her words were true. Even today, when I mourn the loss of a friend or relative, I think of what my Aboriginal foster mother said to me all those years ago. When I calmed down, she started to tell me that like animals and plants, humans die too, from sickness, accidents and old age. I then brought up the subject of the death of my mother, saying that she too was a young woman when she died. I asked her what had caused my mother's death. I was met with a wall of silence. She said, "When you grow older we will tell you."

Mummy Nora was very proud of the way I laid out the two remaining babies. We left the three babies and I helped her lay out two old men, the rest she left to her usual helper who came in after lunch. Several weeks later, I was devastated when I had to lay out a twelve-year-old girl, exactly the same age as myself. My foster mother was with me and as usual I burst out crying. She just let me cry until I couldn't cry anymore, then she said, "Ngumballa, we work now," and gave me instructions on what to do.

After I had finished, she added, "Ngumballa, I am proud of you. You are one of my good workers. I will tell the gudiyar sisters when they come back to put your name on the list along with the other women whose job it is to lay out the dead." Being entrusted with this task was an honour and I was grateful for the training I had received. The tribal people were very proud and happy that one of their young girls had learned how to do this important task. Mummy Nora taught me how to lay out the bodies in the way the missionaries had taught her. While she was laying them out she told me about how the tribal people did it in the bush. It surprised me how different the two ways were.

One day, we heard one of Mummy Nora's boys yell out, "I'm gonna die. I'm gonna die." Mummy Nora and one of the old men ran down to him as again he yelled, "I'm dying." He had been bitten by a snake.

"You'll live," said Mummy Nora when she saw that it was only a water python. But he continued to believe his end had come, and as they carried him up to the hospital he cried and said goodbye to everybody. For months afterwards we girls had many laughs about his 'deadly' snake bite.

Because of the war I found that I learnt much more about my people and myself than I would have if the strict domitory system had continued. I was able to see how families functioned. I could talk to the village people and the camp people without government and church restrictions. I learnt to relate to people better. I became conscious that despite my disabilities, I could use my intelligence to help people even if it was just being there when they needed someone. The relative freedom we had during the war gave me and the other dormitory girls and boys the opportunity to learn tribal Law, something every dormitory child longed for.

# Eight

## *"Messengers from God"*
### ⮎ *The missionaries* ⮌

I enjoyed my war-time school days both as assistant teacher and as pupil and, though inclined to be a bit mischievous, I was an industrious student. Towards the latter part of the war, Reverend John Best came back to take over as superintendent, chaplain and teacher. He asked Coralie to continue to teach.

"Will Connie be helping too?" Coralie asked him.

"Yes. If you would like her to," he said.

"I'd like her to," she told him.

I was so excited to hear this that I felt like jumping about – not that I could, for fear of breaking my bones.

Reverend Best was one of the few missionaries who we knew was genuinely caring for the people that he was ministering to. As far as I can recall, he used none of the cruel punishments that we had got used to on the mission. He was also one of the very few missionaries who was not patronising. He talked to us person-to-person, not as white to black. He didn't wait for a fight to break out in order to talk with the village people. He would walk around in the afternoons and talk with them about family and children.

He didn't go to see people so that he could expound Christianity to them, but simply to get to know them . When he came to the dormitory compound, the girls would run to grab his hands saying, "Sit down under the gum tree here, Father." He would sit down on the ground and then say, "Now who would like to tell me something." On these occasions everyone would want to talk at the same time, especially yours truly, so he'd say, "Hang on, hang on, one at a time."

Reverend Best spoke our English. He sat down with us. He listened to us and these things reminded us of tribal ways. He was full of vitality but he didn't preach fire and brimstone in his sermons. They were easy to listen to and full of real love for the people.

As I was growing up, I was always taught that a missionary was someone who was sent by God to teach us not only to read and write but also to love, help and be kind to each other. There were a few missionaries who fitted in to my image of being 'messengers from God' who gave up their homes in the south for a time to show concern for the welfare of the Aboriginal people. I came to the conclusion that there must be two types of missionaries. The first type were missionaries who really did God's work. There were few of these. The second type were missionaries only in name, who were more interested in establishing their own superiority than in portraying Christianity. They came to 'educate', and to 'make Christians' of us 'ignorant heathens'. Though the second type came to Forrest River under the missionary banner, I felt that they used it as a weapon to dominate and manipulate us.

One of the first type was Mary Jamison (nee Willington), a teacher and a missionary who really did God's work. For me she was the very best of the genuine missionaries and was truly a 'messenger of God'. Love came out of her for everybody. Though she was a teacher, if people were sick she would go to the hospital and see if she could help. In times when the whole community would be struck down with the flu, measles, chicken pox, mumps and any other sickness, Miss Willington was always there to offer her services. All the people had the greatest respect for her. She became known as the munnaburra (beautiful) lady.

She encouraged me to take up music. By teaching me to play the piano she opened up a whole new world of pleasure for me. I had been playing the hymns for church long before she came to Forrest River. One day she said, "Connie, you can't learn to play that way. You have to learn scales."

I said, "Why can't I just play by ear?

"Connie, you could become a very good pianist."

Miss Willington began by showing me the basic principles of music. I would have none of what I called 'the do – re – mi business'. I wasn't going to go up the scales nor down so she had to be content with a rather unorthodox student.

A priest who taught at the school, Father Dick Cranswick, and his wife, were also what I called real missionaries. We used to call Father Cranswick 'John the Baptist' because we always thought of him as a saint, a holy man. He used to invite some of us around after school to learn to sing. He didn't say, "You must come around to the school," but rather he would say, "Who would like to come round to the school and learn to sing?" He taught us how to sing descant and how to harmonise. He also began to break down some of the mission taboos by getting us to sing with the boys. Our first reaction was to say, "Oh no, we can't come and sing with the boys." But he was determined. "Yes, you can come, as I am teaching you all to sing."

"But Father, we can't! That's not allowed!"

"While I'm the superintendent, and the chaplain, it is allowed."

One day I said, "Father, can we take your kids bush?"

Without any hesitation he said, "Yes, you can take them." So Maryanne and Thurston, the wild one, came walkabout with us and we taught them to track and to love the bush. Unfortunately he was not there long as his skin was very sensitive to the sun. Many was the time we would have to put on cold rags and calomine lotion to ease the pain of his burnt face and back.

Miss Patricia Gregory was a teacher who took a personal interest in each child and always made sure that everyone fully understood what she was trying to teach. For her efforts to bridge the gap between the government's missionary education and our tribal heritage, we felt the greatest respect for Miss Gregory and gave her the co-operation our grandparents would have given to their tribal elders.

Miss Gregory was a person who spoke her mind to the superintendent and other staff in the defence of her pupils. The older dormitory girls who were working in the staff kitchen often told us about these incidents. It seems that one of the male missionaries who was not very well liked by the people commented, "That boy should not be in school. Pat, you are wasting your time trying to teach him." The boy in question was a quiet little fellow who hardly ever spoke.

Miss Gregory replied, "That boy takes in more than you give him credit for. He is quite intelligent and while I am teaching here I will give all my pupils every opportunity to reach their full potential."

We asked the girl, "What did the gudiyar fellow do then?"

"Nothing. Miss Gregory shut him up all right."

"Good," we said. "That fellow thinks he knows everything about Aborigines."

In June 1946, a letter from Miss Gregory was published in the Australian Board of Mission Review. It included the following,

> ...The children at present are suffering from a kind of very infectious sores and my school is not so much black as striped! They are all adorned with bandages, which they take much delight in unwinding and winding on again dropping them down in the dirt meanwhile. So it's no wonder that the sores spread!

> I am beginning to realise the difficulties here, but also the opportunities. I love the children, and long to be able to make their lives a little better than their parents can hope for. Why shouldn't they become an independent and flourishing community? If only we white Australians realised the debt we owe them and really made an effort to help them instead of salving our consciences by doling out rations of tea and flour and dreadful-looking clothes we wouldn't be seen dead in ourselves...

There were very few matrons that I got along with. One matron that stands out in my mind as a gracious Christian lady was Sylvia Andrews (later Eddy). She was kindness itself. Though she was nearly deaf she helped us, listened to us and tried to understand our problems. She was one of the few matrons who believed that she needed to sit down with the girls in order to know them.

Matron Andrews found me a pen friend, Cynthia Burgess (now Barnacle), who is still a friend today. I found that I could share my feelings with Cynthia even though we lived in different states. When I was unhappy Cynthia would write back to me and say we will pray about your problems, and ask God's help. I trusted Cynthia even though I hadn't met her. She would send me cards and gifts every Christmas. She also sent things when there was no special reason. The first time we met was in 1958 when I was on my way to Adelaide to visit my brother, Colin. Cynthia and her husband John and their children are my closest friends. I believe God finds and sends us good friends, and I believe he found Cynthia to be my friend when Matron Andrews gave me her name and address.

One afternoon, Matron Andrews took the girls for a walk down the river. Marjorie Reynolds and I stayed home as we were on kitchen duties. After they left, I thought I would do some snooping around. I went into matron's room, looked around and there in the top drawer was her camera. It opened and closed like a concertina, so we called it her concertina camera. I was fascinated so I took it out and started taking photos of anything and everything. Then Marjorie said, "Matron and the girls are coming back."

"Marjorie, do you know how to close this camera?"

"No. You're the one that is fascinated with the camera." So I forced the camera shut and broke it. Sadly, I put it back and closed the drawer. I went back into the kitchen and waited. One of the girls had caught a barrumundi so matron decided to take a photo. She found her broken camera, walked out and said, "Where's Connie?"

I felt remorseful because I had done something wrong to a very dear lady. She did not bawl me out; she didn't send me to the superintendent's office. She simply sat me down and spoke to me and explained that what I had done was wrong and that the camera had cost her a lot of money. I was terribly upset and cried to think that I had done something wrong to her. I was not used to being treated so gently by a matron.

There were also 'so-called missionaries', who came to Forrest River. They were the most arrogant, racist people I have ever known. Some of them were more like soldiers, running the place military style in order to make us 'civilised'. I often wondered what kind of God it was that would send people like this up here to belt

60

Cross on the 'jump up' at Oombulgurri (formerly Forrest River mission).
A memorial to the twenty-three Aboriginal people killed and burnt by police in 1925

1938: Five years old, being a cheeky child as usual and not wanting to have my photo taken, I covered my face with my hands.

L to R: unknown, Coralie Roberts, Violet Edwards, Meena Ahwon, Vigil Evans, Eileen Mitchell, Mrs G. V. Johnston, girl in front of Mrs Johnston unknown, Betty Johnstone, Molly Pierce, , unknown, Ivy Mills, Hilda Meehan, Miss E.Hahn, child in front, Connie McDonald, Joyce Evans, Susan Clark, Daphne Clark, Daffodil

1949: Uncle Robert Roberts (Unjumarra) has just caught a freshwater crocodile at Stevenson's Hole

1950: Mana Coaldrake fitting dormitory girls with dresses
L to R: Ursula, Susan, Mana Coaldrake, Mary, Lovie, Dorothy

1948: Fifteen years old, dressed in my waitress uniform

1957: I am standing with Mrs Mary Jamison, Paul, Ronald and Philip beside our bus at Tennant Creek on our way to Queensland

1957: My first view of Yarrabah jetty

Yarrabah Bay where the skipper
and I often strolled

Mr and Mrs Jamison on the beach near Yarrabah with Paul, Donald, Philip Ian and me

1958: With Lorna Schrieber, my great friend. In the background are palm leaves drying ready for weaving into baskets and mats

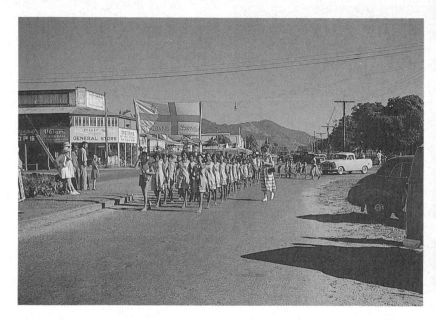

1959: Yarrabah school marching through the main street of Cairns to win the march past plus thirty-six awards and cups

1959: Yarrabah, a group of schoolchildren with the Christmas tree

the life out of us. It was not a God I wanted to know about. When I compared these missionaries with the tribal people we were supposed to avoid, I wished we were allowed more communication with our tribal people.

It made me angry when some gudiyar missionaries would tell us that we were all pagans and that we had to get rid of our heathen beliefs, become 'civilised' like white people and learn to think and eat like them. It always puzzled me how such people could call themselves missionaries. They seemed to have the idea that they were 'boss' of the mission with their motto being "We say – You do – That's it."

One of these missionaries was a matron of the girl's dormitory. I found her very hard to like as she was always running us down and taunting us with racial remarks such as, "I don't know why we bother to try and educate you blacks" or "You blacks have no brains" or "We are just wasting our time trying to civilise you savages." Eventually I became so exasperated by her insults that I responded with a few of my own opinions. All the other girls were amazed as they heard me blurt out, "It's white people like you with your stupid attitudes towards Aborigines, who should not be sent to mission reserves! You should stay in your comfortable homes with your money and riches! As far as I can see from your performance as a matron, I don't think you are a missionary in the true sense at all!" The matron was so shocked at my outburst that she sat down and cried.

This utterly bewildered the other girls and they said, "Connie, look what you have done to the matron." Some of the girls felt sorry for her, and took her back to her house. In the meantime, she had sent for the superintendent. Two hours later, I was called to his office. I told him that I was fed up with matron's unkind comments about Aborigines. He asked me to quote the remarks so I said, "Matron is always saying, 'I don't know why we bother to come up here to try and educate you blacks.'"

The superintendent asked matron if this was so and she told him that it was. And so he asked me, "Why do you object to matron saying these things?"

I answered, "Wouldn't you if you were me? Maybe you think that because you and the matron are white that you have the right to treat us with contempt. I thought that you people were sent here by God to bring his word to us so that we can become Christians. What I've read of Jesus so far in the Bible is that he was a compassionate man, always helping those who were ill, lonely, hungry and those who needed his love. My understanding is that this is what you Christian missionaries were commanded to do when God called you to come up here to Forrest River Mission to do his work. We didn't ask you to come."

Both the superintendent and matron were astonished at my reprimand. So were the girls when I got back to the dormitory and told them what I had said. They thought I was 'proper cheeky'. My punishment for talking back to matron was no walkabouts for two weeks and for the next four months I had to pull up the weeds that were growing around the girl's dining room. This punishment was more a pastime than a deterrent to me. It became a regular pastime because of the frequency of my punishments. And the girls' dining room had the neatest grounds on the mission.

Whenever we went walkabout with the missionaries, the practice was that as soon as we returned the girls would be told by the missionaries, "You have to wash my feet." I didn't mind washing Miss Willington's feet. I could wash her feet any time. But when we were nearly home one day after a particularly exhausting walk, the matron of the time said, "Connie, I want you to wash my feet."

Now if the matron had said, "Please, Connie would you wash my feet?" I would have done so. Because I had been ordered, I replied, "Yes, I'll wash your feet, if you'll wash my feet."

"Aborigines wash white ladies' feet but white ladies do not wash Aborigines' feet."

"Oh well, that's it. You can wash your own feet."

"What! For being so insubordinate I am going to tell Father when we go home."

"You can tell him. We'll both tell him," I assured her.

When we arrived home, we both went to the superintendent's office. I seemed to be forever coming up against authority and so spent a lot of time being called to the superintendent's office or the teacher's office.

"What is it now Connie? I want your version." So I told him all about it. Then he said to matron, "Has this always been a practice?"

Before matron could answer I said, "Yeah. For as long as I can remember. Even when I was five years old, I was washing all these white ladies' toes. It has always been the practice for Aboriginal girls to get down on our knees and wash gudiyar feet."

At that moment his wife came in and said, "I wish somebody would wash my feet."

I laughed but matron didn't find anything funny in her comment. I thought to myself, "Boy, am I going to cop it!" but aloud I put on a bold face, "What punishment now, Father, is going to be meted out?"

"Nothing. No punishment. And this washing of feet has got to stop."

"Good!" I said in surprise. "I suppose the gudiyar people think they are being like the Lord Jesus Christ, but they got this washing of feet back to front. Jesus washed the feet of simple people, not the feet of high fallutin people."

So I went back to the dormitory and announced to the girls that they would never again have to bend down and wash gudiyar feet. Some of the girls were pleased at the news and some were upset as they often received privileges like apples or lollies for the feet washing.

It seemed to me that missionaries like that matron somehow thought that they were God themselves and so required us to treat them as all powerful and almighty. All the time I was adding up these experiences and one day it dawned on me that they were not gods or even angels they were just ordinary humans like me. And I began to see that there were many Aboriginal people who were messengers from God.

The Aboriginal people showed me what the word love really meant. From the little contact I did have with the tribe, especially during the war, I learnt much about love, family life and how to care for the earth and look after all living things. In the tribal situation, I found that every one was kin to everyone else and caring was required of everybody. Before an animal was killed there was

63

a prescribed ritual and even when you were eating it there was more ceremony. Some missionaries told us that these rituals were pagan but I found them spiritually uplifting.

I can remember Aunty Louise and Uncle Robert Unjamurra taking us walkabout and catching fish for a meal. They told us that the fish were sacred because they had life and that even though we took their life it was only because we needed it in order to nourish ourselves. They made it abundantly clear to us that we couldn't kill the animals just because we were humans and could do anything we liked. They told us that the Great Spirit knew our needs and that we should not feel sad or guilty as the Great Spirit forgave us when we used those things for our food. And we learnt too that was why the land was sacred to Aboriginal people. In telling us about Wandjina, Aunty Louise and Uncle Robert appeared to me to be true messengers from God.

My cousin, Freda Chulung, and her husband Clem were one of the couples who helped to keep the mission going. They were totally in charge whenever the rest of the community went on the annual walkabout. All through my childhood I saw Freda and Clem as people who had the strength and ability to carry out the duties that were given them and I admired and looked up to them.

Freda and Clem and Freda's sister Rosie and her husband Gerard were both very close and loving couples. They never missed church on Sunday; their children were well mannered. All of Freda and Rosie's children grew up with a belief in their ability to look after themselves. Gerard was the skipper of the mission launch and Clem was one of the trusted overseers to the superintendent. Clem was a quiet man who had a kind face and an unusual way of walking. Freda and Clem seemed to want to live their lives without being dominated by government and mission regulations. They believed that the mission punishments were too harsh and insisted on handling the problems of their children themselves. Cousin Freda had the idea that you could talk to children rather than punish them. After the war both families left the mission to live in Wyndham to get a better education for the children at the high school. Their children then went on to such jobs as nursing and station hands and today most of them have good jobs with the government.

There were many other older people who I looked up to as people who inspired me to be what I wanted to be. The mission Aborigines gave me an example of dependability and education and the tribal Aborigines taught me to be me. They taught me to understand what it meant to be fully human.

The period during the war when we were without missionaries had been a happy time. Observing my people taught me that we were capable of running our own lives. It gave me a glimpse of what life must have been before the gudiyars came. I emerged with more faith in myself and in my people and with a capacity to look on the missionaries as less god-like than I had been led to believe. Having a rebellious nature enabled me to see more clearly what the government system was doing to us and to realise that some of the missionaries treated us like animals or convicts.

As I grew up I gradually realised that the mission was dealing with different cultures. Some of the people who came from the stations around the Kimberleys did not seem to want to have a knowledge and regard for traditional tribal ways. These people found it easier to understand what the missionaries were on about and were less likely to be put down by them.

On the other hand the people who still had strong tribal attachments were more readily submissive to the regulations of the mission and the government. Though I could see that they had a pride in themselves and their culture they chose to keep that pride to themselves. Outwardly they did what the missionaries wanted but inwardly they were vastly different.

I wondered where I fitted in to all of this. As I knew I was an ubergarge (of mixed race), should I grow up to follow gudiyar ways or should I lean towards my tribal ancestry? I was and I still am proud of my Aboriginal culture but I wanted to become an educated member of the wider society. I was able to resolve this in my mind by telling myself that we are all human beings whether tribal, mission or station Aborigine. I decided that I was first and foremost a human being.

# Nine

## *"Only a ngumballa"*
## ∼ *Entry into womanhood* ∼

Every Thursday morning, the chaplain would come to the school for religious instruction. We found these religion lessons rather boring. One Thursday, the chaplain had a surprise in store for us. After roll-call he said, "I have a particular topic to talk to you about. Very important." I thought, "It can't be punishment. No one has been naughty."

"The topic is – the human sexual organs and human sexual intercourse!" Everybody looked at each other, not really knowing which way to look. "We'll start with the male reproductive organs," and he drew a diagram on the board.

Some of the boys and girls lived with their parents and knew all about this kind of thing. In the tribe they were told about these things as they approached puberty. For the boys, their lessons on the facts of life came as part of their initiation and around twelve the girls were taken out bush to see when a child was being born. However, the gnarnie like me, who were growing up without parents, and who were very naive, were all eyes and ears.

After telling us all the proper names for the sexual organs, he asked us to tell him the tribal names for them. I put my hand up to say, "I don't know what they call those things. I don't even know anything about it." The boys thought I was putting my hand up to answer the question. They made signs to me indicating that I would be in trouble from them if I did. I put my hand down and nobody uttered a word.

"You are not going to learn if you don't tell me," the chaplain told us.

One of the boys put up his hand and said, "We know everything but it is against the law to talk about these things in front of the girls."

"Do you know about how babies are made?"

"We tribal kids from the bush – we know. We don't hear mini-earthquakes and unusual sounds at night for nothing."

Again I put my hand up. "What mini-earthquakes and funny noises?" I asked. By this time I could see that the boy in question was on the point of having apoplexy but I added, "Is that how they make babies?"

"Gee you're dumb," said the boy. "How did you think we came into being?"

"Well, by the Flying Doctor."

Everybody laughed and the chaplain called off the session and didn't discuss sex with us again. I guess he learnt that day that in the tribal situation sex is only spoken about between members of the same sex, as a sign that it is sacred. I was none the wiser.

Puberty brought us girls a blouse and bra. We found it quite hysterical to think that we had to bridle our ngabaloos. Our first demonstration on how to wear a bra was conducted under the strict supervision of the dormitory matron who explained to us how to put what, where. I was the model for the other girls because I was well endowed. There I was, standing up in all my glory, with just a pair of panties on. Every time I was told to put you know what, where, there was a peal of laughter from the other girls. After some time I finally got the ngabaloos in only to find that my breathing was somewhat restricted, so I pretended to faint, which only made the girls laugh louder. Matron was not amused. I was told to go back to the dormitory.

The introduction of petticoats, some time later, caused something of a rebellion. We were told that ladies always wear petticoats and that it was unseemly to see panties through a dress. "Where are the ladies?" I piped up. "I'll see you later, Connie," said matron. And she did. I pulled up grass around the girls' dining room for a month after the introduction of petticoats. And I still had to wear my petticoat.

Living in the dormitory meant that all we were taught was

religion and the three Rs. We didn't learn about our bodies, about sex, about menstruation. When I was twelve, I woke one morning and was shocked at the red, sticky substance running between my legs. I thought, "Something is wrong with me. I must have a disease." I couldn't tell the other girls or the matron when she came. When the girls left for church I hung back. Matron said, "Come on Connie. You'll be late for church."

"I'm not going – to church or school or anywhere."

Matron said, "I haven't got time to argue with you. I'll see you after church."

Once they were gone, I hung out my blanket, washed myself, washed my dress, hung it out to dry and waited. As soon as church came out I went straight to a person that I could trust and that I knew would care, Sister Drage at the hospital. Nancy Drage was a wonderful person. She wanted to go out and mix with the people but she was told, "You don't do that. That is not allowed. We missionaries are just here to bring the word of God."

"Is there anything wrong, Constance?" she asked.

"Yes. I've got a disease."

"What?"

I opened my dress and she saw what it was, put her arms around me lovingly and said, "Look at me, Constance. Do you know what? You are no longer a child. You are now a young woman and your body is changing. This is going to happen every month," and she explained what was happening to me. I was amazed. Nurse Drage told it all to me so beautifully that I looked on her at that moment as if she was my mother.

I said to her, "Nurse Drage, I know all about ngabaloos and woorgoo but this goolie, I don't know nothing about it." And in my confused state, I was talking to her in my native tongue and then in English. She seemed to understand.

"Constance," she said tenderly, "I'll tell you something – if you muck around with boys now you can become pregnant, that means you can have a baby." I thought to myself, "Possibly, this is what my mother would have said." And I wished that she was there.

I suppose no one had told me about menstruation because the senior girls thought it was matron's responsibility. Since I was eleven, I had been sewing up lawn pads and there was a shelf with my name on and my pile of twelve pads alongside the shelves with the names of all the senior girls. Matron had said to me, "You will need these." But that was all she said. After this episode the matron and all the matrons after her explained to the girls about the changes in their bodies. As well as that I made it my business to explain puberty to every dormitory girl when she reached ten years of age.

It wasn't long after the end of the war that I turned thirteen, the age that mission children had to leave school. I continued my work as a teacher's aide but I was no longer a student. The mission continued to suffer food shortages and though I enjoyed my teaching duties I didn't have any energy and found it very hard to sleep. Eventually my appetite disappeared, my stomach became quite distended and I began to suffer severe abdominal pains. The nursing sister at Forrest River arranged for me to go for treatment to the Native Hospital at Three Mile near Wyndham.

Without any proper examination or even questioning me about whether I had ever engaged in sexual intercourse, the matron of the Native Hospital assumed I was probably pregnant. I felt proper yirrbarra at this assumption. More than that, I was very angry as I knew it was impossible and I said to the matron, "How can this be?"

The doctor's examination soon revealed that I was suffering from severe malnutrition and that I was in need of wholesome food. At this bit of news, my anger turned to triumph and I glared at the matron and said, "So much for the supposed pregnancy."

A couple of years after this incident, I was asked to go through some hospital files while I was helping out at the mission hospital. I came across my file and, being of a curious nature, I wanted to see what was written about me. To my horror, there it was, a 1945 entry, standing out like a beacon, "Constance McDonald – pregnant." I was more than angry this time. I confronted the nursing sister and asked, "Who put this entry in here?" She didn't answer. I assumed it must have been her and so I asked her if she would put it right but she refused. I got the card out of the file and tore it in half and I wondered how many other records of Aboriginal people had distorted the truth.

For the next few weeks I stayed at the hospital, where I had three meals a day with lots of fruit and vegetables. My health soon picked up, so did my appetite, and my distended stomach slowly returned to normal. On my previous visits to the hospital for broken bones, I always went straight back to the mission after treatment. However, this time I was moved to one of the cottages in the hospital compound after I had spent a couple of weeks in hospital so that I could continue to recover.

The hospital compound looked like a small mission, the only difference was there was no church building. There were eight cottages, four for female patients and four for males. The cottages looked something like mission dormitories, with cement floors; two blankets but no beds or mattresses; two buckets, one suspended from the ceiling with drinking water in it, and the other on the floor with a toilet seat over it and a candle for each person. There were two toilet buildings, one for the women and one for the men and two shower rooms. I tried to imagine what it would be like waiting for a shower if all thirty-eight dormitory beds were occupied. Fortunately, in all my stays at the hospital over the years, this never happened.

The Native Hospital operated like an annexe of the mission. Nobody was allowed to leave unless relatives came and asked the manager if they could take them out.

I shared a cottage with two married women and a fifteen-year-old girl from Forrest River. The women were pregnant and had been sent into Wyndham from the mission because the nursing sister thought they were going to have difficult confinements. The girl was waiting to have an operation on her ear.

The cottage patients and Aboriginal workers of the Native Hospital compound were issued monthly rations which consisted of flour, tea, sugar, velvet soap for washing and carbolic soap for body hygiene, powdered milk, a large government store handkerchief, either blue with white dots or red with white dots and a block of tobacco .

After I received my first ration, I asked a woman from one of the cattle stations if tobacco was only given to adults and children in their teens. "No," she replied. "Last month my sister was down here with her nine-year-old daughter and the little girl was issued with the same rations as everyone else."

"What! Tobacco too?"

"Yes. The same rations."

I was aghast. "Does your niece chew tobacco?"

"No," she said. "My sister wouldn't let her kids chew tobacco."

This made me even more angry. I decided to do something about it. When I lined up for the second issue of my rations, I confronted the manager about giving tobacco to children. I said, "Why are you giving tobacco to children?"

"Government policy."

I said, "Government policy nothing. For your information I don't chew tobacco...never have and never will. And you can't make me."

He looked at me straight in the face and said, "All blacks chew tobacco – whether they are adults or children. What you do with the tobacco is your business." I walked off with my rations leaving the stick of tobacco behind. The manager called me back and said, "Connie, you will take your issue of tobacco or you will be punished. I shall get in touch with the Native Welfare."

The ration queue was held up. The people were amazed. They had never seen such boldness from one of their lot towards the gudiyars. I heard them whispering, "Fancy talking like that to the gudiyar. And she is only a ngumballa too." This gave me courage. I was beginning to enjoy the confrontation with this gudiyar in front of such a stunned audience. Standing to my full height, I said, " If you punish me by getting in touch with the Native Welfare, I will report you to the Archbishop of the Church of England in Perth."

He looked at me in disbelief. "You wouldn't."

"Oh, wouldn't I? You carry out your threat and I will carry out mine."

By this time news had spread around the compound. Aboriginal people from the cottages, the hospital, as well as any workers who could, had gathered around to witness this unusual event. At this point the manager asked Hector, the Aboriginal overseer, to

71

take over giving out the rations. As he was about to leave I said to him, "What's the matter? Don't you want to further this discussion?"

"No, that's the end of it," he said.

There was silence for a while, then Hector said, "Lot's of bad things been going on here girl, by that manager." The others nodded in agreement. "Yes, our people have been treated bad. We need someone to talk for us."

I walked off after telling Hector to give the tobacco to whomever he chose. He gave it to an old man from Hall's Creek and in return the old man gave him his handkerchief to give to me.

As I thought about the incident, I became aware that even though these people were from different stations, they were my people too and were looking for me to be a spokesperson.

Curfew for the patients was the same as for the dormitory on the mission. We were all locked into our cottages from seven o'clock at night until the morning. This was government policy, I guess, probably because they didn't want us to escape! Each morning the manager unlocked the doors at six o'clock and we were allowed out to have a shower.

The manager always greeted us with, "Good morning. How are you black gins today?"

He expected us to reply with, "All right, boss."

I objected to calling him boss and answered, "I'm perfectly well, thank you, manager," to which he replied, "You call me boss like all the rest of the black boongs. You're no different from them.

I replied, "You may be the boss, but your right title is manager."

He got angry with me and said, "You call me boss like all the other blacks. "

In my usual impertinent manner, I said, "You are the manager of this place and I will address you as such." And so I called him 'manager' for the length of my stay.

A week after the tobacco incident, one of the women who was in my cottage went into labour at about six in the morning. I said to her, "You got pain?"

"Yes," she said. "I think the baby is coming."

"You are lucky," I said.

"Why?"

"The manager is coming to open up."

When he opened the door I said to him, "Good morning. I'm glad to see you."

"Why?"

"This lady is in labour. And I am ready to go for my shower."

He walked in and ordered her loudly, "Get up. What's the matter with you? Don't you want to work today?"

The woman continued to lie in the corner without speaking. I said to him, "Don't speak to her like that."

"We are not going to have another confrontation are we, Connie?"

"That all depends," I said as I ran to help her up. "Can't you see this woman is in labour?" He stood and watched while I struggled and all of a sudden he kicked her saying, "Get up you black gin."

I dropped my towel and toiletries on the floor and said to him, "You have done it now. Aren't you going to get this lady to the hospital? As you are the only one that gives orders around here, why don't you call some of the men to take her to the hospital. Get a stretcher and take the woman to the labour ward."

He was dumbfounded. Not only was I talking back to him, I was ordering him around. When he had finished opening all the dormitories, he sent a young fellow to the hospital to fetch a stretcher.

With all the commotion Hector arrived and said, "What's wrong now? You and boss in argument again." He looked at me as if to say, "What kind of a bull ant's nest is this ngumballa stirring up now?" but he said, "Boss in trouble now?"

I said, "Yes, Uncle, he is in proper trouble now – big trouble."

"Are you going to tell them big boss down Perth."

"Yes," I said. "Big boss church people."

Then he looked at me and noticing his concern, I said, "Uncle, you won't get in trouble. If any one gets in trouble it will be me."

"You can write letter?" he asked. "But you not allowed have paper to write letters. Where you gonna get paper."

"Don't worry. I'll get paper and pencil."

"I'll get writing paper and pencil for you. Tomorrow."

Then I went to tell the matron of the hospital who was also the manager's wife. I told her that Daphne was in labour and that I had had an argument with her husband and I told her that I was going to report him to the authorities in Perth. I apologised to her for doing it as she was the best gudiyar matron that ever worked in the Native Hospital. She felt for the Aboriginal people, loved her work and we knew that she was appalled at the atrocities that were going on in the Kimberleys.

As the matron went across to the hospital the manager told me that he wanted to see me at the Big House, as his home was called by the Aboriginal people.

I said, "I will come if my friend, the young girl from the mission, can come with me." He said it was all right if my friend came, so after breakfast we made our way to the Big House. All he said to me was, "Do not tell anyone what happened this morning or you will regret it."

I said to him, "Are you threatening me? You are already in trouble for what you said and did to Daphne. The police will be told about your threat to me, so be careful."

He said that he was finished with what he had to say to me and so my friend and I went back to our cottage.

The next night, I wrote a letter to the superintendent of the Forrest River Mission, one to the minister of Native Welfare in Perth and one to the Archbishop of the Church of England in Perth. My next task was to post the letters. As on the mission, all letters we wrote were read and if they were found to say anything critical they were not posted for us. If you wanted to get a message to someone you had to send them blackfella style or use the 'bush telegraph'. At the mission we had various schemes for getting letters out but at the Native Hospital I had not worked out a way to send letters. But I knew I would find a way.

# Ten

## *"That drover fella"*
### ❧ *My father* ❧

Next day a group of us were sitting in front of the cottages, chatting with Hector and his wife. Talk moved from one thing to another and of course to where we came from. I said to one of the women, named Rosie, "Where you come from Rose?"

"From Lumbunya Station."

"Do you know a man called Duncan McDonald?"

"Oh yes, that drover fella. Why?"

"People tell me that I am his daughter."

We talked on. Then I ventured my usual question. "Do you know anything about my mother?"

"No. The only woman I know is the one Duncan is married to now. He is married to a young girl called Maisie."

"Where Maisie from?"

"From Simpson Desert, on the Western Australia border. What your mother name?"

"Enid, known as Biddy," I replied eagerly. "Did you know her?"

"No," she said. The tone of her voice showed me that she did know but did not want to become involved. "Anyway if you want to know these things you should ask your father."

"Father! I haven't even met my father so how can I ask him? Anyway, how do you know my father?"

"Good stockman, that fella. He bin drove cattle from the Kimberleys to the Northern Territory and Queensland. He works for the cattle and station owners and he bringim cattle here to the Wyndham meatworks."

Suddenly we heard a car engine. We looked up and saw a green Model-T Ford turning into the compound. Hector casually glanced at me and said, "There father, bilong you?"

"Where ?" I asked

"In that car. That car bilong Duncan McDonald."

I could hardly contain my excitement. Someone had told my father that I was at the Native Hospital compound and here he was. The bush telegraph had worked well. His car stopped in front of the manager's house. I watched as a short man hopped out. Hector nudged me and said, "Yeah, that Duncan all right. That father bilong you."

The manager's house was built on stilts and there was a bell at the bottom of the steps. The short man walked over to the steps, rang the bell and out came the 'boss'. I heard him say, "Hello, Duncan. How are you?" After chatting for a while, the manager called out, "Connie McDonald, will you come over here?"

I stood up and went over, thinking to myself, "This must be my father. We have the same surname."

The manager then announced, "Connie, this is your father, Duncan McDonald." My father put his hand out and eagerly I extended mine. As I shook his hand, I said, "Pleased to meet you, Mr McDonald."

"What's this 'Mr McDonald' business? I'm your father."

Pleasantly surprised, I burst out, "I've always wondered who my father was. I've heard all sorts of things about you and I've always hoped to meet you one day. And now I have."

He turned around to the truck and spoke to the young woman sitting in the front seat. "Maisie, would you come over here please? I want you to meet my daughter."

Out jumped this young lass. I thought to myself, "That couldn't be my father's wife. I'm thirteen going on fourteen – she must be seventeen, no older." My father said, "This is my wife, Maisie."

So I greeted her, "How are you Maisie? Pleased to meet you." Maisie, who was extremely shy, hung her head and asked my father if she could go back to the car. He gave her leave and she climbed in and sat there quietly listening to our conversation. My father asked the manager if I could spend the weekend with them. The manager replied, "Yes, as long as you bring Connie back here by four on Sunday afternoon."

Hardly able to believe what was happening, I asked my father to wait while I went back to the cottage to collect a few belongings for the weekend. On my return, he opened the car door (one thing about my father, he was chivalrous). I sat beside Maisie as we drove back to Four Mile where my father and Maisie were staying with Uncle Sandy, Aunty Molly and their nine-year-old son, Alan.

Next day, my father announced at breakfast that he wanted to leave early to go into Wyndham. Maisie and I hurriedly ate our breakfast, Maisie telling me, "When Duncan says he wants to leave early, he means early."

Fortunately we were already dressed. We left Four Mile at seven, stopping every now and then for me to be introduced to relatives, and arrived in Wyndham at nine. My father was going to the post office to draw out some money to give to each of us. I asked my father to post my letters about the manager. "What's all this about?" he said.

So I told him I didn't like the way the manager was treating the people. My father looked at me in amazement and said, "What are you fussing about? It happens all the time."

This shocked me. I said, "Don't you care? What would you do if it happened to me?"

He looked at me and said, "I'd kill him."

"Well, father," I said, "you know how I feel." My father agreed to post the letters as he knew that if I posted them word would get back to the manager and I would be in big trouble. He then told us to go and buy what we wanted, left us and went down to the Wyndham wharf to see if he could get a casual job.

This was the first time I had money of my own and my first real experience of shopping for myself. It was an exciting adventure, buying pretty dresses made out of something other than flour bags or khaki. Maisie and I made a bee line for the shops starting with the three Chinese shops, Gee Yong Yet, Lee Tong's and Fong Fan's. Maisie took me to where the dresses were, we looked at them but she wasn't impressed with what we saw so she bustled me off saying, "Let's go to Mrs Flinder's shop." Here she chose a couple of dresses for me. The first was a yellow dress with black tulip patterns. When I tried it on, Maisie was delighted. She said, "Mrs Flinders, doesn't this dress suit Connie?"

Mrs Flinders replied, "My word, Connie, you do look nice in that dress. Yellow does suit you."

"You're not saying this because my stepmother says so?"

Then she looked at us both, and said to me, "Did you say this young lass is your stepmother?"

"Yes," I replied.

"Goodness," she exclaimed. "I thought you were sisters!" Maisie and I hugged each other and laughed. We bought dresses, underwear, combs, ribbons, hair-oil and hankies and a pair of shoes each.

That night we went to the pictures. While my father was buying the tickets, Maisie and I sauntered into the theatre parading our new dresses. Looking around, I chose what I thought would be good seats on the left side. While Maisie and I were waiting for my father, the usherette came up and I said, "We'll have those seats there."

She replied, "You can't sit there. Whites only this side – blacks on the other side."

At that moment, my father came up and said, "Who are you calling black?"

Turning beetroot, she said, "Is this your family?"

"Yes," he said, "of course this is my bloody family."

"Well," replied the girl, "you can have those seats at the back, over there in the corner."

My father, riled, stood his ground, "If we can't have those seats we'll leave." Maisie chipped in quietly, "Duncan, we'll take these seats here on the right." However, my father insisted that we sit where I had first chosen and so we did. This was my first taste of segregation. I was appalled. After we sat down, I whispered to Maisie, "Why didn't you tell me about this here seating arrangements, one for blacks and one for whites." Speaking in her quiet way, she replied, "I was trying to tell you but you are just like your father. You wouldn't listen."

78

We waited to see what would happen. The manager didn't come, we were not ordered out and the police were not contacted. We enjoyed the film, and I learned that I was like my father.

Over the next couple of weeks of my hospital stay, I learnt more about how alike we were. My cousin Alan often said to me, "Gee, you talk like your father." Like him, I wanted to find out about things. I wanted to find out about him, the family, his work, travelling and all that business. He wanted to find out all about the mission and why it was they didn't let him have me and why they didn't send me away for proper schooling. Both of us would tell it like it was. If my father said, "I am leaving at seven," he meant it. If I planned to leave at seven, I did. I found this amazing because I had never been brought up by him in any way.

I was thrilled to be spending weekends with my father. Never before had I been with my very own family. I wasn't sure how to act. I kept on waiting for someone to tell me what to do. Family life was quite different from life in the mission dormitory. In the family, I was not told what to do and what not to do all the time. In the family, I felt that people loved me and that it was all right for me to relax and be myself.

My father and Uncle Sandy were well educated. Their father, James McDonald taught all his children at home. They spent much of the following three weeks educating me about life and about the importance of becoming a supporter of the Labor party. "McDonalds," they said, "always vote Labor." This was all new to me as political issues were never discussed on the mission. I listened intently to them and found that I was inspired by their stories. They explained to me how the two-party system worked and told me that Aboriginal people not only had no right to vote but had no rights period.

"The only way your father and I can vote is to get citizenship rights. We have applied to the government of Western Australia many times but we are always knocked back," said Uncle Sandy.

I didn't understand what they meant by citizenship rights but their revelations distressed me as I believed that every human being had rights. I began to think more deeply about politics and began to see the magnitude of the political hold over my people. At the same time I started to realise that my McDonald heritage was a politically active one. After the picture show incident and the lengthy discussions with my father and uncle, I decided that I would educate myself so that I could fit in to the white community.

One day, while I was sitting in the hospital compound a convoy of government vehicles arrived unexpectedly. It was nearly three weeks after my father had posted my letters complaining about the manager and I hadn't thought any more about the letters or whether they had got to their destinations. While we watched them approaching us, Hector said, "Who are these people?"

I said, "They are government people from Perth. "

"How you know?"

"Only government people travel about in cars like that."

Ten minutes later, I was called over to the manager's house. I was introduced to representatives of the minister for Native Welfare and a representative of the Anglican Archbishop of Perth. I was pleased to see that the superintendent from Forrest River was also there, as he was a very understanding man. Pointing to my letter he said to me, "Is this true?"

"Yes," I said.

Then he produced a petition from the Forrest River Mission that had been signed by former Native Hospital patients who had had experiences like mine. The officials asked me many questions and then we joined the people who had assembled outside to find out what was happening. At first, the people were reluctant to say anything, so I said to them, "Now is your chance. Tell your stories."

After a long time, the woman who had the baby came forward and spoke about what had happened to her. Then the others came forward, including Uncle Hector, who had witnessed many incidents. "All the time, this happen," he said.

The man from Native Welfare questioned the manager, "Is this so?" Unable to deny it, the manager agreed that the stories were true. His employment was then terminated and he was told to leave within two weeks.

I was pleased with my efforts at being someone brave enough to speak up for my people. I decided that my actions had proved that I had the ability to be politically active in my own right.

# Eleven

## *"Forget about that tying the knot"*
### ∽ *Maisie* ∽

While convalescing at the hospital, I went on a picnic with my family. I had been on many a picnic with the mission people, but this was my first family picnic. I didn't know what to expect, how to react or how to cope with this new experience with these people who were my family.

Uncle Sandy asked us where we would like to go and Aunty Molly said, "What about we all go to Twelve Mile where those lagoons are. We can hunt for duck and geese eggs. It is their laying season." We all thought this was a good idea and so we loaded up the two cars. Uncle Sandy, Aunty Molly and their son, Alan, in their car and my father, Maisie and me in our car. We passed plenty of game, wild turkeys, kangaroos, wallabies, wild ducks but we didn't stop to kill any as it was eggs we were planning to hunt. On the way out, Maisie began to open up to me and was eager to find out what mission life was like. It became clear to me that my father had told her very little about me and that she thought it wiser not to ask him too much.

On our arrival at Twelve Mile, Aunty Molly carefully scanned the area until she spotted a clump of shady trees and scrub. "That looks like a nice spot. We could have our picnic there," she said.

The men spread the tarpaulin on the ground and we women collected some wood for a fire. Nearby was a little flowing stream of cool clear water which we used to fill the billy. Aunty Molly made the tea and poured it into enamel mugs. Handing me a new green mug she instructed me, "Each person has their own mug and this is to be your mug every time you visit us." Putting the sugar down in the middle of the tarpaulin, she added, "Help yourselves

81

to sugar, I have to fetch something from the car."

She then produced a tin tray covered with a tea towel which she removed to display sandwiches and Sao biscuits topped with vegemite, cheese, pork and plum jam. As custom demanded, she offered the tray first to the men, making sure they had as much as they wanted. Only then did she put the tray down in front of us women. It seemed to me that Aunty Molly was a superb organiser of picnics. I was soon to find that she was a clever organiser of other things as well. As soon as we had eaten, Aunty Molly picked up the mugs, took them to the stream to wash them and then announced to the men folk, "I think you men had better go out and do the hunting while we women stay here and talk about women's business."

"Yeah, that sounds all right," they said and off they went in the direction of the lagoons taking young Alan with them.

"What now?" I wondered to myself.

Aunty Molly then explained, "I got a few things to do here. I have to sort out the food and arrange things for when we have lunch. Then I'll have a bit of a rest. While I'm doing that I'll leave you two together so that you can talk and get used to each other and then the next time you two meet you won't be so shy of each other."

Maisie and I sat down on the tarpaulin and I began with, "Where do you come from?"

"From the Simpson Desert, on the Western Australia side – Gordon Downs."

"Oh!" and I paused, then said, "How did you meet my father?"

And so Maisie told me their story.

"I met him on one of his droving trips. One day I was cutting wood and I cut my toe," and she showed me the scar. "Anyway, I nearly cut it off and was bleeding badly so my mother and father took me up to the station manager's who arranged for us to catch a little plane into the hospital. I was very frightened as they stuck the needle in and stitched up my toe.

"My parents then took me down to the township to buy some food and clothes and everything else. Duncan and the other drovers were in town as they had just finished delivering cattle. They saw us go into the shop and a little while later they came in. All of a sudden Duncan looked at me and I looked at Duncan and he walked over."

I interrupted Maisie, "Wasn't he afraid – with your parents there?"

"No. As soon as he walked over my mother and father went around to another side of the shop pretending to look at other things."

"What happened then?"

"He said, 'Hello,' and asked me if I was married and I said, 'No, I am not married. I am only a young girl?' "

"Did you ask him if he was married?" I asked.

"No," she said. "I don't ask questions?"

"Well, you should have." Again, I interrupted her story with my questioning. "By the way, how old are you now?"

"I'm seventeen, nearly eighteen," Maisie replied. "When Duncan found I wasn't married, he told me that he wanted to marry me. I was really shy and surprised so I reminded him that he had only just met me. 'Oh well,' he said. 'You just think about it. We are staying in town for a little while then we are heading to Alice Springs.' "

"Where did my father stay in Alice Springs?"

"He stayed with a relative down at Havertrees Gap."

"Where is Havertrees Gap?"

"That's where they've got a big reserve where all the Aborigines live. They were put there by Welfare because Aborigines are not allowed to live in the town. Anyway your father then said to me 'How long will you be here?'

" 'Not too long,' I replied. 'Just a couple of days and then we're going back home.' So Duncan told me to come back to that shop so he could see me before I went ."

"Did you tell your parents what my father said?" I asked.

"Yes. When we were going back to where we were staying, my mother and father said to me, 'What was that Duncan McDonald saying to you?' So I told them he wanted to marry me. My father was really shocked. 'What! Marry Duncan!' Even though I knew nothing at all about Duncan I couldn't help replying, 'What's wrong with him Dad?'

"'Plenty!' My Dad was so rattled he could hardly speak.

"'Well, I don't know about these things but I think I'd like to marry him.' Then my mother said, 'Duncan is a good worker. He droves cattle; he works very hard; he earns a lot of money and I think he can take good care of you.' So my mother and I were talking women's talk and she said to me, 'If you think that you would like to go with Duncan, you go.'

"The day before my parents and I were to go back to Gordon Downs, we went back to the shop where I first met your father and there he was. He said to me, 'Well Maisie, the boys and I are leaving now. Are you coming with me? Did you ask your parents?'

"Now it was Duncan's turn to be surprised, 'Yes I did and they said I can go.' I already had a few things packed and Duncan said, 'You don't need clothes. I've already bought a case of things for you.' I kissed my mother and father goodbye and I went with Duncan."

"Weren't you sad to leave your parents, your brothers and sisters?" I asked.

"Yes," she said, "but to my mind, Duncan seemed a good man who would look after me and care for me."

"And has he so far?"

And she said,"Yeah. He's a very good man."

"So what happened then?"

"Well, I thought I would have to ride a horse and so I said to Duncan, 'I don't want to ride a horse,' but Duncan said, 'Don't worry; I've got two trucks, a big one for the horses and a smaller one for transport for us and the stores.'"

"Weren't you scared going off like that to a different part of the country?"

"Oh, yeah! I suppose so but we travel about a lot so it didn't really worry me."

"But to Alice Springs, Maisie? The Northern Territory is a long way from the Gordon Downs!"

"Yes, I know. But I wasn't frightened because I knew Duncan would look after me. Anyway, when we got to Wave Hill, Duncan popped in and asked the sergeant of police if he would marry us. He said he would, so we were getting ready and Duncan changed his mind. He said, 'Oh, its a bit of a hassle; let's forget about it.' So he went to the police sergeant and said, 'Forget about that tying the knot, Maisie and I will just live.'

"So the policeman said, 'Please yourself. But I want to tell you something. You are to look after this girl because she is only seventeen years old. If we hear that you have been mistreating her you will be in serious trouble and she will be taken away from you by the courts.'

"'Don't worry about that, sergeant, I'm aiming to look after Maisie.' So that was that. I was glad to be on my way after all that fuss and bother."

"Were you frightened?"

"I wasn't frightened, until we came back to Wyndham and Sandy's place. I hadn't met your father's brother and I was wondering, 'Will they like me, will they want me and make me welcome?' I was so scared; I was hiding behind Duncan. Your Aunty Molly came and said, 'I'm Molly, Sandy's wife. Come on, don't be frightened. Welcome to our place,' and she kissed me, and then Sandy came and shook hands with me. I wasn't frightened any more because your Aunty Molly is such a lovely person. During the next couple of days, we went into Wyndham and Duncan started introducing me to his other relatives?"

"Like who?"

"George, and Ivy Carter and their family, the Talbots."

"Oh, I didn't know my father had so many relatives. The only relatives I knew about were his brother Sandy and Sandy's wife, Molly and their son, Alan," I said. I thought I would try to bring up the subject of my mother, so I said to Maisie, "Did my father tell you anything about my mother."

"Yeah, he told me that he had been living with your mother."

"Did he tell you what her name was?"

"Yes, he said her name was Biddy and that she was a young girl like me."

"And did he tell you that he had a daughter?"

"Yes. He said that Biddy had a daughter by him and that her name was Connie. When I asked him where you were he said that you were on the Forrest River Mission and that the missionaries were taking care of you because when your mother died, they took over looking after you. He also told me that your mother was only fifteen when you were born."

" Did my father ever go to visit me?"

"No, he never went to Forrest River when I was with him. I used to keep saying to him 'Why don't we go and see your daughter?' But he would reply, 'I am not allowed to go to the mission.' And when I'd ask him why he would say, 'It's got nothing to do with you. It shouldn't worry you.' And so I didn't pester him any more."

"Maisie," I said, "Did he tell you anything about my mother, where she came from, who were her people, what was her tribe name and why she died?"

"No, I don't know anything. I don't press Duncan on these things."

"But you might have wanted to know what my mother was like."

All she could tell me was that my father had told her that my mother was a very pretty young lady, and that unfortunately she had died when she was quite young.

"Have you ever seen a photo of my mother?"

Before answering she hesitated, I said, "Why are you frightened to answer ?"

"Because Duncan would know I told you."

"Don't worry. I'll stand by you. I'll tell him that I was pestering you."

"Yeah, your father has a photo of her. You ask him to show you. Sometimes he gets a sad look in his eyes when he looks at her photo."

"Does that worry you?"

"No. She was Duncan's woman and she had his daughter. I don't worry."

And so we talked on till Aunty Molly came and said, "Do you two know each other now? Are you getting on well?"

"Oh yes, Aunty Molly, we are getting on real well," I replied enthusiastically.

"That's good," said Aunty Molly. "What about we make a cup of tea?"

By this time it was getting towards lunchtime, we were feeling hungry and there was no sign of the men. So Aunty said, "What about we have some damper and syrup and a cup of tea and some of these chicken's eggs that I boiled up and a bit of meat?"

The first thing I asked my father on their return was, "Do you have a photo of my mother?" And he did have a photo, taken by an old box brownie camera. He pulled it out of his wallet and showed it to me, saying, "That was your mother."

Looking at it, I protested, "It can't be. That's just a little girl."

He became angry and said, "That was your mother." I was bewildered and I started to think that maybe the reason no one wanted to tell me anything about my mother was because she was so young. I decided to accept things as they were and try to get to know my father better.

Soon after the picnic, my hospital stay ended and I returned to Forrest River, a changed person. I withdrew into my own thoughts as I reflected on the happenings at the Native Hospital. Seeing the photo of my mother had had a traumatic effect on me as before that I hadn't realised that she was so young when I was born. On the other hand, it made me feel that she had been a real person. I stopped imagining what she might look like and pictured her as I had seen her in the photo.

I was happy that my father had shown me the photo. It made me feel a little closer to him and to realise that whatever the situation was that brought them together and made them my parents, there was no point in my being resentful. At the same time I sensed that my father was struggling to come to terms with my very existence.

When I returned to Forrest River, the tribal people and the missionaries noticed the change in me straight away. All around the mission, the village people were saying "What's wrong with Connie?" Tribal people were saying, 'What's wrong with that ngumballa?" I no longer needed to fantasise about what my mother looked like or how old she was and gradually the questions about my mother became less frequent. Instead I began to focus more on myself and on my future. I became a quieter and more reserved person and remained that way until I left the Kimberleys.

I could see more clearly who I was and what I could become. I felt a deep sadness because I knew that the current system meant that neither the training nor the opportunities were likely to come my way.

I used to dream that someday, somehow I would be given the chances I needed. In one of my imaginings, a government official would arrive at Forrest River and say, "Connie, we are giving you the opportunity to become whatever you want to be." I would then say to him, "I want to go away to teachers' training college and become a trained teacher." He would say, "It will all be arranged." I always felt so happy as I contemplated this prospect and then sad as I realised that it was a hopeless dream. The impossibility of my situation did not deter me from continuing to hope that eventually I would find my rightful place in this world, be it as a teacher or in some other role.

Another of my dreams had me living with my father and Maisie, going to school at Wyndham where there were gudiyars and Aborigines learning together. In this fantasy, I would be a happy child in an ordinary family. Dormitories did not exist. I would see myself listening to my father's droving stories, cooking meals with Maisie and going on family picnics. My rebellious streak was still there but I was becoming more of a thinker.

A couple of months after I first met my father and Maisie, he wrote to me saying that as there were no jobs in Wyndham, he was going back to Alice Springs. His letter said that he was pleased he had met me and that he hoped that we would meet up again some day.

I was pleased to receive my first letter from my father. Deep down, I didn't dare to expect that this meeting with him would lead to something more permanent. Still, I carried that letter around with me for many years hoping that this was not to be the end of our association and that someday he really would accept me as his daughter.

# Twelve

## *"There was no life in the bones"*
### ❧ *Anthropology* ❧

The government often sent doctors, dentists, eye specialists, naturalists and anthropologists to the Aboriginal reserves and missions. The police were also included in these intrusions into our private lives. We were observed, examined, researched into, measured, photographed, sampled, questioned and written about as though we were not human beings and didn't have any feelings of shame or emotion. Government and mission policy was that any white people coming to the mission for whatever reason were not to divulge any information about their visit to the 'natives'. I found this policy quite disturbing and often wondered about the future of myself and my people.

When I was in my early teens, we had a visit from anthropologists from Sydney. We were told that these men were scientists and the purpose of their visit was to study the Aborigines and their culture. I was very curious about what all this meant. Three days after they arrived, they were taken up to the old people in the camp who were of particular interest because they were still living in a semi-tribal situation. I guessed that they would be spending the whole day with the camp people.

I decided that this was my opportunity to find out what these city gudiyars were on about. Having coaxed a couple of friends to stand watch for me, I managed to sneak away from the dormitory and stealthily went through the bushes to the anthropologists' house. I crept in the back door and began foraging around for some information. It took me a long time as I took care to put everything back in its right place after I examined it. A large cardboard box caught my eye. On one side it had the words 'Anthropology Items'. I quickly opened the box and saw a folder. I was about to open the folder when I realised that that if I didn't move on, I would be caught. Reluctantly, I closed the box and made for the door.

A couple of days later my curiosity got the better of me. I went to the dormitory matron and said, "I want to watch those gentlemen do their work."

"I'm glad you are taking an interest in what the scientists are doing. Perhaps you may learn something about yourself and your people." I thought, "Bingo, matron! You have hit the nail on the head. That is exactly what I am aiming to do. I want to find out all about anthropology." But I said, "Thank you, matron," and hurried off down the road feeling very pleased with myself for pulling off such a smart one.

This time I knocked innocently on the front door. One of the anthropologists opened it. "I have permission from matron to come and watch you at work. I want to learn something of what you are doing."

He was amazed but invited me in. On the verandah, they had set out various items on trestles and each item was marked fragile and classified. In one corner there was an empty trestle and under it were four cardboard boxes. He introduced me to the rest of the team and then said, "Connie, would you like to help put some of the things out on the trestles?"

"Yes."

"You can start with those boxes under the table, beginning with box number one."

I opened the box and eagerly looked in. To my horror, I saw a human skull. Terrified, I let go of the lid and screaming loudly rushed out the door. The three men jumped up and followed me wondering what had happened. Matron was standing on her front verandah, watching all the commotion. As I passed her house she called to me to come and talk over the problem. "You look as if you have seen a ghost."

"I did."

"What do you mean, you did?" she asked.

"Well one of them gudiyars asked me if I would like to help," and I told her the story, ending with the announcement that I had seen a human head.

"You mean a skeleton of a human head?"

"Yeah, whatever. I did see it and I got a big fright and I'm not going back to those anthropologists any more. They had dead people's bones in their house."

Trying to pacify me, matron said, "There was no life in the bones. They would and could not possibly hurt you."

But I am an Aboriginal and had often been told by our tribal people that when you died your spirit was still there while your bones were still visible and that your spirits stayed in the bones until such time as the tribal elders sang them on their way to their final resting place. As I stood there I remembered a time years ago when we were on walkabout. I had been wandering through the bush with an older girl and I noticed that she was hanging back well behind me and seemed very quiet. She knew where we were heading but I hadn't learnt. Then I came upon a forbidden thing. I turned around and said, "What's this?"

Then, as a spear landed right in front of me, the girl said, "It is just a warning. You go any further and it won't be in front of you, it will be through you." We went back home and the tribal people got the bones and put them together like a jigsaw puzzle. They had a big ceremony and then buried the bones in the ground.

It didn't matter what matron said to me. My curiosity for anthropology came to a very quick end.

# Thirteen

## *"Service with a smile"*
## ∽ *To Alice Springs* ∽

In 1948, there were some changes at Forrest River. Our new superintendent was the Reverend Keith Coaldrake. He was trying to get away from the harsh regime by introducing more humane ways of dealing with the people. He encouraged many of the young men and women to go and live with their parents. This made the people very happy as they were a family once more. On his arrival, he officially appointed Aunty Louisa and Uncle Robert to the mission staff and he instructed that hessian dresses were not to be used for punishments any more.

One day, matron called out to me, "Connie McDonald, the superintendent would like to see you now."

I walked in. "What have I done now?" I said.

"It's not what you've done, Connie. Sit down and listen to what I have to say. A couple of months ago the missionaries and the staff all got together and had a meeting."

Because he was still only new to the mission, his perception of me was of someone who had a halo and was sprouting wings. Little did he know that I was a rebel at heart. He had no idea of the problems I had caused previous missionaries. "We are impressed with your enthusiasm about helping in the school and Miss Willington thinks that you will make a good teacher. Not only that. From our observations, you are very intelligent and we thought that you might like to further your education."

"What!" I interrupted, in astonishment. "Go back to school?"

"Yes, isn't that your intention? You told Miss Willington one day you wished you were back at school to learn some more."

"That's right!"

He smiled more broadly, "Your wish has come true. We have applied to the Native Welfare Department in Perth for permission to send you over to Alice Springs."

"But I've already left school."

"That doesn't matter. Do you want to further your education?"

"Yes, I do. When will I be going?"

"In January next year. Everything has been arranged. We've got in touch with the deaconess running the hostel for Aboriginal boys and girls at Alice Springs and they have a vacancy and would be pleased to have you."

Astounded at this wonderful news, all I could say was, "Oh that will be good. How long will I be there for?"

"For two years."

I couldn't believe that something like this could happen to me and I could hardly contain how I felt.

"Everything will be organised for you. The mission will buy you a case and any things you might need. Miss Willington is going to help you to make some dresses and get things arranged."

I went back to the dormitory and all the girls gathered around me and said "What did Judja (father) want you for?"

"I'm going to Alice Springs," I proudly announced, knowing that neither I nor the others knew where Alice Springs was.

"But what do you want to go to Alice Springs for?"

"Judja said that all the staff had a meeting and they want me to go and finish my education."

"What do you want to finish your education for? You're not going to get anywhere."

Soon after that Reverend Coaldrake went into Wyndham and bought some rolls of material which he gave to Miss Willington. I picked out the materials I liked, and for the next few months Miss Willington and I sewed dresses and nighties on her treadle sewing machine.

I was excited as I packed all these new clothes in my brand new port. By this time word had got around on the 'bush telegraph' and everyone on the mission and in the village knew of my plans. On the first Sunday in December, Reverend Coaldrake announced that I was going away to school to further my education and asked the people to pray for me that I could learn more and one day be able to help them back on the mission.

All the people were saying, "What's she going away for? Doesn't she want to stay? She belongs here. Who does she think she is? Does she want to be a black whitefella?"

These comments didn't hurt me because I was used to hearing this kind of thing. I knew of others who had given up wanting to improve themselves because they couldn't face such criticisms from their own people. Because I saw myself as being on my own and not really belonging to anybody, it was easier for me to ignore the criticisms.

I was glad to have the support of Coralie Roberts, the assistant teacher. She arranged a farewell party for me at the Dadaway Lagoon. She told all the children to lay bullrushes on the ground to represent a table. As the sun went down and the cool of the evening came, we sat down to a sumptuous meal of bush food and mission fare. Coralie then stood to make a speech.

"We should all be pleased that Connie has been given this opportunity to go and further her education. We must all be grateful to God and pray for her."

Finally the day came to leave. It was the beginning of the school year in 1949. The launch was there at the jetty. I stepped on board with all the passengers. Everyone from the mission came down to the jetty to farewell me. As the launch left the jetty, Coralie's encouraging face stood out like a beacon. She stood as though she was the only one there, waving to me with great joy as the children jumped up around her.

Aunty Dudgulla, Mummy Nora and her family were all there weeping. Everyone else just stood there, and I guess they were probably still trying to come to terms with my decision. The only ones besides Coralie actually waving goodbye were the missionaries.

Never before had I felt so free as I looked back at the disappearing mission with its gaol-like dormitories that to me symbolised punishment and domination. While I was glad to leave Forrest River and the dormitory system, I knew that there would

94

still be dormitories at Alice Springs and that I would still be under gudiyar rule. I knew that I was still a ward of the state and under government regulations and I knew that wherever I went I was still not really free.

Nevertheless it pained me then, and it pains me today, that I was given an opportunity that Coralie, with all her abilities, should have had. Coralie would have made a wonderful school principal. In 1989, when I spent a week with Judja and Marna Coaldrake in Samford, Queensland, he said, "You'd go far and wide to find a person like Coralie. She was a good girl. If I had come to Forrest River when she was young, I would have arranged to send her away for more education."

That night, I stayed with a family in Wyndham but as I was so excited I found it very hard to sleep. At three o'clock, I decided that, as I couldn't get back to sleep, I would stoke up the copper ready for the morning baths. The mother heard me and said, "Ngumballa, what are you doing?" I replied, "I'm going to have a bath so I'll be ready." She couldn't talk me out of it so she went back to sleep . As I sat around waiting for the water to get hot, I heard the rest of the family sleeping. Later, when the father sat down to the breakfast I had prepared he said, "Girlie, you were up very early."

"Well, I don't want to miss the plane."

The airport was at Six Mile and we had to catch the airport bus. Some of my friends caught the bus too, so they could wave goodbye. Uncle Sandy, Aunty Mollie and Alan came in their car. At the airport, we were laughing and crying until I looked around at the various planes and asked an Aboriginal worker, "Which one is the plane to Alice Springs?"

Pointing, he said, "That little one."

"That little thing? It's smaller than the Flying Doctor's plane."

"Oh yeah, yeah. Ernie Connellan's Airways from Alice Springs."

"How many passengers does that little plane carry?"

"Six, seven at the most"

The pilot then said, "All aboard!"

To me, the trip to Alice Springs was like going to the other side of the world. A real adventure! I climbed aboard and positioned myself right up near the front of the plane. The pilot announced, "We are on the bread-and-mail run. That means we will land at every station." It meant too that we picked up and dropped mail, passengers, food and other items. No sooner were we up in the air than we seemed to be landing again.

The plane landed first at Ivanhoe Station where they had just had some rain. The aerodrome was right next to the homestead, so we all walked onto the verandah to have morning tea, fresh baked scones and a hot cup of tea. I tried to count the stations Ivanhoe, Rosewood, Lissadel...but I lost count.

That night we landed at Wave Hill, where we were to stay for the night. The station manager and his Aboriginal assistant picked us up in their truck. On the way, this old fellow from Wave Hill said to me, "What your skin name?"

"Nungulla."

"What your mother name?"

"Biddy. That's all I know, as I don't know where she comes from. My father is Duncan McDonald."

"Tch, tch, tch," was all he said.

"What's the matter? Do you know Duncan?"

All he did was nod his head. "Do you know anything about my father?"

"Yeah, I know plenty about your father."

"Well, could you tell me?"

"No. You're too young. When you grow up, you'll know all about him."

I thought, "Here's this phrase again!"

As we drew closer to the station, he called out to the Aboriginal people in their language, and the manager pulled up in front of the hotel, saying, "You are all booked in to my hotel for tonight." Some Aboriginal women came up and the tribal man said to me, "These are all nungullas. They are all your tribal sisters."

"But," I said, "I'm from a different tribe."

96

"That doesn't matter. Your skin name nungulla, isn't it?"

"Yes."

"Then these are your sisters and they are going to look after you. Girl, you don't want to stay at the hotel. No good people there. No good."

So I went to the desk and said, "Are there any spare beds on the verandah as I am too scared to sleep up in the hotel. If I stay down here these women will look after me." So a bed was made up for me on the verandah by one of the ladies. I felt warm and safe with all those nungulla sisters around.

I was woken early in the morning by Andy's wife, Vera, who was also a nungulla. I asked her what the time was and she replied, "Picanniny daylight," and I thought, "That's about three o'clock." Vera had a large pot of boiling water ready to make me a nice hot bath. "Hop in the tub," she said. There I was being scrubbed up with my nungulla tribal sisters making sure that I had a good bath – washing my hair and everywhere else, at the same time they were nattering away in their language. I thought to myself, "Gee, this is service with a smile."

At around five o'clock, the hotel manager came to the verandah and told me, "Breakfast will be ready early, as you are leaving at seven. You can eat any time you like." Vera then escorted me to the hotel dining room. I was served by an Aboriginal waitress.

Two stops after Wave Hill, I was the only passenger left so the pilot called out, "Are you enjoying the trip, Miss McDonald?"

"Yes," I replied, thinking to myself, "Fancy this fella calling me Miss!" I felt it an honour to be called Miss McDonald and I could sense that this man had a genuine respect for me.

During this leg of the journey we struck a storm and the pilot called out, "Miss, are you frightened?"

"No," I yelled back.

"Well, would you like to come and sit in the front then?" I scrambled up the front to sit with him thinking to myself that this was really adventurous.

"Do you know where you are going?" I asked.

"No," he informed me, "and if the lightning hits us we are finished." I thought to myself, "He is talking like a black fella." If we inquire about an Aboriginal person and they are no longer alive, we will be told in the Kimberley lingo that, "They are finished."

We continued along in the dark for about an hour and a half until at last there was daylight again and the pilot enquired, "Were you frightened?"

"Oh no," I said. "I thought that was the most adventurous thing that has ever happened to me."

"Just as well you were the only passenger this time."

"Why?" I asked.

"Well, Miss McDonald," he explained, "during storms I've carried passengers that were screaming and begging me to land, crying and saying their last prayers."

"Were they really?" I asked, genuinely amazed and almost sorry I had missed out on witnessing such drama. "I thought it was just wonderful!"

"I'm glad to have had a passenger that actually enjoyed riding out a storm," he laughed and added jovially, "I think most of my passengers in storms must have been Roman Catholics."

Puzzled, I said, "Roman Catholics! Why Roman Catholics?"

"Because they sit in their seats reciting lots of Hail Marys," and he laughed louder.

Our journey continued with several stops until we approached Alice Springs around four. I didn't sleep a wink in the plane as I didn't want to miss anything. Often as we landed, we would see kangaroos and emus running across the countryside frightened by the noise of our little 'five seater'. I felt very important when the stockmen waved to us as we came into view.

As we flew over the Alice, I was overwhelmed by the beauty of the hills and ranges dazzling in the afternoon sun. I had never seen such a variety of colour and texture. I remembered the rugged beauty of my own Kimberleys but here was something totally different. The pilot flew over the town, circled round and dipped the wings so we could get a bird's-eye view of the township. Whereupon he flew out over the McDonnell Ranges, dipped again and said, "Going to St Mary's Aboriginal Hostel are you, Miss McDonald?"

"Yes," I replied, not taking my eyes off the breath-taking views.

"There it is there," he said as the plane descended.

Boys and girls and even adults were running out to the playground and waving at us. They had all been told that Connie McDonald was on that plane.

"Is anyone coming to pick you up?"

"Yes," I said. "Deaconess Heath, Sister Eileen."

"Oh yes. I know Sister Eileen very well," and looking out the window as we came to a stop, he said, "There she is over there standing beside the grey ute with a young girl beside her."

I picked up my case, disembarked slowly and walked over to Sister Eileen and the girl. Sister Eileen took my case from me, shook hands and introduced herself, "This is June Bostock (later Satour), one of our senior girls." As Sister Eileen drove in to St Mary's, all the children ran down to meet us chasing alongside while they called out, "Hello Connie! Welcome Connie."

I was very taken by this warm and timely welcome, coming as it did at the same time as a strong rush of homesickness. No sooner had we climbed out of the ute than the tea bell rang and the students were lining up, hungrily chatting outside the dining room.

"Would you like to have a shower before tea?" asked Sister Eileen.

"Yes, I would," I replied wondering if all this lining up meant I was out of the fat and into the frying pan. Feeling refreshed by the shower I put on clean clothes and a brave face and followed June to the dining room. As soon as I walked in Sister Eileen said, "Attention please everyone! I want you to meet the new girl. This is Connie McDonald from the Forrest River Mission in Western Australia and I would like you all to make her welcome."

Sunday was always a special day at the hostel with roast meat and vegetables for dinner and icecream and gramma pie for sweets. I ate as much as I could but I was very tired and was relieved when Sister Eileen suggested I might like to go to bed. Once more, the senior girl escorted me to the dormitory where I dropped onto my bed and went straight to sleep.

We had to get up early, do our chores before morning service and then line up again for breakfast. Then we finished off our chores before morning prayer. I didn't have any chores that morning because Sister Eileen wanted to take me into Alice Springs to buy school shoes and books. The school bus came and all the other children climbed on and went off to school. I was dressed in my uniform, a white blouse and blue tunic. Proudly, I told Sister Eileen that I would buy the shoes myself as I had some money.

Equipped with all my new belongings, I accompanied Sister Eileen to meet the principal of my new school, Alice Springs Public School which was attended by all the children in Alice Springs, black or white. The huge playground and the large number of children overwhelmed me but in the playground I met my cousin Fay Andrews (now Hampton). The principal showed me to my classroom where my teacher, Miss Roberts, said to the girls and boys, "Meet your new classmate. Miss Connie McDonald. She has come all the way from the Church of England mission in Forrest River, Western Australia."

In unison, the class said, "Hello Connie," and I said in a tiny voice, "Hello, boys and girls."

# Fourteen

## "The three Rs! That's all they want us to learn"
### ∾ St Mary's Hostel ∾

The first few weeks at St Mary's I was homesick, longing to go back to the life I knew at Forrest River. Then one day, I noticed a green Model-T Ford coming into the hostel grounds and I knew straight away that it was my father. He went in to see Sister Eileen who knew him very well. I was excited to think that my father was taking the time to come and see me.

Sister Eileen called out, "Connie, would you like to come over here. Your father wants to speak to you."

I hurried over and, as before, I put my hand out to shake my father's hand but, to my amazement, he not only took my hand but drew me to him and embraced me. I felt wonderful, and thought that maybe he at last realised that this was his child he was embracing and not just someone who had his name.

My father had come to see if I would like to spend the weekend with Maisie and him. I had heard Maisie talk about Havertrees Gap and how it was a reserve on the outskirts of Alice Springs. We pulled up in front of a big house. A man and his wife came out to greet us. My father introduced me to them but I was so shy I couldn't talk.

He took my arm and said, "Come round the back. We have a room where we stay when we are in Alice Springs. Maisie is there." I was amazed at how mature Maisie had grown. She was expecting their first child and I was really excited at the prospect of having a brother or sister. Almost every weekend after that I visited them. I always appreciated the fact that my father would send a note to school with my cousin to tell me when he was in town.

Having been brought up on the mission, bonding was very difficult for me. I was suddenly confronted with the fact that I had to play my part in developing a bond with my father and I didn't know where to begin. I would ask the girls at the hostel, "How do you love your mother and father?"

"It's only natural," they would say.

I listened to my father's droving stories and Maisie's stories about her childhood and the hopes they both had for the new baby. When Maisie went to bed, my father and I would often talk for many hours, especially on political issues. By all this listening, I gradually came to understand what belonging to a family meant. Here at last, were two people who loved each other and who included me in their love. Although I had received love as a child on the mission it did not seem to me to be real love. I would think, "These people are just loving me because they have to." I did not realise that love was a real thing until my visits with my father and Maisie.

My father did not bring up the subject of marriage and children with me because he could see that I had my own views on what I wanted to do with my life. One day I asked him what he thought about my getting married in the future and he said, "It's your business. It's your life. Only you can make that decision."

When my father spoke about politics, however, he did not digress from any important views that he wanted me to learn. He seemed to think that politics was very important and that everybody should know how the country was being governed. I often plied him with questions like, "What about Aboriginal issues?" or "What standing have we in the white community of today?" He would say, "As I said before, Aborigines are not allowed to vote and have no rights, full stop."

At the hostel, I would bring up the subject of politics and the boys and girls would say, "We aren't allowed to talk about those government things." They thought I was a rabble rouser but this didn't stop me from putting political issues to them. I would say, "You fellas want to stay in one place. You don't want to grow?"

Maisie would often say, "You are getting more and more like your father," and sometimes she would get annoyed and moan, "I wish you were more like your mother." But I was proud to be told that I was like my father. At least it meant that I had an identity. It was uncanny how alike we were. We thought the same and we had a similar temperament even though our personalities clashed occasionally.

We were talking at the hostel one day and my friend June told me, "We came down here to learn the three Rs not to learn about government things. We hate the word government."

I said, "The three Rs! That's all they want you to learn! The government don't want you to go any further. Well, I'm gonna learn more than the three Rs. My father says its important for me to learn about the government because I might find myself working for them one day. I'm going to make my father proud of me." Then I asked them, "What are you going to do in the future?"

The girls all said, "We want to find a good husband and get married and have children."

"There's nothing wrong with that," I told them.

Most of the boys then piped up and said, "We want to be good stockmen and maybe one day we might own the stations."

"You fellas are in the dreaming."

June then asked, "What are you going to do? Are you going to get married and have children?"

"Maybe some day. I'm going to make a way for myself in this here white society first."

June replied, "Connie, you are in the dreaming," and they all laughed.

Some time later, I found out that quite a few of the fathers of these boys and girls were interested in politics, but they didn't talk about it like the McDonalds did, because they feared a backlash from the white society. Occasionally my father would ask if he could take a couple of my friends for a picnic with me and he would talk to them about politics. They would say, "Yeah, that's what Connie told us."

The political discussions between my father and I were often fiery. I can't remember what any of our arguments were about but I do remember feeling sorry for Maisie having to listen to us. My father always harped on about how I needed to listen to what he had to say. One night he said, "Connie you need to know all about politics so that you can hold your own in the white society. Let's face it, you are not going to live on Forrest River all your life. The day will come when you leave and you will need to stand on your own two feet."

In my usual cheeky manner, I said, "What two feet?"

"Are you trying to be funny?" he shouted.

"No father," I replied.

At that moment, Maisie appeared. She called out, "Duncan, you come to bed. And Connie, you go to bed too."

My father went meekly. So did I. For the first time in my life I quietly did as I was told. Later, as I was lying in bed, I thought to myself, "Maisie is being a mother to me. She loves me." Maisie, even though she was so young, had accepted me as her daughter. Until that night, any correcting of me was left to my father. That night life changed for me, dramatically. Maisie became my mother.

Next morning, Maisie knocked on my bedroom door and said, "Connie, breakfast is ready." I opened the door and walked into the dining room. Looking at both of them I said, "Good morning, father and mother." Maisie immediately got up off the chair, came to me and embraced me, weeping, "I didn't think that you would ever call me mother."

My father stood there stunned. After a while he came over and put his arms around me and Maisie. He didn't say a word but we were all crying. I thought to myself. "This is it. We are united as a family." As well as having the profoundest respect for Maisie, I began to love her deeply. I realised that maybe at last humility was possible for me.

One morning before school, when I was sitting reading a book in the lunch shed, my cousin Fay came calling out, "Connie, Connie, Aunty Maisie's in hospital. She's had a little boy and his name is Colin."

"True?" I said. I was so excited that I hugged her. "Now I have a little brother that I can call my own."

Colin's birth changed my outlook on life. I doted on Colin during my stay in Alice Springs. I felt that I was not alone any more. Maisie seemed to sense that I needed to bond with my little brother. She would bring him up to the school at lunchtime several times a week. Usually she would bring a few treats for me as well but I was not interested in them so much as in Colin. Nursing Colin, and visiting my father and Maisie started to bring out in me the love I didn't know I had.

By this time Maisie and I had become good friends and she was beginning to understand me well. I began to wonder whether my mother would have been like Maisie – whether she would have given me the same kind of love that Maisie was giving me now. "This is the first time that we have seen you change from being a stern person to being someone who can show love," she told me. "Duncan has noticed the change in you since Colin was born. He said to me, 'Connie's not so quiet now. She really loves her little brother.'"

For the rest of that first year at Alice Springs, I saw quite a lot of my family especially my father. My time with him was precious. Even if I was feeling sick, I would go out with him when he came to get me. He strengthened my confidence in myself and my resilience and encouraged my ambition.

Life at the hostel in that first year was hectic. We seemed to be involved in one adventure after another. The first winter I spent at Alice Springs was terribly cold. I didn't know that winter away from the coast could mean such low temperatures. By August, my feet became frost bitten and I found it very difficult to get about. The slightest knock to any part of my feet made them bleed and become extremely painful. They became so delicate that I was unable to wear my shoes and socks. Sister Eileen took me in to see the doctor who said,"You will just have to keep this lass at home, bathe her feet and keep them well covered in this ointment." This meant I had to do my lessons at home for a while.

Apart from this minor inconvenience which made me think from time to time that Forrest River was never like this, I thoroughly enjoyed my stay at the hostel, participating in everything that I possibly could: games, any sports that weren't too strenuous for me, walkabout with the other girls on the weekends, hunting for rabbits and things not far from the hostel.

There was one sad event at Forrest River that caused me great distress and made me long to be back home with my people. One day, a telegram arrived from the Reverend Coaldrake telling me that Coralie Roberts, the Aboriginal assistant teacher, had died. I was shocked. In my mind I could see her on the foreshore, waving and smiling at my good fortune. I didn't go to school but stayed at the hostel and cried and cried. I didn't ask God why. I would not be able to understand how someone with so much vitality, a peacemaker, a teacher and a leader could be called 'home' at such an early age.

Three weeks later, a letter arrived from Reverend Coaldrake explaining to me that the nature of the illness was not known at that time. (The nature of the illness that caused her death, a type of congenital arthritis, was revealed to me in 1989 when I spent a week in Brisbane with Judja and Marna Coaldrake.) The whole mission was shaken by what had happened. In many ways, I don't think it ever recovered from this terrible tragedy.

The mission trained me, but Coralie, by the way she went about things, showed me the kind of person I could become. She didn't have to say anything. I knew I was a different personality from her and that I could not emulate her, but I wanted to be like her and I was determined to make the best of the education she had prepared me for.

Three months after my arrival, Sister Eileen asked me if I would like to join the girl guides. The first time I went away with the guides, we camped at the foot of Mt Gillan, on the Friday after school  The next morning all the guides except for June and I set off to climb Mt Gillan. We chatted happily about her life at Daly Waters and my experiences at Forrest River Mission. All went well until June started telling me ghost stories. It was then that I realised we were completely on our own. I thought to myself, "If any terrible thing should happen, June will be able to run away or get help but what can I do?" Both my feet were in bandages to protect them.

I said to June, "Will we go and follow the girls?"

"No," she said. "We can't. They're gone."

I looked up towards the summit but could not see any movement. "I don't care," I said, "I'm going to follow them," and I started walking.

I knew that if I kept on walking June would follow me. And she did. It was a hard climb. I had never done anything like it before. We were covered with scratches and bruises and I started to cry. "Well," said June, "you wanted to come."

When we had almost reached the top, I suddenly lost my footing, slipped and fell. As I slid down, the bandage on my right foot somehow came loose and caught on a ledge. There I was, suspended in mid-air, upside down like a fruit bat. I was 'proper' scared. "A ghost could easily get me now." Then I looked down and realised how far we had come. I thought, "Constance, if this bandage breaks this is the end."

Meanwhile June stood at the top, crying and screaming for help. Forgetting my own fears I decided I had to tell her what to do. So I said, "June, stop that crying and go and get me a long sapling, longer than you." In a state of panic, she rushed towards a young gum tree so I yelled out, "Not that one."

"Why not?"

"Because it breaks easily. You ought to know that." (Even from my upside-down position, I still managed to be in command.) June soon found another sapling that looked pliable. "Put it on the ground and put your foot on it and break it." With all these orders I think I was showing my potential as a future captain of the girl guides.

After June had managed to bring me to safety we both sat down, put our arms around each other and bawled our eyes out. By this time, the rest of the troop had arrived back at the camp and a few of them had set out to search for us. When they found us, the guide captain asked why we had left the camp.

"There were too many ghosts down there and I didn't want to stay there," I said.

"Connie," she said, "ghosts only come out at night, not during the day."

Under my breath I said, "You're not an Aboriginal." And we went back to camp. Not long after this dramatic inauguration into guiding, I was appointed a guide lieutenant and was known thereafter as 'Lefty' McDonald.

My music training continued but even at Alice Springs I hated scales. I thought to myself, "Boring, boring, boring." I didn't like reading music. I guess I was lazy. Whenever I could get away with not playing scales, I didn't play them. Mrs Schroeder was always coming out from the curtains saying to me, "Connie, get back to your scales." I always tried to avoid her.

Marie Burke, the hostel cook who came from Roper River, loved each of us as if we were her own. Marie was a big woman and I was afraid of her because to me she was a formidable figure. What Marie said was word. She caught me once or twice playing tunes like *Waltzing Matilda*. One day she said, "Connie, you should know better. Do your scales."

Beneath Marie's resolute exterior, there was a heart of gold and I knew that if I had any problems I could speak to her about them. Marie was the one to bridge the gap between black and white. She would often talk to us and encourage us to have more confidence in Sister Eileen and white people in general. We girls in the senior dormitory were puzzled by her efforts to bring black and white together (even though I had been trying to do the same thing with my own people and the missionaries at Forrest River).

"Why she do that?" we'd say to each other. We found it hard to fathom why she was telling us these things when we knew full well that she had come up against unfair missionaries when she was growing up. Wherever we had been brought up, all of us were very bitter about white people because of all the atrocities and massacres to our race that we had heard about from our people. I could see what Marie was trying to do and I pointed out to the other girls that we should listen more to her. I realised that Marie was preparing us for the outside world because, like my father, she was aware of the enormity of the struggle ahead of us.

I looked on Marie as a special friend and our friendship continues to this day. Even so, I was overwhelmed by the welcome she and her daughter Wendy, gave me when I visited her in September 1992. Marie kept on saying, "I didn't believe that I would ever see you again."

That first year at Alice Springs was a good year for me as, apart from my feet, I didn't get sick and didn't break any bones, so I considered myself rather lucky. After growing up with broken bones it now seemed to me that maybe I was at last getting better and that the promise of growing out of osteo-genesis imperfecta at adolescence was actually going to come true. I said to the sports teacher, "Can I please take part in the sports and if I fall down and break my leg then it's tough cheese."

He asked Sister Eileen, who said, "It's better to let her play sports than to mollycoddle her."

When the annual sports day arrived, I took part with the rest of Stuart House, proudly wearing my white blouse and red tunic, the Stuart colours. The Stuart boys wore white shirts and red shorts while Todd House wore blue shorts or skirts. I was delighted as we marched from the school to the sports ground and overjoyed when it was announced that Stuarts had won the march.

One of the hockey team from Stuart House was sick, making them a girl short. The sports teacher said, "Connie, you could take her place; you wouldn't have to run too far . We just want some one to contest the hit-off. You can leave it to the rest of the girls to run for the goal."

"Yeah, yeah , all right!" Words failed me! Connie McDonald playing hockey for the Stuart House team! The game went on and I was thoroughly enjoying myself, when I heard the girl from Todd House team that was playing opposite me, a gudiyar girl, whom we'll call Anne, pass remarks like, "I can beat that Connie any time; she can't even run."

I didn't say anything until we started our next hit off after a goal. As we 'Hockey oned' I muttered, "I heard what you said! You are going to cop it for that!"

So we started again, "Hockey one; Hockey two; Hockey three" and our hockey sticks got caught. (I was doing it on purpose.)

"This is your last chance you two girls. If you can't do it properly we will have to get two other girls," said the umpire.

"Hockey one .. Hockey two ... Hockey three..." and I missed the ball intentionally and hit the girl on the shin. She fell down screaming, "Connie hit me! She meant to hit me!"

"No, I didn't!"

"Yes, she did! She meant to hit me!"

"We will do it again," and the umpire called another girl over.

"Mary you take Anne's place." I liked Mary, and we got the game under way without further incident. Anne was taken to the sidelines where her leg swelled up and she looked very sorry for herself. When I returned to my house I told the rest of the girls what I had done.

They told me that that girl didn't like Aboriginal girls so I said, "Oh well, I gave her what for. I hit her on the shin."

All the girls laughed and said, "Good on you Connie." I didn't take part in any other games because the sports teacher considered that I was too dangerous. For the rest of the day, I sat on the sidelines and barracked for Stuart House.

Eventually the bus came to take us Aboriginal children back to the hostel. We sat, red and white Stuarts on one side and blue and white Todds on the other. We sang, boasted of our winnings and swapped stories of the day. I piped up, "We won the hockey."

"Yeah, because you hit our captain on the shins."

"Well, she was passing rude remarks about me and so I gave her what for."

When the bus pulled up at St Mary's, Sister Eileen was there to meet us. She said, "Connie McDonald, I would like to see you in my office."

"Uh oh," I thought. "That girl's parents must have rung up."

"What's this I hear about you fighting at the sports ground today? Anne's father rang up and told me that she now has a sore shin."

"I wasn't fighting."

"Tell me what happened."

I told her all about the hockey match and my revenge.

"Well," said Sister Eileen, "You mustn't do that."

"If anybody passes remarks about me and about my skin or my appearance then I will just knock them over."

"Connie. Little ladies don't do that."

"I'm not a lady. I'm a girl. I'm Connie McDonald. If anyone says things about me and they are close at hand then I will belt them."

"Oh Connie. You had better ask God to forgive you for doing that naughty thing. I don't think the Lord would like that."

"I don't think the Lord would like that white girl passing remarks about me."

"Connie, go and change out of your sports clothes, do your homework and then come back and do your music and let there not be another incident like this again. This is the second time you have done something like this." She was referring to what I had done to one of the boys in my class who had made snide remarks about me. I threw my pen, the old type with a sharp nib, at him with such force that it was stuck in his right arm.

"You have got to learn to curb your temper."

"Yes, Sister Eileen," I said. "It's a Scottish temper."

"Well, you've got to learn to curb it or it will get you in trouble. You can go now."

The senior girls immediately questioned me about what Sister Eileen had wanted. "Oh, she was just talking to me about that girl I hit with the hockey stick."

Nita said, "Yes. They shouldn't pass remarks about us Aborigines. If she had said that to me, I would have hit her too."

We were all agreeing except for one girl who said, "That's not the right way."

"Just keep quiet. You're just saying that because you have a white father. You think like them."

Then Ivy, who was a peacemaker and very well aware of my bad temper, said, " Connie, What about you and I, we go and have our baths first."

At evening prayer time, Sister Eileen asked us to express our sorrow for anything we had done wrong during the day. She prayed that we might be sorry for any person we might have injured or hurt. I thought to myself. "I'm not going to say sorry." I don't know what God thought of me but Sister Eileen couldn't have been too impressed. As we were supposed to be praying quietly to ourselves, I could see Sister Eileen looking around checking to make sure everyone was praying. She looked at me kneeling at the organ without even closing my eyes and she knew that I wasn't saying any prayers.

Sister Eileen was unlike other gudiyar missionaries. She always listened to what we had to say, didn't believe in degrading punishments, didn't talk at us or down to us but simply spoke with us helping us to sort out our problems ourselves. I always felt at ease with Sister Eileen and had no trouble speaking openly with her. She accepted that some of us were rebels (including me!) and saw her task as being to direct that rebellion rather than to crush it. She was a strict and efficient missionary, who was mother, friend, confidante and spiritual leader all rolled into one. She was quietly spoken, sensitive to the racism that surrounded us and always telling us that we should hold our heads up in adversity and be proud of not only who we were but of what we were.

Her quiet sense of humour must have helped her cope with many difficult situations. One day when I was practising my music, I became bored with playing the same old scales. I started to play *Waltzing Matilda* by ear and was merrily tinkling the ivories when all of a sudden someone tapped me on the shoulder. Turning around, I nearly fell off the piano stool. There standing directly behind me was Sister Eileen with a smile on her face. She looked at me and I looked at her sheepishly.

"I don't want to go reading them crotchets and quavers and scales and all. Are you going to punish me?" I asked.

"No, Connie, you can become a good pianist, maybe a concert pianist," she replied and left the room. This was her way of saying, "Get back to your scales."

Another time when I was doing my music practice, Sister Eileen came in to the lounge room and said, "What on earth are you playing, Connie? Are you playing the piece of music you are supposed to be learning?"

She came over to look at the sheet of music. "I see it is the right music. Why doesn't it sound right?"

"It might be because I was playing the music with only the white notes."

"And what about the black notes?"

"I did that too."

"How did that sound?"

"Terrible."

"You know Connie, you can't play the piano with only the white notes or only the black notes."

"Why?"

"Because it is both of them that make the harmony."

This was something new and quite profound. It set me thinking. "Why isn't it the same with us human beings? Whites and blacks?"

"In time it will be," she assured me. "These things take time."

"Why?"

"Do you trust me?" she said.

"Well," I hesitated and then said, "No, I don't suppose I do." So I put the same question to her. "Do you trust me, Sister Eileen?"

It was her turn to hesitate. She seemed amazed that I should ask the question of her. For a moment our eyes met, as she struggled to find her answer. I suddenly sensed that here were two human beings, meeting as equals, to try and fathom one of life's great tragedies, racism. It dawned on me that if I had spoken to one of the missionaries at Forrest River in the same way I would have been accused of being insubordinate. From that moment on I realised that between us there was a bond of trust.

It was harder for me than for the other children to come to terms with 'authority' because of my rebellious nature. Sister Eileen knew this and she was careful in the way she spoke to me about things. Gradually I realised that her authority was totally different from what I had experienced at Forrest River and that she knew more about what was going on in my head than anyone else. At times I wished that she was my mother but I daren't let myself get too close to her.

Everyone at the hostel loved and respected Sister Eileen. She was what I would call a missionary in the true sense of the word.

# Fifteen

## *"I'm going to confront this man"*
### ❧ *Delmore Downs* ❧

At Christmas, the Aboriginal children from the hostel used to go home for the holidays as most of them lived around Alice Springs. The first year I was at the hostel, Sister Eileen said, "Connie, we are not sending you home for Christmas. You can stay with your father and Maisie and Colin."

"No, I can't because they are on a droving trip to Wyndham."

"In that case," she said, "You'll have to stay here."

"That'll be real good," I said.

"You won't be by yourself because June Forrester will be staying here too. I will take you out as often as I can. You can bring all your things over here to the main house and you can have one of the rooms here so you won't be in the dormitory by yourselves." The main house was where Sister Eileen and all the working women lived and where all the little junior boys and girls were looked after.

During the first week of the holidays, I was outside the main house sitting under a gum tree contemplating the future when Sister Eileen came up to me and said, "Connie, I want you to come and pack a few things and get ready. You are going to a sheep station."

"Why?"

"The wife of a sheep station manager by the name of Mrs Holt, from Delmore Downs Station, has just had a baby boy here at the Alice Springs Hospital and her eldest boy is not quite two yet. Mr Holt has asked me if I have any girls who could go and help his wife. I told him that I had a girl who might be interested."

On Thursday night, Mr Holt rang to say he would be picking his wife up from hospital the next morning and would come and get me then.

Mr Holt and his son Donald arrived to pick me up; Sister Eileen gave me a kiss goodbye and I climbed into the ute. Mr Holt said, "Donald, this is Connie. She is going to look after you."

Donald ignored me until his mother came out carrying his new little brother. As she climbed into the truck, Donald suddenly clambered onto my lap. Mr Holt looked across in surprise at us and said, "I see Donald has a new friend." From that moment he followed me everywhere.

It was a long drive to Delmore Downs. By the time we arrived at about two o'clock the following morning we were tired, stiff and weary of Donald's crying. We all had a cup of tea, a slice of toast and then went to sleep. Next morning, when I looked out the window I noticed that way down past the shearing sheds was a group of gunyahs. From where I was I could see that they were solidly constructed of iron, timber and leaves. In the Kimberleys, I had only seen traditional gunyahs made out of branches, various types of bark, leaves, spinifex and grass, tied together with strings made from treated bark.

"Mr Holt," I inquired "What are those?"

"They are the homes of my Aboriginal workers." I was to learn that these gunyahs were permanent dwellings except when someone died. Later, I was told that though the Aboriginal people chose to live separately, they were treated the same as the other workers. Mr Holt, who was a fair man, paid every worker a fair wage whether they were Aboriginal or white and perhaps even more important he tried to teach them how to budget their money. One day I asked him if I could join his budget class. "Why?" he asked.

"I want to come and learn all about how to handle money."

He was amazed at this. "Didn't they teach you at Forrest River?"

"No," I said. "Don't forget Forrest River is a mission. Everything is handed out. We worked because we were told to, not for money."

Mr Holt was aghast. "You are more than welcome to attend my classes but I could teach you at home if you like."

"I want to learn with the other people," and whenever I could make time from my work, I joined the class.

I was surprised at the vastness of Delmore Downs. It reminded me of the cattle stations I had seen in the Kimberleys except there was not a sign of cattle anywhere just sheep, sheep and more sheep. My job was the normal duties of a housemaid plus looking after and caring for Donald. I did the cooking and the ironing and the washing, fed the chooks, collected the eggs and most important I had to keep Donald away from the creek. At the back of the house there was a creek that flooded every time it rained. Donald was my biggest worry as I only had to turn around for one minute and he'd be gone. To my great relief, I managed to keep him out of trouble.

Another part of my job was to give out the rations to the Aboriginal people who worked on the property. One person I remember with delight was the goat lady. Every day this intriguing old lady would come to the house to collect her food for lunch and then off she would go taking about two hundred goats out to graze. To my astonishment, she would call them by name and they immediately followed her for their day's roaming.

I couldn't talk her language so we communicated using signs. My years of learning sign language from the tribal people at Forrest River came in very handy. Good morning was an ordinary wave of the hand; I want a drink was putting your hand to your mouth with your forefinger joined to your thumb looking something like a cup; food or damper was putting all your fingers together over your thumb and then pointing them into your mouth; tobacco, was two fingers joined to your thumb and put first to your mouth and then behind the ear. This was because when they chewed tobacco every now and then they would take it out of their mouth and put it behind the ear.

On Christmas Eve, Mrs Holt said, "We have to get ready now because we are going to McDonald Downs station to my family to celebrate Christmas." We were talking away and she said, "That's funny your name is McDonald too. How do you spell your name?"

I said, "M c D o n a l d."

116

"That's the way we spell our name. I was Jessie McDonald before I married," and she continued, "You'd like my people."

I felt very much at home at McDonald Downs. It was the first time I had Christmas dinner with gudiyar people, apart from the missionaries. This was different. It was a family affair and I was thrilled to find that I was accepted as one of the family. We had a wonderful Christmas dinner, slept it off in the afternoon and I received lots of presents. After a few days, we returned to Delmore Downs but in many ways it was still like Christmas. Never before had I been treated as well as I was by the Holt and McDonald families.

Mr Holt paid me every week for the work I was doing and I began to feel quite rich. Unlike many Aboriginal household helpers working on other stations, I was paid a fair wage for a sixteen-year-old. Mrs Holt had a room that had lots and lots of materials. She took me in there one day and said, "Pick any material you want and I will make you some dresses." And she did, lots of them.

One morning, Mr Holt announced that the shearers were expected in two days and that my duties were going to multiply. Instead of rising at six, Mrs Holt and I were to get up at four in the morning to prepare breakfast for about ten shearers. After cleaning up the breakfast dishes, we had to prepare smoko then lunch, smoko and then dinner. It was all a new and exciting experience for a sixteen-year-old girl who had the preconceived notion that only men and boys worked on stations. But was I tired after two days of blending the new schedule with my normal duties . The manager in charge of the shearers was a tall gudiyar man married to an Aboriginal woman. They had five children, the eldest of whom was a girl aged twelve. None of the children had been to school as their father believed he could teach them all they needed to know. No one yet had been able to convince him to change his mind, not even his mother. Mr Holt asked me if I would talk to him.

One night after tea, I went over to the their tent, followed as usual by Donald. I was approached by the eldest girl. I said, "Hello. My name is Connie McDonald."

Straight away she said, "You must be Duncan McDonald's daughter."

117

She was very shy but we got talking and she said, "Donald is big now. How long are you staying with his family?"

"Until school starts again," I said.

"I wish I could go to school."

I thought to myself, "I'm going to confront this man." He looked as though he was over six feet tall but I wasn't going to let that worry me.

Looking dejected, she said, "It's no good Connie, he won't listen to anyone."

She entered the tent and informed her father that I wanted to see him. He opened the flap and she introduced me to him, telling him that I was Duncan McDonald's daughter. I was impressed by her father's physique. He was so straight and tall. He introduced me to the rest of the children, telling me their ages, and he took me over to his wife and speaking in her language told her who I was. She responded with a smile.

"What is it that you want to see me about, Connie?" he said as soon as we were seated on the floor.

Coming straight to the point I said, "I understand that you don't want your children to go to school. Why is that ?"

"I can teach them all they need to know. Besides their mother needs them."

By this time I was quite enraged, "These children should be at school. You are depriving them of an education."

"I never had much education and it hasn't hurt me."

"Your children have the right to go to school. With a bit of education they might really do something and become famous one day and you'll be pleased."

Immediately, he stood up and said, "And who do you think you are telling me about my own kids?"

I, too, stood up, "Well, anyway you think about it." Pointing to his oldest daughter, I said, "Those children, especially your daughter there, want to go to school real bad."

I was so sure of myself that I told Mr and Mrs Holt all about it. They asked, "Did he give in?"

"No," I said. "But I have a feeling that those children will be starting school in the new year."

When the shearers left, a week or so later, I spoke to the young girl reassuring her with, "Don't you worry. Things will sort themselves out. You'll all be going to school when school starts next year." But as she left I felt very sad.

Unbeknowns to the shearer and his family, I had a strong ally to whom I was going to talk. It wasn't Mr and Mrs Holt, Sister Eileen or the shearer but the Divine Master.

At the end of the holidays I returned to Alice Springs feeling very rich with my overflowing bank account, my brand new dresses that Mrs Holt had made me and new pants, singlets and bras that she had bought me. It was a very sad moment when I had to leave the family. Donald was so upset he wouldn't say goodbye. I realised that it would probably be the last time I would ever see them.

I had been very happy at Delmore Downs. Back at Forrest River, I always felt that all the Aboriginal people were never trusted to do anything on our own but at Delmore Downs, Mr and Mrs Holt trusted me completely. I was pleased to be trusted by these gudiyars. I found that in myself I could cope with whatever responsibilities were given to me and that I could give my all to any situation. Because of their trust, I began to believe that I would be able to put to full advantage all the training I was receiving at Alice Springs.

On the first weekend after school resumed, we were sitting round when we saw a truck drive up to the hostel. I knew straight away it belonged to the shearer and his family. He hopped out and looked around to find me.

"Well, Connie, you are responsible for this so I expect you to look after these kids of mine, especially my eldest daughter."

"I will," I beamed as she and I put our arms around each other and hugged and kissed like long lost cousins.

"Oh Connie, I'm so glad to get the opportunity to come to school." Sister Eileen gave me the job of helping her with her homework so we became good friends. Today she is a highly respected leader of her people. Her father would be very proud of her.

# Sixteen

## *"I can't fathom these missionaries"*
### ⌒ *A new status* ⌒

In October of 1950, my father sent me a note to tell me that he would be taking me out for the weekend because the family would shortly be going back to the Kimberleys. As my two years at Alice Springs were coming to an end, I could not be sure when our paths would cross again. By this time, I felt that I was secure in this relationship with my parents and that I was totally accepted by both of them.

On the Saturday, we went to Simpson's Gap, an idyllic place for a family picnic. There I was with my father, my mother and my little brother. After lunch, my father went for a little walkabout and my mother and I chatted while I played with little Colin.

I said to Maisie, "Mother, do you think that father would let me come and live with the family because next year I will turn eighteen and I will not be a ward of the state. I would dearly love to come and live with the family."

She said, "I don't know about Duncan but I would love you to come and be with us. But I think you had better ask your father."

When my father came back, I said, "Father, I've got something to ask you. As I'm turning eighteen next year, I want to know if I can come and live with you and the family? Now that I have found you, I would very much like to live with you and be part of the family. You must have known that I always wanted to be with you."

He seemed to be amazed at my question. After giving it some thought he looked at me and said, "Connie, you are an adult now and you can look after yourself."

I felt as though he had stabbed me in the heart, but aloud I said nothing. I felt totally rejected.

Looking at him, Maisie said, "I can't make you out. This daughter of yours that you always wanted to get from the mission, here she is, asking to come and be with us, and you answer her that way." She was distraught. I told her, "Don't get too upset as you are breastfeeding Colin, and you don't want to lose your milk."

"Well, I can't get over what Duncan has just said to you."

On the way home to Havertrees Gap, nobody said anything. It was like a cyclone had blown through our lives. I said, "Father, take me back to St Mary's."

"But you have another day here?"

"I think not, father."

Then Maisie piped up, "What! After what you said to her you want her to stay another day?"

I went into my room and packed up my belongings. "When you are ready to take me," I said, "I will be waiting in the car." I then asked Maisie if she knew why he would not have me with them. She replied, "I have no reason for it."

Maisie and I embraced, in tears, and then she picked up Colin and followed me to the car. I embraced and kissed her again, kissed Colin and stepped into the car to wait for my father. Maisie leant over and said, "When Duncan comes back from the hostel he won't find me here." Then my father came out and got into the car. Maisie promptly walked round to the driver's side, "When you come back, Colin and I won't be here."

He said, "Aren't you going to come and see Connie off?"

"No. We have said our goodbyes already." And then and there, she left him and stayed away for quite a while.

I was puzzled. Why had my father built up all this family closeness only to reject me. I was just returning to what it had been on the mission. From then on all trust for everyone went out of me. I relied only on myself and as much as I wanted to see Maisie, I decided that I didn't want to see my father again.

The West Australian government and the mission staff thought that after two years in Alice Springs my education was complete, so Sister Eileen told me that I would have to

121

return to Forrest River. With a little sadness, I packed my bags. I had grown quite fond of Alice Springs. I had made many friends not only with the Aboriginal children at the hostel but also with some of the town children. On the other hand I was happy to be going back home as I was a little homesick.

As we were unable to catch a plane from Alice Springs at that time, I had to begin my journey on the same bus that took the boys and girls home to Newcastle Waters, Daly River, Banka Banka and the outlying stations around Alice Springs, staying overnight in Newcastle Waters. Once on the plane, my trip was quite unlike the one to the Alice two years earlier. It wasn't the milk-and-mail run. It was a faster, smoother, safer and, to my disappointment, more uneventful trip.

The plane landed at Six Mile aerodrome, Wyndham, at seven in the morning. As he drove me into the town, the airport bus driver, one of Mummy Nora's sons, told me that the launch was already in and that they were waiting for me.

I asked him what time the launch had arrived and he said. "This morning, early, at three."

"Boy," I said, "the captain and the crew must be busy loading on stores."

"Oh no, they came in for the stores last week. This is a special trip to take you home."

I thought to myself, "Gee, I must be important."

When we arrived in town, a cousin of mine told me that the postmaster wanted to see me. He handed me a telegram which read, "Welcome home Connie, we are all anxiously waiting to see you again," signed 'staff and people'. I was touched by the telegram and felt that at last I belonged.

Uncle Sandy and family were waiting for me at the Wyndham jetty and as usual they had quite a few parcels to give me. The launch with its passengers then proceeded on the full tide down the Gulf. When the mission came into view, I was amazed to see people lining the banks of the river. Everyone from the mission was there to greet me, even some of the old tribal men and women from the camp. There were shouts of "Welcome home Connie!", "Glad to have you back", lots of waving and tears with children jumping up and down and trying to get a better view of me. I was overcome by this show of affection for me by my people.

It was neap tide, so about half a mile before the normal landing place the captain cut the engine and the crew threw ropes to some of the working men on the river bank. They, in turn, pulled the launch close into the bank, making it easier for all on board to disembark. One of the crew helped me off. I was immediately surrounded by a barrage of noisy well-wishers who all tried to guide me up the very narrow path to the waiting truck, a beaten up old red Chevrolet.

Back at the compound, I was confronted with some unexpected news. The chaplain's wife told me that I was never to live in the girl's dormitory again, and that I was to live at the mission house with them until a house was built for me. In an instant, I became a member of the mission staff, as assistant teacher, and I was to be addressed by all and sundry as Sister Connie.

The news hit me like a blow from heaven. I wasn't ready for this sudden change to my life. It was hard for me to comprehend the responsibility which it would bring. However, I did realise that though it would be difficult for me personally, it meant that at last, I, as well as my people, were being recognised as human beings. It seemed that at last God had answered my prayer, the prayer I had composed when I lived in the dormitory one day after I had been punished, and a prayer that I had prayed every day since then. The prayer reads as follows:

*Dear Heavenly Father*

*Please help these missionaries and all other white people to see us as human beings, and that we are your children too, and that you gave your son Jesus to die for all men, this includes the Aboriginal people. Help us, as you've always done in the past to love our oppressors, as I know you know that my people and in fact the Aboriginal people throughout Australia are suffering under white man's rule. Maybe someday you may call me, unworthy though I am, to help fight for justice for my people, and I thank you Lord, for loving and giving us the strength and dignity to carry on under the Australian Government's cruel and atrocious system which we find ourselves in. Lord hear my prayer and let the cries of your oppressed people come to you.*

*I know in my heart Lord that as you have and will answer my prayer, so too Lord, the day will come when the white people will come to realise that we too are human beings just like them and will treat us as such.*

*Thank you, Lord for listening to your humble servant. Amen.*

I say this prayer every day even today, and God gives me the courage, strength and dignity to carry on with my life.

Unfortunately, my people, especially the dormitory girls, did not take kindly to my becoming a member of the mission staff because this meant I ceased to be one of them. To me, of course, this was not true. I was still Connie McDonald, the same girl who had left the mission two years earlier for Alice Springs. They feared that I would become flash and not want to associate with them any more, and they assumed that because I had had a little more education, it would set me apart from them.

Though I was made a member of the mission staff, the people considered that I was a missionary. I tried to point out to them that I was not a missionary in the true sense of the word and that a missionary was someone who was called by God to do his work and who had been to a special college to be trained. They would not listen. This depressed me because I have a great love for my people and I found it difficult to explain that it was not my idea to become a missionary. I told the dormitory girls that I had been looking forward to coming back to live in the dormitory again but this was not to be.

I stayed with the chaplain and his wife for two months until a building was found for me. It was a building that was attached to the nursing sister's quarters and was used as a maternity ward. It was decided by the authorities that as accommmodation was hard to come by the building was to be renovated and painted and would become my home until such time as a house was built for me. The mission carpenter, a gudiyar, and his Aboriginal apprentices were called in to fix up the house. I had all my meals at the staff dining room with all the unmarried white staff of both sexes and I also shared the staff shower room. I was apprehensive about living alone and found it very hard to settle down as years of dormitory life meant that I had always lived with a crowd.

124

While I was away at Alice Springs, Mary Willington, who was still teaching, had married Bill Jamison, another gudiyar who worked on the mission. I was told how she had thrilled everyone because she not only had the wedding at Forrest River but also asked Uncle Robert Roberts Unjamurra, one of the mission elders, to give her away. Her own father was sick and unable to be there so he wrote a special letter to Uncle Bob asking him to be 'father' for the occasion. Uncle Bob told me that he felt honoured as he walked down the aisle with Mary and she described it to me later as the 'holiest and most reverend experience' she had had. It is likely that never before in Western Australian history was a missionary 'given away' in marriage by an Aboriginal elder.

I learnt a lot about teaching from Mrs Mary Jamison. She never lost her temper. When I was helping her teach, I was the one who used to get mad with the children. Sometimes I would smack them and tell them to use some commonsense but Mary always had a different way of dealing with problems. Her way was to sit down with the child and talk to them. Needless to say her way was more effective than mine and slowly I followed her example.

When night came, I'd be thoroughly scared. The Aboriginal people knew about this fear because each night after the evening church service, I would go and visit the village people – a different family each night. As the night wore on, I dreaded the thought of going back to my place, so more often than not the family whom I was visiting would make up a bed for me, then early in the morning before anyone was awake I would sneak home. This went on for quite a while until in time the fear vanished.

The biggest room in the sister's quarters was turned into a maternity ward, and I can tell you it was cooler and more pleasant a place in which to give birth than in the old maternity building which had been used for so long. It was also convenient for the nursing sister to keep a close watch on her charges.

When a woman was in labour and came in to have her baby, the sister would wake me up, and ask me to go and tell the superintendent to start up the generator so the lights could be turned on. Invariably, these little babies decided they would arrive from midnight on into the small hours of the morning. I would get up put on my dressing gown and slippers and hot-foot it to the superintendent's house. The possibility of falling over in the dark or of treading on snakes, scorpions, jagged glass or wood made this quite a dangerous journey. I carried a torch and sometimes a hurricane lamp. When everything was over and a new baby had been safely delivered, I would congratulate the mother and go back to bed. Each time as I rolled into bed, I would feel like Sir Edmund Hilary and that I had just climbed Mt Everest again.

There was a standard joke between the women who were pregnant and myself. They would say to me, "We will try to have our babies in the mornings and in the early afternoons so that you can get your beauty sleep at night." We'd all laugh together. I can even remember two women who did oblige, one a young mother gave birth to her first child, a little girl, at three in the afternoon and another mother had her sixth child at eleven in the morning.

Not all nurses were as kind as Nancy Drage. One night while I was living in my little house next to the maternity wing, I developed a very bad migraine so I knocked on the door of the nurse's quarters and told the current nurse about my headache. This new nursing sister was really mad at being woken up and grabbed a big tin of tablets without looking at what they were and gave me some. Next morning, I didn't seem to be able to feel anything and when I looked in the mirror I discovered that I was swollen all over. I was furious. I rushed over and knocked on her door again.

"Come and see what you done." She came to the door and looked rather shocked when she saw me. "You didn't look at the label on that tin did you? What was it that you gave me?" She refused to answer me so I said, "I'm going straight up to the superintendent to tell him what you did."

"Oh," she said "I thought I gave you..."

"Well, you didn't bother to look. I'm going to make a big song about this and if I die you are going to be up for murder."

So I went off, my face burning, my tongue and lips getting thicker by the minute, "That nurse down there," I blurted out as clearly as my contorted mouth would let me, "she tried to poison me!"

I told him the story and begged him in vain to get in touch with the Flying Doctor to find out what kind of poison it was and what

126

could be done for me. As he went down to ask the nurse what she had given me, I said, "If you don't find out what it was she gave me I will tell the Flying Doctor all about it next time he comes. If I'm alive to tell him."

Close to tears, very frightened of what might happen to me, and bewildered by their lack of concern, I went down to Aunty Louise and Uncle Robert.

"Ngumballa," they said, "what's wrong with your face?" I told them.

"No more trust gudiyar's medicine. What did they give you?"

"I don't know and they don't care."

And so they looked after me in the tribal way.

Soon after that the nurse was replaced for a short time by another nursing sister. She was a lovely person. Like Nancy Drage, she wanted to go out and mix with the people. She was told by the powers-that-be that "We missionaries don't do that." Yet when we heard about missionaries that went to Africa, it seems they did go with the people, they would sit with them and get to know them. I think the Baptists might have done that with the Aborigines but certainly not the Church of England. They were told that they were not allowed to go to the people. You are there just to bring them the word of God. How can you take the word of God to people if you do not go and sit with them?

While I was assistant teacher, there was a visiting missionary at the school. One day he told me that he wanted to see me at his house at two o'clock sharp. After lunch, when I thought it would be pretty close to two o'clock, I went and asked matron if it was and she said, "Yes. It is five past two." I went to the house and he greeted me with, "You're late."

"How could you expect me to know when its two o'clock when I can't tell the time?" I joked.

"Well, you had better start learning now. Come in anyway. We have to sort all these books out."

We started to separate out all the various reading books and arithmetic books into their piles. He asked me what I thought of all the members of the staff. He went through each individual missionary asking me my opinion. So I told him what I thought of them.

"Who do you think is the best missionary?"

I told him who I thought was the best missionary. He agreed, then he asked me about the Aboriginal staff members. I told him that I thought they were doing well and that I admired them.

After we had been working for a while, he said, "You can sit on the chair there if you like." I noticed that when he bent to get a book, he looked up my dress. So I said, "What are you looking up there for? The books are not up there, all the books are down on the floor."

His reply astounded me. "Have you ever slept with any man?"

"No. Certainly not. Why should I ?"

"You're eighteen – you should. Do you want to try now?"

I was shocked. "You should know better than to ask that question. You're a missionary. You're a staff member."

He locked all the doors so I went to the window. I was really scared. "I'll scream and run out and tell all the people."

"Well," he said, "you are never going to know, are you."

So he let me go.

I did not dare tell any one about what he said as I knew that if I told the missionaries they would simply accuse me of lying and if I told the people, the reaction would simply be, "You must have been asking for it." Knowing that I would not get a good hearing from either side, I told no one.

I didn't feel any shame for what might have happened because he would have overpowered me with his strength and I would have been powerless to do anything about it. I was quite astounded that a 'messenger of God' would try to seduce a young Aboriginal girl. Fortunately, he left the mission soon after that. Years later, while attending a church function in Perth, I heard a voice say, "Hello, Sister McDonald." I looked up and who should I see but this same man who was by now a priest in the Church of England. I didn't say a word but walked straight past him. Maybe I shouldn't have but I did not want to be anywhere near him – and he knew!

A couple of days later, the superintendent wanted to see me.

"It seems that you don't like some of the missionaries," he said.

"Did that fellow tell you this?"

"Yes."

"Well, he asked me, 'What do you think about the missionaries?' so I told him."

"You didn't give me a very good assessment, did you?"

"No. Anyway, I was just answering his questions."

"Most of what you said is lies," he said.

"Oh, don't give me that." But even though I was on the mission staff, I was duly punished.

When I first found out that I was to be made a member of the mission staff, I had expected that I would have the same status as the other missionaries. After all, the people on the mission were told to call me 'Sister Connie'. After these experiences, I began to think that maybe I was being used as a token mediator or as a stepping stone to reach the rest of the people. I felt angry. I got to thinking, "These missionaries, they try to make themselves God. They make me a member of the mission staff and yet I am not allowed to voice my opinions about anything. They may as well let me go back and live in the dormitory. I can't fathom those missionaries."

# Seventeen

## *"Where this one come from?"*
### ∽ *Learning my culture* ∽

While Uncle Robert and Aunty Louisa were on the mission staff, the three of us took the dormitory girls to Booral on their annual walkabout. We camped where acacia bushes surrounded a freshwater stream. As soon as we arrived, Aunty Louisa reminded everyone about how to use the river so that all living things in the river would be preserved. We were to take drinking water from upstream of the camp area, we were to wash well downstream and clothes were to be spread on the rocks to dry.

Between the drinking and the washing areas was the place for fun. The girls began diving from the rock ledges into the pools, splashing around or moving off a little to do some fishing. They even found bathing fun, as on walkabout we didn't use carbolic soap, but lathered our skin with dried out acacia shoots and then lay on the warm rocks to dry.

While Uncle Robert went kangaroo hunting, Aunty Louisa took the primary girls goanna hunting and yam and berry gathering. I stayed behind at the camp to look after the little ones.

After lunch, the little girls and I were sitting under a big jungerrie tree when we saw two of the older young girls coming back to the camp. They were cousins aged ten and twelve. I could see that the ten-year-old was quite distressed and as she came closer I could also see that she was holding her right hand. Telling the littlies to stay where they were, I hurried to meet them. Running through my mind were all sorts of possibilities. "What's the matter?" I said. "Have you been bitten by a snake or spider?"

"No, Sister Connie," she said, "but look at my hand. It's all white."

It was also rigid and her long fingers were bent like claws. They looked like the talons of an eagle. I tried to straighten her fingers but nothing happened. I asked her how long her hand had been like this?

"Since yesterday. What's wrong with me, sister? Please tell me?"

I took both girls into my tent, sat them down and then I told the anxious girl to close her eyes and stretch her hands towards me. I took a safety pin from the first-aid kit so I could give her a pain test. I jabbed her right hand and fingers with the pin but she did not move or make a sound. Then I jabbed her left hand and fingers and she immediately jumped away telling me in no uncertain terms that I was hurting her. I then repeated the test with her eyes open so she could see the results for herself.

"Why didn't my right hand feel anything, sister? And why is my skin all white?" she asked. And then she laughed and said, "Am I going to turn into a gudiyar?"

We both laughed but her cousin stayed serious and said, "This is not funny."

"I know it's not funny," I said. "When did you realise that something was wrong?"

"About a week before we came on our walkabout."

"Why didn't you tell the nursing sister?"

"I was frightened to."

"Why didn't you ask the dormitory matron if you could come and see me?"

Looking into my eyes, she asked, "Have I got leprosy?"

Looking at both of them I explained, "Yes, my dear, I'm afraid you have. The whiteness on the skin is a sign of leprosy. We shall have to send you back to the mission."

She stood there looking into space. I tried to speak to her but there was no answer or movement and I realised that she was in shock.

So I said to her cousin, "Stoke up the fire and put on the billy and we'll have a cup of tea." We walked back to the the littlies and sat under the jungerrie tree waiting for the billy to boil. I explained to the girls about the signs and symptoms of leprosy. "I've read a lot about leprosy in the hospital medical books and although the leprosy has taken hold of you, there are new medicines that can cure leprosy much quicker than in the old days. You are young so the chance of making a full recovery is promising."

She listened to me but could not take in what I was saying. The little girls could see something was wrong so I explained to them that though she was sick she would get better one day.

When Aunty Louisa and the rest of the girls came back to the camp, I explained to them all what the young girl was facing. Not long afterwards, Uncle Robert came back carrying a big red kangaroo over his shoulders. As he put his load down, his wife told him the news and he came over to me looking worried. "Is this true, ngumballa?"

"Yes, uncle. We have to send her back to the mission tomorrow and then she will have to go to the leprosarium at Derby."

"Then we send smoke signals to the old people in the camp. They tell the mission that the girl's camp needs help."

While the kangaroo, goanna, fish and yams were cooking, all the girls, including myself and the littlies, went to gather plenty of firewood to make a large fire so that we could send a message as we were sixty miles from the mission. We made a huge pile of kindling, logs, leaves and grass .

Once the message sending was over, we all sat down to a feast of bush food. I coaxed the young girl into eating something as it was going to be a long night and I knew that no one was going to be able to sleep. In the meantime everyone except her cousin moved away from the girl. After supper I conducted the evening service and prayed for the girl that she would be comforted in her time of separation from her family. Everyone was crying so much that I stopped the service and we went to our tents.

I quietly said to Judy, "You don't need to worry. Bring your blankets and you and your cousin can come and sleep in my tent next to me." I was sad to think how rejected she must feel. "How can my own people reject someone," I thought and put my arms around them both. "Sister Connie, aren't you frightened you might get leprosy too?"

I explained, "The others are frightened because they don't

132

fully understand about leprosy. I understand about leprosy because I read all about it in the medical books at the hospital."

"I'm glad you read the books," then she paused for a while and quietly said, "Will I get better or will I die?"

This question nearly blew me out of my tent. I put my arms around her and gave her a big hug. At first she drew away from me but I kept my arms around her and after a bit she relaxed and put her head on my shoulder saying, "Sister Connie, I thank God for sending you here because you love and care about us. You help everybody on the mission, even though some people don't like you because you are now a missionary."

I interrupted, "I am not a missionary but a member of the mission staff. A missionary is someone God calls to do his work and he hasn't called me yet."

Then she looked at me and said, "Maybe God did call you. Maybe you didn't hear him. And I'm glad he called you."

I was so overcome with emotion that I pulled her to me and embraced her and we both cried. I thought to myself, "Thank you, dear Lord, for giving me this opportunity of helping one of my people." It was the first time I had ever in my life reached out to care for any one. I thanked God that I was able to break out of the barriers of my mission upbringing so that when I saw that a young girl needing someone to care for her, right at that very moment, I was able to be that person. Her profound statement set me thinking. Sometimes we are so pre-occupied with our own importance that we don't hear God. Maybe God did call me.

She continued, "You know sister, when you became a missionary, all them people were jealous. There were murmurings in the village and in the dormitory. They all think you are flash."

"I know, Judy. It doesn't worry me."

"You went to Alice Springs and had some more education. You're strong."

"Well Judy, it seems to me that you have to be strong and stand up for yourself if you are going to get along in life. So that is what I do."

The next morning, the two cousins and I rose early and went a long distance down to the lower reaches of the stream so we could get cleaned up without stirring up the fears of the rest of the camp. After breakfast we all assembled near the jungerrie trees as usual for our morning prayers. Just as we were singing the last hymn, I saw Uncle Robert kneel down and put his ear to the ground. Then he stood up and walked over to me and said, "Ngumballa, the truck is just coming round the bend." I looked up and sure enough there in the distance was the old red Chevrolet truck.

I was relieved to see Marna Coaldrake sitting in the front seat. I knew that she was a person who would take care of the girl without any fears for herself and without plying the girl with questions. I took Marna into my tent and explained everything to her. Then she came out and organised everything showing a gentle and compassionate side that nobody had seen before.

When the truck was ready to leave, I called Uncle Robert, Aunty Louisa and the girls to come and say goodbye. The littlies came and shook hands but no one else moved.

"Isn't anyone else going to say goodbye?" But they remained motionless.

Even though I realised why they didn't want to come close, I was angry at their insensitivity. I became even angrier when the two men who had come out on the back of truck insisted that they sit in the front for the return journey leaving Marna and Judy to sit on the back. Furious, I said, "Get this truck out of here now."

As I waved goodbye, tears streamed down my face. Several years later when I was coming back from a visit to Perth, I called into the leprosarium at Derby. The girl rushed up to me and I put my arms around her. She was one of the lucky ones. She only spent eight years at the leprosarium!

I slowly resumed my contact with the community at large. I had enjoyed my first tribal experiences which had been established during the war and I felt glad that once again I was in a position to talk to my people. As a full-time teacher's aide and community worker, I was able to give the rest of the staff a better insight into the feeling of the people and a deeper understanding of our culture. This was hard because the missionaries' and the government's sole purpose was to make us think and talk like gudiyar people. For as long as I can remember we were always told that we were to forget all about our Aboriginal culture and that we had to learn the whiteman's ways. It was like telling Umba the kangaroo that it had to run and lay eggs like Wearie the emu.

I developed the practice of regularly visiting the tribal people at the camp with my Aunty Dudgulla and listening to their stories. I told them, "I don't know nothing because them gudiyar bin bring me up. You can tell me now. And don't get frightened of them gudiyars because one day I might write books."

I wanted to learn about the tribal ways of giving birth. I said to Aunty Dudgulla, "Teach me. I want to learn 'em."

"Ngumballa," she said, "you learn 'em all these things." So she told me how tribal women gave birth in the bush. They scooped a little hole in the ground, filled it up with special, sacred leaves and the mother just squatted over it. She did not have to push against gravity. The older tribal women always knew if a woman was going to have difficulties. I said to Aunty Dudgulla, "How you tell?"

"You look at which way they warra (walk)," she said.

One day King Peter Warriu said, "Ngumballa. You big missionary now. You educated. You learn everything. We respect you. But all these things no good if you don't be you." In other words, he was telling me to put snobbery aside and not to be flash. I wasn't going to tell him that I wasn't a missionary but a member of the mission staff. Who was I to argue with the King of the tribe.

A great honour was bestowed on me by King Peter. On the weekends I would go and talk to him. He was very pleased that I wanted to learn and he told the tribal people, "She all right. She bin fight against gudiyars. You bin tell'm story now." So they began to train me in tribal culture and law though they told me nothing about men's sacred things because if a woman ever knew about such things she could be sung to death. They took me out bush and told me all about our culture – about what the stories were and what they meant and about how to live with nature. King Peter Warriu instructed one of the tribal women to teach me under cover of dark. When she had finished what she had to say she would be gone and, though I listened carefully, I never knew who she was.

One day, I was talking to a tribal uncle and I asked him in our language, "Where did the Aborigines come from?"

His answer was, "What do you mean – where did we come from? We belong here. Our people have always been here. This is Aboriginal country."

Speaking in our language as best I could, I said, "White man's law says Australia was once joined to Asia and that Aboriginal people bin walk through that way."

At this, he became very angry and said, "You listen here, ngumballa, this here land belong to Aboriginal people before white people came and for all time. This was our land. We obeyed the laws of the Great Spirit and nature. Our children were happy. We were happy, and we had plenty of food and shelter. Then the white man bin come and bugger'im up everything."

When I echoed his sentiment saying, "Yeah, them whitefellas bin bugger'im up everything," he became angry with me and said, "I am elder. You are still ngumballa. Don't you swear. Just because you live like gudiyars and they bin grow you up, don't think you can swear. Tribal children are taught that swearing is wrong and any child who swears is punished. You must take notice of tribal Law and not swear until you are a ngoowahlee." He then went on to talk about the tragic disintegration of the Aboriginal culture. I was glad I didn't have a spear through my foot for asking such a silly question. I learnt some sad but important lessons from a man who had seen the violation of his land and the dispossession of his people and had found himself helpless to prevent such tragedies.

Now that I considered that I was close to being an adult, I again plied the questions, "Who is my mother? Where did she come from? Which tribe did she belong to?" Even then no one gave me answers to the questions I asked. They did, however, tell me some stories. The stories raised even more questions for me.

Ever since the war, I had suspected that I was a blood relative of Aunty Dudgulla. I asked her if this was so and she told me that she was my mother's sister. At Forrest River, it was the custom for the tribal elders to come and see all babies on the mission. Aunty Dudgulla told me that three other babies were born around the same time as me and that soon after my arrival we were all placed on view for the tribal elders' approval. Apparently I created quite an interest, as I was different from the other three babies with fairer skin, very tight curly black hair and deformed legs and feet. When the chief of the tribe saw me he said, "Where this one come from?"

Another elder promptly replied, "From wrong side of the gunyah!" It seems I was a barrel of laughs even from the day I was born. The phrase, "Where this one come from?" made me feel that I was an alien in my own country and that I did not belong to anyone.

When the tribal people died it was the custom to perform a smoke ceremony. I had to smoke their place out. I had to burn all their clothes. I remember the first time I did it. Someone had died and I was sitting in my little house when a young girl came up to me and said, "Sister McDonald, mummy and Aunty Marjorie want to know if you will do the smoking?" Only green leaves could be used for a smoking. So I collected some green leaves to put with the clothes. There were some fairly new clothes but even they had to be burnt. The girl's Aunty Marjorie told me, "Now you do that, ngumballa. Once our sister bin touch 'em they have to be burnt. Everything. This is law.' "

The chaplain came down and I said to him, "It is up to us to support the smoking. Nobody can live in that place any more. You can't break these laws."

"But," he said, "they're all Christians now. They shouldn't need these things any more."

"You can't knock something down like this that has been handed down to my people for thousands of years."

"But Sister McDonald, you are encouraging practices that are of heathen influence."

"I have been given the privilege of doing all these things and I am learning too. I'm not going to forget my culture just because you want me to be a Christian."

He thought for a bit and then said, "You are very smart and the things you challenge me on – you make me think."

I made the fire the way I had learnt from Aunty Dudgulla. First I made sure that it wasn't a windy day as a smoking must be done on a calm day. This was because I must not let any ashes blow away. She had shown me how to start the fire so that the flames were contained in the house and so that everything was burnt to ashes. The fire burnt straight up as it was supposed to and soon the clothes and thatched roof were alight. The walls which were made of mud brick were blackened but not burnt. I collected the ashes in a hessian bag making sure that I didn't miss any. I then gave the sacred ashes to the family.

My part was finished. It was up to the family then to decide what they would do with the ashes, whether they would throw them on the river, bury them or whatever. The old people of the tribe would then organise a big song and dance that the mission people could not attend. The house was not occupied again by the same family and three months later the tribal elders chose another family to rebuild the house.

During this time, I didn't care what the mission thought. I was glad to be learning about my Aboriginal heritage. I said to myself, "I am a member of staff and no longer a dormitory girl, so come what may I am going to go and find out things." I could see that here was my chance – maybe my one and only chance and I believed that if I came up against the mission bureaucracy I would come out on top. My yearning to learn about my culture was so strong that nothing would stop me.

I often visited Mummy Nora's family during this time. I would go and sit and listen. Eileen, Mummy Nora's daughter, told me one time that her mother had seen the potential in me from when I was a very little girl. "My Mummy – you were favourite with her. Mummy would say 'This little girl we will grow up because she is proper clever. We look after her.' " I wondered whether Eileen might have felt a bit neglected but she never complained.

I was sitting with Mummy Nora one night when she said, "No good having arguments with these missionaries."

"Well," I said, "I'm not taking any notice of them. If this is our culture, then this is our culture. You tell me more, Mummy Nora."

"You, proper cheeky one," she laughed.

# Eighteen

## *"A right and proper person"*
## ⤳ *Leaving the mission* ⤳

Three years after I came back from Alice Springs, the Western Australian government decided that it was time the school at Forrest River became part of the state's education system. In 1953, the first government-trained teachers arrived: Miss Edna Thomas (now Gray) and Miss Leita Turner (now Bell). Miss Thomas became the headmistress. When the change took place, the government had to decide whether to continue to employ me, as I was not a trained teacher.

I was not worried about my employment. I knew I had no qualifications to teach and I would accept their decision. Maybe I would leave the mission and find employment elsewhere. My uncle Sandy often told me that if I left the mission, he would find me a job in Wyndham. However, the government decided that I could continue teaching. I was happy with their decision as teaching was what I had known all my life and I enjoyed it. I also enjoyed the training in lesson preparation that the new headmistress gave me.

I usually spent my holidays in Wyndham either with Uncle Sandy, Aunty Mollie and Alan or with my friends, the Macales out at One Mile Gully. The Macales had a daughter, Ruth, who was around my age, and who had been a great friend of mine during my dormitory days (and still is). Her father had been the head stockman at Forrest River but he took his family to Wyndham when his wife died after the war and never returned. Ruth and I would often talk about what life had in store for us. One day Ruth looked at me seriously and said, "Connie, you must leave Forrest River. You have gone as far as you can go there. The longer you stay there the more dependent on you the people and missionaries will become."

I was amazed and said, "But Ruth, I feel a sense of duty to the mission and to the people. So I can't leave."

"Well," said Ruth. "If you stay on there you will never grow. Not only will you not grow mentally and emotionally but you won't grow spiritually."

Then it hit me. The chaplain needed me to play the organ for every service. The school needed me because I understood the children and their families. My people needed me to give them help and advice. From an early age, I had helped care for the sick, especially in epidemics of flu, measles and chicken pox. I told the mission staff about anyone who had leprosy or tuberculosis. And more often than not it was I who cleaned them up, especially the tribal patients as no one would touch a person with leprosy. I had come to believe I was indispensible. I said, "You are talking sense, Ruth."

"Well," she said. "When you go back to the mission think about it," and she emphasised the word 'think'.

The mission had instilled in me that I was here to serve and that I really didn't have any other options. While the 'Christian' part of me was saying, "You are here to serve your people," the rest of my being was urging me to think about myself. Ruth's words started a slow awakening in me that made me more conscious of my own potential and my rights to lead my own life. I started to think about leaving the mission and finding my way in the wider world.

One day I said to the headmistress, "Now that I am twenty-one, I am able to leave the mission and travel Australia."

She said, "You can leave the mission but the only way you can travel throughout Australia is to get your citizenship rights. You know about the twentieth parallel?"

"Yes, I already know about the twentieth parallel business but I thought I'd be able to get out of it." Aborigines from the Kimberley could not officially cross the border from Western Australia into the Northern Territory nor go further south than Derby without special permission. It reminded me of the dingo fence I had heard about that prevented dingoes from wandering into new territory.

A couple of weeks later, Miss Thomas said, "I have a form for you to sign."

"What for?"

"It's for citizenship rights."

"What's this here 'citizenship rights'? Explain it to me."

"It enables you to be exempt from the Native Welfare Act. That means you can travel anywhere in Australia without having to get permission from the Welfare."

"Oh good," I said. "Now I'll be able to travel to Perth, Sydney and even Queensland." And without thinking about it any further I signed the form. Months later I received a letter from the Native Welfare Department informing me that my application had been approved and a date had been set for me to appear before the magistrate in the Wyndham courthouse. On the sixteenth of December, 1954, eleven months after I turned twenty-one, I had my first appearance in court.

There were two of us waiting in the hall of the courthouse for our citizenship rights, Keith Chulung and myself. An Aboriginal police tracker came and sat with us while we waited. I think he came to give us moral support as he knew what Aboriginal people were up against when they went to court. Though we knew we were there for an entirely different reason from the usual one for our people, I was still glad that he was there to give us confidence. Neither of us properly understood what the whole process was about.

We were both excited as we knew that having citizenship rights meant that we could go anywhere we liked. We laughed and joked about the twentieth parallel saying we would now be free to go beyond the bounds of government restrictions. Each of us, though eager to gain our citizenship, hoped that the other one would be called to go in first. Then Keith said, "Here come the big wigs." He pointed to a rotund gentleman and said, "That one is the magistrate."

I said, "He looks more like Father Christmas to me; he's so large and jolly."

141

As they passed us they smiled and nodded. I was shocked – important gudiyars smiling at three Aborigines. I thought, "Gee, things are looking up for my people."

Ten minutes later, the clerk of the court came out and called, "Mr Keith Chulung, will you come in." This left me worrying about what questions they would ask and whether I would be given my citizenship rights. I might have left if the police tracker had not been there. To reassure me, he said, "Ngumballa, everything will be all right."

Eventually the door opened and Keith came out smiling and holding out his citizenship card. He looked as though he had won the Melbourne Cup. The clerk of the court said, "You can come in now, Miss McDonald. This way please."

I looked back at the police tracker who gave me a big smile. I composed myself and walked in while the clerk held the door open. I felt most important.

The clerk told me where to stand and the magistrate put his hand out towards me. I didn't know what to do so the clerk whispered to me, "His worship wants to shake your hand." I couldn't believe it. But I put out my hand and he shook it. Then he said, "Name?"

Bowing, I said, "Constance, your majesty."

The clerk whispered, "Your worship."

"Surname?"

"McDonald, your worship," I said, bowing again.

"Where were you born?"

"Four Mile, Wyndham, your worship," and I bowed again.

The clerk whispered to me again, "You don't have to bow."

"I see here in your file that you completed your education at Alice Springs."

"Yes, your worship."

Then he said, "What is your reason for applying for citizenship rights?"

This flustered me, "Well, your majesty..."

Quick as a wink, the magistrate said, "Young lady, address me as your worship."

"I understand that getting my citizenship rights will let me travel anywhere in Australia and I will not be under the Native Welfare Act any more. I will be free to come and go as I wish."

Then he made his official declaration, "Miss Constance McDonald, we, the government of Western Australia and the Native Welfare Department deem that you are a right and proper person to be in receipt of citizenship. Your record shows that you have not been in gaol or in trouble with the police on the mission or anywhere else. Your conduct record is one you can be proud of. All Aboriginal people should follow your example. The departments concerned are pleased that you be given full citizenship rights."

At this, I interrupted him, "Your worship, why should I have to be given citizenship rights in my own country. I was born here."

"It's the law," he said.

"Hogwash."

"Excuse me, what did you say?"

"I'm just thinking out loud. What law, your worship?"

"The government's law."

By now, I was well and truly in an argumentative mood, so I enquired further, "How many laws have you got for Aborigines in this land?"

"Miss McDonald, we are not here to talk about the law. We are here to give you your citizenship. Do you want it?"

"Yes, your worship."

He stood up and said, "Congratulations, Miss McDonald," and shook my hand. "Now you have the same rights as white people. You can drink."

"Well, I don't drink and I don't aim to start now!"

He invited Keith and me to the sergeant's house for a cup of tea. I walked out thinking to myself, "Freedom at last." It felt better than getting a knighthood. But I still wondered why I needed it.

In 1955, Miss Sally Gare, a government-trained teacher, was sent to Forrest River to take over my teaching job. After all those years of teaching, I was now officially unqualified to teach. I felt as though I was in a vacuum. I wanted to leave but somehow I couldn't bring myself to do it.

I stayed on at the mission as general assistant to the missionaries and continued to learn as much as I could about tribal ways by going up to the camp whenever King Peter requested my presence. I did not get along well with the chaplain of the time. Every time he and I crossed paths, it was like the saint and the devil, he, of course, being the saint. He didn't seem to like an Aboriginal person showing any intelligence.

One of my duties was to play the organ for all the services. I had to play for morning prayer, I had to play for evening prayer, I had to play everything for Sundays. When he tried to order me around all the time I would say to him, "I'm not a dormitory girl any more but a free citizen. You can't boss me around. If I don't want to come and play the organ, I won't."

After years of being at everyone's beck and call to look after the sick, supervise the dormitory girls, organise the roster for cleaning the church, play the organ, speak up for my people who were not getting a fair go, give them advice on difficult situations and still not feeling as though I was an accepted member of the Oombulgurri tribe, I felt as though everything in my life was tumbling down. I asked myself, "Why am I doing all this when people could do more for themselves?" But I continued on.

One day, I was summoned to the superintendent's office.

"Connie, we are going to excommunicate you. You can go to church but you cannot take the sacrament." This was all very well, but he didn't tell me why I was being excommunicated. Keeping up my usual brave front, I said, "When is this to happen?"

"This week."

I did know what the word 'excommunicate' meant but I thought, "I'll make him think I don't know what it means." I didn't want to show him how intelligent I was, so I decided to make him think that I was dumb. I went home to my little house where I had been reading about the Tower of London. The word excommunication was just like the word execution, so I thought I'd have some fun at my own expense; after all it was me who was going to lose my head. I laughed like crazy to think of the trick I was playing on him.

It seemed funny to me that they would excommunicate me but still want me to play the organ. So next Sunday I went up to the church, played the organ for the service and then waited, wondering when they were going to excommunicate me and wondering what it would involve. For a month it continued. When people commented saying, "You aren't going to communion." I said, "Oh, no! I'm waiting to be excommunicated," and I added for good measure, "They're going to chop my head off!"

All the people were really upset about this. "Why? What you done?" they asked.

"I don't know."

No one said anything but there was an uneasiness on the mission because the people were worried about me. So I decided to explain to them that the word excommunicate meant I was cut off from the church not that my head was cut off.

It seemed strange to me that an ordinary fellow like the superintendent of the mission was going to do the excommunicating bit. The Articles of Religion in the Book of Common Prayer 1662, now known as the Australian Prayer Book 1978, state emphatically in Article 33 of excommunicate persons: "That person which by open denunciation of the Church is rightly cut off from the unity of the whole multitude of the Faithful, as a Heathen and Publican. Until he be openly reconciled by penance, and received into the Church by a Judge that hath authority (thereunto)." Therefore my excommunication was invalid and a farce because the faithful of the mission did not know about it and there was no public announcement on the matter.

I thought to myself, "I'm a free person now. Nobody is going to tell me what to do." The missionaries were very wary of me after that. It became policy to never ask Constance anything. I didn't go to church, I didn't play the organ, I didn't visit the village people, I didn't teach. I just worked as a nanny for the Jamison's three boys and continued my visits to the camp at night. I was unable to find out what it was all about and to this day I do not know why I was excommunicated.

Then one day I packed all my belongings, told the superintendent I was leaving and caught the launch to Wyndham. When I arrived, I didn't know where I was going to live. I stepped on to the jetty with all my luggage when a couple of kiddies came running up to me and the eldest of them, a boy of about twelve years, offered

145

to carry my case. He asked me who I was and I said, "My name is Connie McDonald."

"Oh, you must be Uncle Sandy's daughter."

"No, I'm Duncan McDonald's daughter." I then asked him what relation he was to my father and Uncle Sandy.

"My dad's a relative of your uncle and father," he informed me.

"Is he really?"

"Yes," he replied "You can ask me mum."

"Are my father and Maisie in town?"

"No. All the family have gone to Hall's Creek and won't be back for a while."

He then told me to follow him to his place. His mother put her hand out to me and said, "I'm Ivy Carter. My husband George is a relative of your father. Where are you going to stay?"

"Well, I was thinking of going out to Uncle Sandy's place but now that they are on holidays, I don't know where I am going to stay."

"You are welcome to come and live with us if you wish," she said. And so I did.

As soon as I walked into their house I felt at ease and knew straight away that I was going to fit in with the family. Five o'clock arrived and so did George, Ivy's husband. As soon as he came in through the door, he shook my hand, saying, "I knew straight away that you were Duncan's daughter, because there's no mistaking."

He and his wife had three children and they lived in the town opposite the gudiyar hospital and quite close to the foreshore. It was only a small house, with two bedrooms, a kitchen and a small room which was converted into a shower room, and, of course, there was a loo in the back yard. The children's bedroom was divided in two by a partition, the girls and I occupied one side of the partition and their son the other side. The parents had their own bedroom. We ate our meals outside the house because there was no dining room and when it rained we just had to squeeze into the kitchen and sit wherever we could find room.

After being with the family for two weeks, I told George and Ivy that I felt that as I was staying with them it was only right that

146

I should find a job so that I could pay my board. The mission had never taught us to manage our affairs. Even though I had been paid as a teacher's aide, my salary was always administered for me. Fortunately my Uncle Sandy had instilled in me the importance of standing on my own two feet and working for a living. They both agreed to help me find a job, though George said that as I was family he didn't expect me to work. George explained that it would have to be domestic work as I was not trained.

All my relatives always made me welcome. Every time I came to Wyndham you would think the queen was visiting by the way they prepared for me. I did not try to set myself apart but I had had more education and I didn't get into drinking and gambling. My cousin Alan tells me that as a teenager he often wanted to go across to the mission to see what it was like over there, but his parents would say, "Don't you go over there. You'll end up like Connie, indoctrinated by the mission."

Before I left Forrest River, a young policeman had come up to arrest one of the mission staff, a matron, originally from England, who was on drugs. She was taken to Wyndham and charged with fraud. Everyone felt very sorry for her because we realised she was very sick. When the policeman came to arrest her, he had to stay the night at the mission and the matron was locked up in a little room at the mission house. That night was one of our outdoor picture show evenings, so we all took our chairs along and lined them up against the wall and watched the show. While the film was showing, I kept on being hit with pebbles so I turned around and one of the boys pointed to the policeman. As the pictures ended and I picked up my chair, a hand took it from me and a voice said, "I'll carry the chair." It was the gudiyar policeman.

"You can carry it around to the front of the church for me and I'll take it from there."

"Oh no," he said. "I'll carry it home. I know where you live."

"Oh you do, do you?" I countered. As we reached the door I said, "Thank you very much." There was no way I was going to invite him in after the episode I had had a couple of years before with the visiting missionary.

147

One night, when I was staying with Ivy and George we heard the gate squeak so I looked out and said, "Minmint garlu (policeman) here."

George went out and asked what he wanted.

"Can I speak to your cousin?"

So I went out, and on the attack as usual, said, "What's the matter? I never done anything."

"Would you like to come for a ride?"

"No fear. You're a married man."

"If you don't come, I'll tell the sergeant bad things that you done."

"Oh yeah? What are you going to tell the sergeant?"

"Oh, I'll make up a story."

"Well, that's your business."

"Come on. We'll go for a ride out to the Four Mile."

"No. You go by yourself."

So he told me his sad story, "Do you know that when I got home from Forrest River, my wife was having it on with the taxi driver."

"Well, that's too bad. Are you going to do anything about it?"

"No. But my wife wants to divorce me. She wants to marry the taxi driver."

"Good for her. I'm sure you'll find somebody else."

"I want you."

"Don't be funny," I said. "You are being ridiculous. You don't want me. You're just saying that on the rebound. No way."

He began to get quite upset and George came to my rescue. "I think you had better go now, officer. All the kids are asleep here and we want to go to bed."

I went inside and told George and Ivy all about it. "Ah! Proper mad one that," said George .

Next day, I went up to the shop and who should pull up in front of me but the police car. There were a lot of Aboriginal people there and one of them said, "He's making a line for you."

"Don't be funny. He's a married man," I said.

"Not any more!" he replied. In Wyndham, everybody knows everybody's business.

148

I said to myself, "They are not going to know my business because I am not going to go with this fellow." Everywhere I went after that the policeman shadowed me but that was that as far as I was concerned. Maybe I missed something. Imagine me as a policeman's wife! 'Black woman marries white policeman!' Wouldn't that have been something!

After a couple of months in Wyndham, I began to get rather bored with life. An appendix operation had left me unable to do housework or get a job. One night after we had all settled in to bed and were sound asleep, I was disturbed by a voice. As I was half asleep, I thought it was my cousin George, saying, "Go back to Forrest River."

"Why would I want to go back to Forrest River?" I thought it was a bit funny as I didn't get any reply. So I turned over and settled down to sleep again. Once more I heard the voice, "Go back to Forrest River." When it happened again the third time I got up. I was fully awake by now and had no hope of going back to sleep. "Are you awake George? Ivy? kids?" No answer. I got up and made myself a cup of tea. As I was sipping my cuppa, Ivy came out and joined me. "What is the matter? Haven't you been sleeping?"

"Oh yes, I was having a very good sleep until someone woke me up," I replied.

"What someone?"

"I heard this voice saying to me three times, 'Go back to Forrest River.' "

"Well, you are a Christian and you come from Forrest River; do you think it was God speaking to you?"

That morning, when the plane came in from Derby, there was a young woman who had just been discharged from the leprosarium and was returning home. I said to Ivy, "That looks like Olive de Grey." I went up to Olive and we put our arms around each other and kissed and cried for joy because we hadn't seen each other for ten years.

"Did they tell the mission that you were coming home?"

"I don't know."

I sent a telegram to say that Olive was in Wyndham and would need to be picked up. I added to the telegram that seeing the launch was coming in for her I might as well go back to Forrest

River too. We didn't have to wait too long for a reply to our telegram, "Sending boat in tomorrow. Put Olive on boat. You are welcome to come back."

I was pleased to be allowed back, and rushed to tell Ivy the good news. Ivy and George gave me twenty pounds to buy myself some clothes. The boat trip was uneventful except for casual comment of one of the crew which rather worried me, "You got no house any more. The old fellow is living there now."

Next morning, we arrived at the mission. Once again everyone was there waiting. This was a very special occasion as Olive had been at the leprosarium for ten years. The old people cried for joy. Her young son, Neil, who had been born soon after she went to Derby and had been taken back immediately to be looked after by his grandparents, King Peter Warriu and Lydia, stood shyly by as he did not know her. All this excitement about Olive made me feel very strange. It was like I was an immigrant. I was amazed that attitudes could change so much. No one seemed to want to know me. No one came up to me and said hello and I did not know where I was going to live.

Fortunately for me Mr Bill Jamison who was the mission engineer, appeared and said, "You know your house is taken. Well, you are coming to stay with Mary and me and the boys." I settled down to my job of taking care of the Jamison children and made regular visits up to the camp at night to continue my tribal education under the direction of a tribal woman.

One evening after dinner, we were sitting on the verandah enjoying the twilight when the Jamisons told me they were being transferred to Yarrabah, North Queensland. The people I knew in Western Australia all seemed to have one ambition, to go to Queensland, so I was delighted when Mrs Jamison said, "We'd like you to come with us."

"Oh yes," I said, "that's all right but are you going to pay for it?"

She called out to Bill, "Bring out the *Heralds of the King* magazine."

He opened it at the advertisements. I glanced at the page and there was an ad for a kindergarten teacher at Yarrabah saying, 'preferably Aborigine'.

Bill said, "Would you like to apply."

"It won't hurt," I said casually, and sent for the application papers.

When they arrived, I filled in my answers to such questions as 'Are you a communicant? Do you attend Church regularly? What training have you had for teaching? Have you attended College?' and waited for a month before I heard back from them. I didn't think much about it as I assumed someone else had the job.

Then one morning at about three o'clock, the launch came back in from Wyndham. Whenever the boat came in, the Jamisons made a ritual of opening the mail bags. This time it was more special than usual. It was neap tide and Bill had to get the old Chevrolet truck and go down about a mile and a half to meet the launch because there was no water for it to come up to the main jetty. While he was away Mrs Jamison and I prepared for the accompanying ritual – we lit the hurricane lamp and put on the kettle to make the many cups of tea that accompanied the opening of the mail-bags.

Bill opened up the large canvas bag and tipped the mail all over the floor. We rummaged around putting the letters in their right piles. "Here's a letter for you, Connie, from the Bishop of North Queensland. This is it!" he said, handing me a small brown envelope with the Bishop's crest on the back.

I wasn't excited. At least I didn't think I was excited. I opened it up thinking, "Oh well, whatever happens, happens."

*The Board has met. Your application has been approved and you have been accepted.*

I thought, "Gee, in spite of being excommunicated, in spite of not having had teacher training perhaps I will be of some use. I am really starting out in life now; I'm going to Queensland."

The next Sunday, the chaplain announced in church that the Jamisons and Connie McDonald were going to Yarrabah to teach. As I had not attended church for some time, I didn't expect anyone to take much notice. To my surprise, all sorts of people came up to me after church asking me, "Do you really have to go to Queensland?" "Do you want to go?"

"Well," I assured them, "There is nothing for me here. If I

151

stay, I'll be fighting with the chaplain all the time."

I was leaving because nobody had ever said to me that they loved me. I knew that the McDonald family loved me but I wanted more, especially from my father and from the people at the mission. I left Forrest River, a bitter and disillusioned young woman.

Sitting on the verandah one day after I had finished all my packing, I noticed this little old lady coming towards me. It was Aunty Dudgulla. I spoke to her in language and then she told me that she had come with a message for me, "King Peter wants to see you."

I went up to the camp with her (King Peter was not allowed to live in the mission as he had two wives.) King Peter sat down beside me outside his tent and began to instruct me. "Ngumballa, you can tell what all these old people bin tell you about our culture when they take you out bush. You can go everywhere, anywhere, you can do them drawing, but not sacred ones. And when you go other places, don't you draw them sacred things bilong other people. You stick to your own stories and your own drawings. That Law, that tribal Law." I promised King Peter that to the day I died, I would do the right thing. King Peter was making sure that I was clear about the Law and would not encroach on things that were not mine or tell of things I had no right to. At the same time, he was entrusting me to preserve and tell those things that were allowed to me. As Aunty Dudgulla took me home in the dark, I felt sad to be leaving but highly honoured at the confidence King Peter had placed in me .

# PART TWO

## BEYOND FORREST RIVER

# Nineteen

## *"You might meet Slim Dusty"*
### To Queensland

The epic journey to my new life in Queensland began in 1957 on the *Munnumburra* (the mission launch), which took us to Wyndham. Here we were to board the passenger-ship *Koojarra* for Darwin.

Whenever I visited George and Ivy in Wyndham, George would say, "You're missing a good opportunity with that policeman." But I took no notice. The day the Jamisons and I went to organise our baggage for the trip, who should walk on the wharf and ask if he could carry my case but the young policeman.

"Whereabouts in Queensland are you going?" he asked.

"Just Queensland," I replied. I wasn't going to tell him where and have him following me. "It's been nice knowing you."

"Are you coming back?"

"No. I'm going for good. I'm going to travel around. Good-bye." Again I felt a little sorry for him. Perhaps he was genuine.

I knew that Uncle Sandy, Aunty Molly and Alan would be there to see me off but I was surprised to see my father and Maisie also turn up. My father came over to me and said, "Connie, I've changed my mind. You can come and live with us."

I let forth, giving my father the full blast of my feelings. "Bit too late now, father! I am an adult remember, but I'm not eighteen; now I am twenty five. I am going to live my life and I will never see you again. Goodbye." And I went on board the *Koojarra*. I was surprised to see my father cry and wondered whether I should have said it but at that time I didn't feel any remorse.

I realise now that my outburst came as a culmination of all my pent-up feelings about the things my father hadn't done for me and which I had carried in my heart for many years.

The journey took us up the Cambridge Gulf. Imagine the excitement we felt when the captain ordered us on deck. When all were assembled, he told us to line the decks on both sides of the ship to witness a natural phenomenon. As the ship slowed down almost to a stop, we all jostled for a place at the railing and then we saw it. Paul's little voice piped up, "It looks like someone stretched a white string across the water." On one side of Paul's 'piece of string' was the muddy, brown water of the Cambridge Gulf and on the other side was the deep blue water of the Timor Sea. The meeting of these two waters was marked by a turbulence that prevented the mixing of the two colours.

After four days in Darwin, we boarded Tuitt's bus which took us to Tennant Creek. The journey to Mt Isa was long and exhausting and the children were getting cross and tired. We had to stop every now and then to stretch our legs and answer nature's call. In those days, petrol stations were few and far between. Every hundred miles or so, we would pull up at a hotel which was a relief as we could have a meal and freshen up. I was looking forward to seeing Mt Isa as my father and other drovers used to talk about it.

We arrived exhausted and went to our hotel. It was a while before I went to sleep as I had to do my meditation and say my prayers and then I had to see that the boys were comfortable and their mosquito nets were firmly tucked in. At Mt Isa, the tedium of travelling finally gave way to excitement as we felt that we were in Queensland at last. It was liked the promised land. After all, it was the place where you might meet Slim Dusty!

Some days later, we left Mt Isa by train. Although this leg of the journey was as long as all the others, we didn't mind because we had sleeping berths in our carriages. It was not until we were on the train to Townsville that I felt that my spirit was free – free from oppression, free from suppression, free from drummed-in religion and free from the twentieth parallel. I decided there and then that my freedom would know no bounds.

After arriving at our hotel in Townsville, we were summoned to the Bishop's lodge for lunch. By this time we felt that we were seasoned travellers, having journeyed across some of the most remote, inhospitable and sparsely-settled regions of the top end of Australia. The day before we left Townsville for Cairns, I washed my new floral nylon dress and hung it on a line on the verandah of the hotel. After about ten minutes, I went to see if my dress was dry and to my horror the line was empty. I was very upset because my best friend had bought me the dress as a going-away present. Suddenly, something yellow caught my eye on the roof of the house next door. It was my dress. I found Mr Jamison and told him what had happened. He went to the office and the hotel manager asked two of his workers to retrieve my dress. The task was a bit risky but the young fellows managed to retrieve my dress without damaging it. I was glad to have it back all in one piece.

We left Townsville by train in the morning and arrived in Cairns the next afternoon. Coming from the dry Kimberleys, I had never seen such greenery before. It was like entering into a new world of the sugarcane farms and the rainforests.

I had many hopes for my life in this 'new world'.

# Twenty

## *"The way he look at you"*
## ᔗ *Yarrabah* ᔗ

Two boys from Yarrabah were waiting at the Cairns railway station to meet us. They informed us that the mission launch was at the wharf all loaded up and ready to depart. "The tide is on the turn. If we miss it, we will have to wait another four hours until the turn of the next tide," they said. "Besides, the mission people and missionaries are all waiting at the jetty to meet you."

As we boarded at the wharf, we noticed that there were quite a few people returning to Yarrabah. Some had been patients at the Cairns Base Hospital and had been discharged that day, others were men, women and young girls returning for the weekend or on holidays. The men worked on the sugar plantations and the women did domestic work as cooks in private homes and hospitals. The young girls worked as domestics and waitresses on the various islands around Cairns such as Dunk and Hamilton Islands which were being opened up as resorts at that time.

Some of the people told me that they had heard about me from the late Conrad Madigan and the late Louie Greenwood, who were both captains of the mission launch at Forrest River at different times. These gentlemen came from Yarrabah and each had wanted to adopt me but the Native Welfare had vetoed their requests. The department told them that my father was still alive and he would have to give his permission and legally sign me over for adoption. As I talked to the people about the captains I felt as though I already belonged.

When the launch came round Bessie's Point and into Yarrabah Bay, the water changed colour from a deep ocean blue to a shimmering turquoise. I could see by the number of boats that were on the water and pulled up on the shore that fishing was an important part of life in Yarrabah. Looking beyond the shore, I was struck by the density of the forest that was so different from the sparse and lonely vegetation of the Kimberleys. I thought that it looked like the original garden of Eden and I said to Mrs Jamison, "What a beautiful place!"

I will never forget the warmth of the reception when we arrived at Yarrabah. That night they held a corroboree along with island dancing. Each of us in turn was brought to the centre of the gathering and formally introduced by Lottie Maywee, Queen of the Goonjangi tribe.

I was delighted to be back teaching. I loved the children and I found working with them a challenge. One day, I called four-year-old Joe to my desk because he was pulling the hair of one of the little girls. I stood him in front of me, "Why are you doing that?"

He looked at me and said, "You can't punish me."

"Why can't I?"

"Because I'll tell my mother."

"Well Joe, while you are here in kindy, I am the boss and if you are naughty I will punish you."

Joe started to cry as he thought that I was going to give him the cane. So I said, "No Joe, I just wanted to tell you that it is not right for little boys to pull little girl's hair. If you do it again I shall have to smack you." Then the flood-gates opened and he cried even more but he didn't ever pull her hair again.

It was the custom for boys and girls to carry the books for their favourite teachers. One afternoon, a nine-year-old boy knocked on the kindergarten door. It was Lloyd Schrieber, offering to carry my books. He was a bright and intelligent young fellow. He spoke well, his manners were impeccable, he dressed well, he was polite and he also had a sense of humour.

At the missionary female quarters, I invited him in and put the books on the dining-room table. He hesitated before he left so I said, "Is there anything I can do for you, Lloyd?"

He answered, "Teacher Con, I'd like you to come and meet my family."

So I went into my room, titivated myself and we set off.

As we were walking along Lloyd said, "Teacher Con. You will like my family." I asked him how many were in his family. He said, "Granny Lottie, mum, dad, Vincent and Peter are at home and my two sisters Gwenny and Betty are at school at Charter's Towers and of course there's me!"

As we were nearing his home, I began to feel both excited and nervous all at once. Lloyd stood at the bottom of the stairs (all the houses were on stilts) and said, "Granny, I've brought someone to meet you."

We sat down to talk and Granny Lottie said, "We were all wanting to meet you since Dadda Greenwood and Dadda Madigan told us about you and how they each wanted to adopt you and bring you back here." Soon Lloyd's mother, Lorna, arrived and invited me to stay to dinner. The Schriebers became my Yarrabah family and I spent many happy times with them.

The first time I met Lorna I thought to myself, "What a strikingly beautiful young woman! She's too young to be the mother of five children." Lorna had a beautiful smile which I thought was quite captivating. I took to her straight away and I knew that we would become good friends.

When I met Lorna's husband, Stephen, for the first time I was a bit afraid because he is a big man who was quiet and reserved. I did not have much to do with Stephen and his sons Vincent and Peter because they were away working during the week. Stephen was manager of the pineapple and banana plantation and vegetable crops at Jajangee. As I came to know Stephen, I found he was a gentle and loving man and we also became friends. I only saw the two girls of the family, Gwen and Bettina, when they came back home to Yarrabah from Charters Towers where they went to St Gabriel's Anglican School for girls.

Lottie Maywee was a straight-out, no-nonsense person just like myself, but she was also a very loving and understanding person and a very good Christian. I felt that I could talk to her about things which is why I told her about the emnity between my father and me. I was still hurting from the break with my father so I told Granny Lottie about what had happened between us when

I was leaving from the wharf at Wyndham. Granny said, "You shouldn't have left angry."

"Well, friend," I said. "He didn't want me when I was born. He was never there when I needed him. Why should I feel sorry for him now?"

"Listen girl!" she said. "You don't speak like that to your father. Where is your tribal upbringing?"

Stubbornly I said, "I don't want to see him again."

This made Granny Lottie angry and she said, "Don't speak like that about your father again in front of me."

"How would Lorna have felt if her father did that to her?"

Just then Lorna came in and said, "Mum, you've got to understand that Connie's start in life was a difficult one. We were a family. Connie had no family."

Grannie, not to be outdone, said, "It doesn't matter. Connie should respect her father no matter what!" Turning to me she said, "Girl, you mustn't abandon your father altogether. One day, you might lose him and it will be too late. Then you will have to live with the hatred you had for the rest of your life."

"I'll think about it." I said. We had a cup of tea and the subject was closed. Later I went back to my quarters and pondered Granny Lottie's words. I said no more but thought to myself, "Why is Granny Lottie telling me not to abandon my father when it was he who abandoned me?" I began to wonder whether I had been too harsh with him. I felt a deep respect for Granny Lottie for taking it upon herself to speak to me like that about family.

Lorna and her mother helped me through many difficult times. I thank the Divine Master for giving me such good, loving and Christian friends. My friendship with this family will be forever.

All the time I was at Yarrabah, my father and I did not correspond. A few of the dormitory girls wrote to me from time to time, letting me know what was happening on the mission. Sometimes I would get a letter from Ruth Macale (now Oxenbridge) telling me about life in Wyndham. Maisie wrote from Alice Springs, a letter that I kept for many years, because it began "To my dear stepdaughter". In the letter, she told me she was leaving my father and that they had decided to make me Colin's guardian.

Colin, she said, had the same bone condition as me and his continual broken bones had caused Welfare to transfer him to Adelaide for special care. He had been living for several years at a children's home connected with the Royal Children's Hospital in Adelaide and spent his life in and out of hospital. This did not surprise me as, when he was a baby, I would often say to Maisie, "Be careful when you pick him up. Maybe he might have the same thing as I have."

Later, I received a letter from the Child Welfare Department confirming that I was officially Colin's guardian and that all decisions about him had to be approved by me. I was glad that they had made this arrangement as I was worried about what might happen to him. In the Christmas holidays of 1958, I went to see him. I left Yarrabah, where there were no streets, just a few rough roads used by the mission trucks, and arrived in Adelaide with its very wide, paved streets. They were the widest streets I had ever seen, so on my first visit to the Children's Hospital, I was nervous about crossing the main road. The pedestrian lights went green. The cars stopped. My confidence returned. I set off to cross the road, sauntering happily in my usual laid-back Kimberley style. I was only half-way across when I heard the beeps and honks of cars, and the voices of people yelling out, "What's wrong with you?" "Can't you read the lights?"

Not really taking anything in I thought to myself, "Gee, these people are friendly, yelling out to me." So I waved to them and smiled. The more I waved, the more they honked. A motorcycle policeman pulled up and said, "What have we here? Why are you holding up the traffic?"

"What do you mean, officer? I was crossing the road."

"Well, you were taking a mighty long time about it. Where do you come from?"

"Originally from the Kimberley, Western Australia."

"That figures," and he took me to the police station and told me all about lights and walking briskly across the road. From then on I was more careful.

As he grew up, I visited Colin from time to time at the Adelaide children's home and when he was no longer a state ward, he came to live with me for a couple of years in Bexley, New South

161

Wales. Despite our bone conditions, we both enjoyed life and got on very well. He returned to Adelaide where he lived with a family who cared for him until his death in 1987.

A young migloo man lived at the Yarrabah mission house and was skipper of the mission launch. He had fair hair, blue eyes and was tall and handsome. I couldn't help noticing his fine physique and the proud way he walked. I admired him from a distance and often dreamed that I would like to marry someone like him one day. Our paths often crossed on my visits to the mission house or when I went on the occasional trip to Cairns. Most times we merely said hello or talked about the weather. After a while he started to ask me about how the kindy was going and how the children were. I thought it strange that he was so interested in the kindergarten.

The first inkling I had that he had more than a casual interest in me occurred when I went to visit the Schriebers after school. During my visits, Granny Lottie, Lorna and I would often talk about life. On these occasions young Lloyd would make himself scarce, asking permission from his mother to go and play with his friends. On this particular day, as I sat drinking my tea, Granny said, "The skipper is throwing a line out for you girl."

"Don't be funny," I said.

"Funny nothing! We've been watching him and we notice the way he look at you." I thought about how one has to be very careful and discreet about one's behaviour in a close community like a mission because missionaries and teachers were looked upon as people who were beyond reproach. I could remember how the people at Forrest River mission thought about the missionaries. I knew it was the same with the Yarrabah people.

Lorna walked in and Granny said to her, "Tell this girl that migloo skipper is throwing a line out for her."

I looked at Lorna and said, "Is this true?"

"He even tells the fellas that help him down the launch that he is falling in love with you."

"True?" I said, wanting to spin out this very interesting conversation. "I had better ask him."

"Now you listen here," said Granny Lottie. "How old are you?"

"I'm twenty-five."

"Well, it's time you got married."

"What do I want to get married for, Granny?"

"Everybody gets married."

"Not everybody."

"Well, you want to have a family don't you?"

"Someday, maybe. Maybe not."

"Oh you're a hard-headed one. Lorna you had better talk to this girl. Put some sense into her."

"But Granny, I don't feel anything for him. Aren't you supposed to feel something?"

"Well girl, you have to work up to it."

Soon after, I had to go to the hospital in Cairns because I had broken my right foot. It was neap tide so the boat could not come near the jetty but was anchored in the channel at the point. Those, like me, who couldn't walk were taken to a big rock close to the edge of the water by truck and then we were all rowed out to the launch in a dinghy. I was the last patient to go in the dinghy. Imagine my surprise when I saw the skipper himself rowing over to pick me up.

Suddenly it dawned on me that what Granny and Lorna had been telling me was true. He was 'fishing' for me. As the dinghy neared the shore, I didn't know which way to look. He greeted me, "Hello there," and I thought to myself, "That is that look they were telling me about."

I sat on the rock as demurely as I could manage. The dinghy came quite close to shore and I could have stepped into it but he insisted that he would get me safely on board. As he lifted me off the rock, I began to shiver and he said, "What's the matter? You're not frightened by me are you?"

"No," I said. And he gave me that look again. "Put your arms around my neck and hold me tight," he said and I did. "Tighter," he said and I did. "Boy," I thought, "This fellow is really keen on me." This new experience was very frightening.

He said, "You'll be all right, my dear. I'll look after you."

He knew I wasn't shivering because it was cold or because I was frightened he would drop me. My shaking indicated to him that this was the first time any man had held me like that. He assured me that nothing was going to happen to me and he meant

163

it. He rowed slowly to the boat as we sat facing each other in the tiny dinghy. I didn't know which way to look and I thought to myself, "Constance, is this how romance starts?" He must have known that I felt embarrassed because for once I was caught short for words so he began the conversation. "Do you like Yarrabah?"

"Oh yes, very much."

"What are your plans for the future?"

Recovering some of my forthright manner, I said, "If I knew what my plans were I'd tell you."

"Do you think you'll be staying in Yarrabah long?"

"It all depends," I said to him.

By the time I had begun to relax and our conversation had started to deepen, the dinghy pulled alongside the launch. One of the crew, who was Lorna's cousin, yelled over the side, "Hey boss, what happened? I didn't think you two were coming." I was embarrassed but the skipper looked at him with a sly look and smiling, threw him the rope.

He asked one of his crew members to jump in to hold the dinghy steady. The other crew man let the rope ladder down and between the two of them they managed to get me and my broken foot aboard the launch. The young migloo man invited me to sit beside him at the tiller but I declined, saying that I would sit on the top in the fresh air. Once the launch rounded Bessie's Point the skipper called to a crew member to take the tiller and came up and sat very close to me. I thought to myself, "Well, Constance, be brave." We chatted as if we were long lost cousins. As we neared Cairns, he whispered, "When we get to the wharf you stay put."

"Why?" I asked, "Are you going to carry me off again?"

"I'd like to," he replied, "but the ambulance is coming to get you. I'll come to the hospital to see you before we go back to Yarrabah."

As I came out of the x-ray room at the hospital, I saw him again. He came up and said, "How long are you going to be?"

"I don't know," I told him. "They have to put a plaster on."

"Oh well, it has to be hello and goodbye then, because the tide will soon turn." I was disappointed to find that I would have to stay at the hospital but quite confused when the ambulance pulled up

164

outside. I asked why it was there.

"The ambulance men are going to take you back to the wharf."

"But the launch has gone back to Yarrabah. It left an hour ago."

"How would you know?" And ignoring what I said the men put me in the ambulance and took me to the wharf. The launch was not there!

"Where am I going to stay?" I asked.

"We know where to take you," said one of the men.

When the ambulance stopped, one of them opened the door and said, "Here we are." I saw that we had stopped at the police station. A police constable came to the door of the ambulance and said, "What have we here?"

"A patient from the Cairns Base Hospital who missed the Yarrabah launch," said the ambulance officer.

"Excuse me," I chipped in. "I didn't miss the launch. The attending doctor knew that the launch was going straight back and I understood that I would be staying in hospital overnight."

"I haven't seen you before," said the policeman, ignoring what I had said.

"No, you haven't," I assured him. "I am not a Queenslander. I'm from the Kimberleys, Western Australia. You can't lock me up because I'm a missionary and a member of the teaching staff at Yarrabah. Do you want to know my name and date of birth and everything?"

"No."

"You might as well," I said angrily. "I'll tell you something, I have my citizenship rights," and I showed him the card, "so if you lock me up you'll know about it."

The constable went inside and out came the sergeant. He looked at me and said, "Why didn't you tell somebody you had your citizenship rights?"

"Nobody asked me," I said. I felt enraged as this was my first personal experience of the police racism that the Murri people had to live with. He looked to me as though he was feeling rather stupid and I said again, "If you put me in there, you will hear all about it."

Looking very uncomfortable, the sergeant said, "Take her back to the hospital. We can't keep her here."

Seeing me back at the hospital, the doctor said, "What are you doing back here?" I gave him the full blast of my anger, "Didn't I tell you the launch had already gone back to Yarrabah? You know where they took me, don't you? I am not a criminal. Did you realise that I have my citizenship rights and that you should treat me properly."

"Why didn't you tell me?" he said, looking embarrassed.

"You didn't ask. What are you going to do with me now?"

"I guess we'll have to find a bed for you," he said apologetically.

As I prepared myself for bed and tried to calm down, I realised that living on the mission had meant that I had been relatively unaware of the magnitude of the racism that the Aboriginal people had to endure.

Three days later, the launch made a special trip in to pick me up. I was pleased to see that I was to be the only person on board apart from the skipper and his crew. This time, I hobbled from the ambulance to the boat using crutches. I hadn't got far before the skipper jumped off to help me onto the launch.

"Is this a special trip for me?" I asked.

"Yes, my dear, it is."

"Couldn't your crew have come and got me?" (I was doing a bit of fishing of my own.)

"Connie, remember who the skipper is here," he laughed.

While I was deciding where I was going to sit, one of his crew said, "Boss, I'll take the tiller. You have enough on your hands." I gave that fellow a look.

The three men looked at each other and exchanged smiles, "Oh, thank you," said the skipper. Turning to me, he said, "Come downstairs with me so we can have a bit of privacy."

"Do you know what happens to me if I am in a closed-in area of a boat? I'd be sick all over you. We can still sit up on deck and be private. Those fellas are not going to take any notice of us."

He looked at me and said, "You want to bet?" The boys all laughed.

We sat up the front of the launch where I had a full view

of the sea and could feel the breeze. We continued our earlier conversation, only now I was more relaxed. I told the skipper that I liked travelling and would probably leave Yarrabah in a couple of years. I explained to him that my wandering urge came from having been kept on Forrest River Mission for so many years and that now I had freedom I planned to travel .

"Have you ever thought of getting married?" he asked.

"Yes, often."

"Did you have any boyfriends?"

"Yeah, one or two."

"Were any of them serious?"

I didn't want to explain to him that growing up in a mission dormitory, rather than a family, meant that I found it difficult to relate to anybody especially men. Instead I said, "Girls and boys never mixed on the mission until we were adults. We were told that things boys and girls did together were big sins and we should avoid all contact. It was harp, harp, harp, all the time." Then I said, "Did you grow up in a family?"

"Oh yes."

"Was it happy?"

"Yes, just normal family arguments and things."

"You had love, didn't you."

"Yes."

"Well," I said, "that's what I missed out on. Do you see now why I am cautious with men and why I won't let my defences down?"

"Now I understand," he said. "I thought you were just playing hard to get. Do you think we could have a relationship?"

"Oh, I suppose so."

"Well, I'd like to see more of you when you haven't got too much work to do."

"That'll be all right," I said, thinking to myself that this was the first time I had met a man who did not try to dominate me and who was really prepared to try to understand me. Then I remembered my bone condition and decided I should tell him all about it. After I had described it to him, he said, "That doesn't matter. I love you."

167

"True?" I said.

"I do."

"This boat is taking a long time to get home. Has the engine broken down or did they move Yarrabah?"

"Neither," he said. "The crew fixed all this up when we were coming in. We had a pow-wow about things." Eventually the launch arrived at the point. The skipper yelled out, "Drop the anchor here."

"But boss," replied one of the crew. "The tide is full. We can go to the wharf."

"No. We'll anchor the launch here and you two can go."

Quickly I said, pointing to one of the crew, "He can row me to the shore first and I'll wait for you there."

"Oh," said the skipper. "I thought maybe we could talk for another hour or two."

Firmly I said, "No, we've had enough talk for now. I'll wait for you on shore."

As I waited for the skipper on shore, I wondered, "Will I hot-foot it back to the mission or will I wait for him?" Reminding myself that a promise is a promise, I stayed there in the moonlight with much trepidation.

At last I saw the dinghy coming and heard the laughing and jokes of the crew. As I listened to the men's voices and the swish of the oars, I looked around me. The palm trees were swaying in the breeze, the moon was shining on the water and the whole area seemed to be shimmering. The dinghy pulled in and before I knew it he was there beside me.

"Now you can walk your missus home," teased his crew member.

"Excuse me," I said. "I'm not his missus yet."

The skipper laughed and I started to hobble beside him on my crutches while he tried to help me by putting his arm around me. After walking some distance we sat down for a while.

"Why didn't the launch go right up to the wharf?" I asked.

"I wanted to walk you home."

"What, on crutches?"

"I wanted to get to know you."

"Plenty of time for that."

That night I could hardly sleep and I wondered whether he was having trouble sleeping too. This was the first time in my life a man had this effect on me.

The next day Sister Muriel Stanley (later Underwood) sent one of her nurses to tell me that I needed to spend some time in the Yarrabah hospital so that my foot would heal properly. I wasn't surprised when I saw who it was that drove the truck down to pick me up, in fact I was secretly rather pleased. I had a pleasant stay in hospital as the skipper was a regular visitor with fruit and books. Even when the launch arrived too late for visiting hours, the staff would let him in to see me. Whenever I looked out and saw the launch coming in or going out, it reminded me of the first time he and I conversed with each other.

Three weeks later, when my foot was much better, I was summoned to the mission house by the superintendent's wife. She called her cook to put the kettle on and set the table for afternoon tea.

"How many?" asked the young lass.

"Four," was the reply.

We sat on the verandah, looking out on Yarrabah Bay.

"How is your foot?" she said.

I thought to myself, "She didn't ask me up here to talk about my broken foot." So I said, "What is the real reason that you asked me up here?"

She looked at me, smiled, and said, "Of late the skipper has become a changed man."

"Has he? What has that got to do with me?"

She explained, "One night, he couldn't sleep so he came to our room, knocked on the door and asked to come in. My husband asked him what the problem was.

"He said, 'I'm in love with Connie McDonald,' and I said, 'What a good choice!'

"'But,' he replied, 'Connie is playing hard to get. She won't commit herself.'

"'Well, have you asked her to marry you?'

She looked at me and smiled again so I said, "So you know about this supposed romance."

"We've known for a long time how he felt about you and so

we have invited you to dinner on his request."

The young lass came out to say that afternoon tea was ready. We moved into the lounge room. The skipper came out and she told him to sit on the lounge next to me. I thought to myself, "Talk about throwing people together."

We had a cup of tea and then the superintendent's wife said she had to go and organise dinner.

"Why are you going?" I asked.

"I want you both to get acquainted," and she left.

He brought out some photos of his family and of him as a child. I felt sad because I had no photos of my childhood but we laughed and joked especially at his baby photos. After dinner he walked me home and for the following few months we saw each other regularly. Maybe some of the people on Yarrabah suspected that there was a romance going on between us, and maybe they were wondering what kind of wedding there would be.

One Sunday night, I decided not to go to evensong as I was suffering from a migraine. I was lying on my bed in my darkened room when I heard a knock at the door. It was Jessie, a thirteen-year-old girl, sent by Granny Lottie to stay with me. She had scarcely come in and sat on the end of my bed when there was another knock on the door. She called out, "Who is it?"

"Me."

"What do you want?" she said as she opened the door.

"I want to see Teacher Con."

"She has a migraine but I'll ask her."

Jessie said, "Teacher Con, it's the skipper and he wants to talk to you."

I explained to him that I was lying down because I had a very bad headache and he said, "I want to speak to you in private. It won't take long."

"You can speak with Jessie here."

"No, Connie." he said. "I want to speak to you alone." So I asked Jessie to leave.

"Can I close the door?" he asked.

"Yes," I replied, "that's all right so long as you don't do anything untoward. What do you want to tell me?"

"I don't want to tell you anything. I want to ask you something."

"Ask away," I said.

He took my hands in his, looked at me with those eyes of his and said simply, "Connie, will you marry me?"

My head was throbbing and I said, "Did I hear right? Did you ask me to marry you?"

"Yes, I did."

"Well, I'll have to think about it."

"Don't take too long. I want to know the answer soon." By this time not only was my head throbbing but my heart was jumping up and down as well and I began to think "If this is romance, give me more." He sat on the bed, put his arms around me, lifted me up off the pillow and kissed me. My senses seemed to be running every which way. I said, "Hang on, put the brakes on."

"All right, Connie. Is this the first time you've been kissed?"

"Oh no. I've had kisses before from Aboriginal boyfriends back in the Kimberleys but yours has really set off the firecrackers."

"I'm pleased," he said and gave me a softer kiss, cradling me gently in his arms. "Can I see you another time?"

I said to him, "After this kiss you can see me any time." Then I called Jessie and told her what had happened.

She giggled and said, "Teacher Con, you and the skipper are too much. What was it like?"

"Unbelievable," I told her. "You'll find out when you grow up."

We chatted until we heard the last hymn and then I asked him to walk Jessie home.

That night, I couldn't sleep. One of the other women on the mission staff heard me walking up and down, and asked me if I was all right. I told her that my head was throbbing but I didn't tell her anything about my heart. She offered to walk me up to the hospital but I assured her there was nothing she could do, "There is little that can be done when a migraine gets hold of you. You just have to let it take its course." To myself I thought, "There is little that can be done once love takes hold of you..."

I was glad that the skipper had wakened love in me but I was frightened. I didn't know how to cope with this new experience. I wasn't sure whether I wanted to spend my whole life with him and I was worried about how my frail body would cope with the demands of marriage and children.

I had been relishing my new-found freedom when I first met the skipper and marriage was far from my mind. I was intent on a career and travel and I was determined to be myself rather than what other people wanted me to be. His proposal of marriage nearly bowled me over. I wondered, "What will happen to this new freedom if I say yes?  I can see myself, at home, keeping house for a husband, and later on children, and with no career." Sometimes I even thought, "What if I have children? Will I abandon them like my father did me?"

I knew that marriage to the skipper might mean I could travel all over Australia and maybe even overseas, but it wouldn't be *my* travel and it probably wouldn't make me happy. I told myself that freedom and independence meant more to me than being a wife and mother, even the wife of this wonderful man and mother to his children. Yet I was beginning to love the skipper. I wanted to see more of him and my feelings for him were very deep. I had confidence in him. I could sense that he had the most profound respect and care for me. For the first time, I could really love and trust a man. Over the next few months, our friendship increased and our love for each other grew until one day something unexpected happened to me.

While I was meditating, I heard a voice within me say, "I want you to join the Church Army." I didn't know much about the Church Army. I knew Sister Muriel Stanley (later Underwood) who was an Aboriginal Church Army officer working at Yarrabah and the first Aboriginal to be trained by the Church Army. She was also the first Aboriginal to be trained as a nurse in the then Crown Street Women's Hospital in Sydney. I had always admired her as at that time she was the only fully-trained Aboriginal nursing sister in Australia. I often talked to her and I was inspired by the wonderful work she did as matron of the Yarrabah hospital. Until I heard that small voice, I had never been the least bit interested in becoming a Church Army sister myself.

In Australia, the Church Army rule is that when a female officer marries, her title of sister and Church Army officer are relinquished, though she can still work for the Church Army in helping her husband in his Church Army work. The superintendent's wife had been a Church Army sister but when she married she had to relinquish her titles. I prayed and prayed about this message that had come between me and the happiness I hoped for with the skipper. I had to make a decision between my own happiness and what I believed God was calling me to do.

I took myself off to talk to Sister Muriel and told her about my dilemma, "I am not sure whether God is calling me to do his work by helping my people or whether I should marry the skipper."

She said, "Connie, this is your decision. Pray about it and if you are convinced God is calling you then you join the Church Army but if you don't think he is calling you, then marry the skipper. It's up to you."

After my chat with Sister Muriel, I went home much perturbed at the choice I had to make. I knew that this decision was going to change the direction of my whole life and I agonised over it for a long time.

Eventually I came to the conclusion that God wanted me to help my people and join the Church Army. I wept as I realised that I was forgoing a life with the skipper and the chance of becoming a wife and mother. I was angry with the Divine Master because I felt that, after all these years of giving service to him, he had finally shown me what love and happiness is only to ask me to give it all up. However, I was relieved to think that I would not be losing my independence. I felt confused but at the same time I was convinced I had made the right decision. In January 1960, I wrote to the Church Army inquiring about how to join.

For the next few weeks I managed to see very little of the skipper as I dreaded telling him my decision. I prayed, "Lord, you will have to give me the strength and courage to tell the man I love that my life is not going to be spent with him."

Early in February, I received some pamphlets and an application form which I filled in and returned immediately. A couple of weeks later, I received a letter from the Church Army head office advising me that the Board had met and decided to accept me as a student in the following year. Now that everything was confirmed, I knew that I could not delay telling the skipper any longer. I looked out to the bay to check whether the launch was in. Yes, it was moored in the channel. The skipper would be home. "Hello stranger!" was his greeting.

I thought to myself, "After I tell you what I have come for, I will be a stranger."

Looking at my face he said, "Is there anything wrong"

"Can we sit down?" I continued formally, "I've got something to tell you and this is it: the answer to your proposal is, 'No'. The reason for this is I feel that God is calling me to work for him among my own people."

He did not say a thing. I think he was in shock. We looked at each other and then I broke down and cried. He came to me and put his arms around me and said, "If that is what you want to do, then who am I to stand in your way."

Between sobs I said, "To think what could have been." I put my arms around him and we embraced.

Then he said, "Look at it this way Connie, maybe your God is saving you from something." Trying to smile he added, "I wish you all the best."

The superintendent's wife came in and asked what was wrong. I told her that I had given him the answer to his proposal. Putting her arms around both of us she said, "Then I detect that the answer was no. Have you got a good reason for refusing him?" I told her of my plans.

As I walked back home, I thought to myself, "Well, I'm glad I had a taste of romance, if only for a short time. I'm glad to know what love is all about." I promised myself that the experience of this love was something I would never forget.

Not very long after that the skipper left Yarrabah.

# Twenty-one

## *"Now it is alive"*
### ⤳ Jean Olsen ⤳

After I had been teaching at Yarrabah for some time, I realised that the school was in need of a new direction. I put forward submissions for things like sporting activities, excursions and the involvement of local tribal people in teaching about their culture. The Aboriginal helpers were enthusiastic about my ideas but the people in charge did not think my suggestions would work.

I felt disappointed but carried on regardless of the powers-that-be and taught my kindergarten class the way I wanted to. As I had done at Forrest River, I took my pupils outside and asked them to look around them and tell me what they could see. Instead of drawing houses, cats and dogs, I encouraged them to draw mango trees, palm trees, rocks, men fishing and women digging for crabs and oysters. I wanted them to become aware of the surroundings where their ancestors had lived and where they and their families belonged. The kindergarten children and I were learning together. My policy was for me to get to know them and them me.

The rest of the school seemed to be plodding along learning nothing but the three Rs and Church 'morals'. It was always, "You can't do this and it's wrong to do that. If you do wrong you will go to hell." Religion was the main concern of the school curriculum. I thought I had left the little word 'sin' behind at Forrest River but I came to realise that the aim of missions was to impart religion – a religion that controlled every thought and action. This meant that morale was low amongst the Aboriginal staff and pupils. We felt that we were getting nowhere and that the children were coming to school because they had to. They seemed to have an attitude of "We'd better learn what they want us to and then get out quick."

At the same time, I realised that religion had a part to play and that it was the missionaries' duty to teach religion.

This all changed when a new teacher, Miss Jean Olsen, arrived from the Sydney diocese. Jean came to us direct from her four years' training at the House of the Epiphany in Stanmore. Before this, she had to curtail her training as a nurse at Broken Hill because of an accident. She then trained as a missionary teacher and her aim was to go to New Guinea but the Divine Master had other ideas. She was sent to Yarrabah instead.

When told of our new teacher the whole school was excited. We were all hoping that she would become the head mistress, and on her first day at school, Jean announced that this was so.

Jean's stay at the mission was only about eighteen months but what she achieved in that time was phenomenal. Each month Jean had a teachers' meeting. She would ask us to put forward comments on what was happening in the school and told us of changes she was making. She ran the school efficiently, brightening up the rooms with pictures and crafts created by the children. She demanded punctuality and expected us teachers to give of our best. Jean gave training sessions to the teachers' aides and had the first ever open day. She designed a pattern for the school sports in the Yarrabah mission colours of grey and red, and a pattern for the girls' uniform and encouraged the mothers to sew them together.

She started the house sport system for the school and managed to get some of the fathers and grandfathers to make shields for each house. She organised for the Yarrabah school to take part in the Inter-school Sports Carnival in Cairns for the first time. Everyone in Yarrabah was excited, parents, grandparents, children, big brothers and sisters, aunties, cousins, missionaries, everybody. It was wonderful to see the pride in the whole community. The parents used to come and watch them practise marching, swimming and athletics.

The day of the carnival came. We were all on board the launch, looking forward to the carnival when, just as we rounded Bessie's Point, the sea became rough and most of us were seasick for the rest of the journey. The other teachers weathered the rough seas much better than I did. Jean was running from one end of the boat to the other looking after everyone, mopping up messes, and encouraging me to lead them in singing whenever I wasn't leaning over the side being sick.

When we reached Cairns wharf, I thought, "Terra firma never felt so good," and our enthusiasm returned quickly. Jean spoke to the assembled school giving us all instructions about what to do and how to behave. Jean, with two of her class, a boy and a girl, marched at the head of the school proudly carrying the Yarrabah flag for all to see. Each teacher walked beside their class encouraging them to do their best. I was at the end with the kindergarten. Our school was delighted when it was announced that we had won the march past and many of our children had excelled in every sport. On our return to Yarrabah, laden with trophies, we found that the children became more interested in their school work.

Encouraged by this success Jean decided to have a pet parade. She announced to the school, "You can bring along any pets you like, and you can dress them up." There were dogs, cats, ducks, horses, chickens, birds and a large pig. All went well until the dogs got a whiff of the pig. They broke ranks and chased it. All you could see then was a flurry of animals and children and all you could hear was laughing, squealing, squawking, grunting, quacking, barking, miaowing and neighing. There was dust everywhere. Once all the animals had been retrieved, everybody sat down on the ground and laughed and laughed. Jean and I both count it as one of the highlights of our stay at Yarrabah.

Jean gave every one at the school a sense of pride in themselves. She was someone who had the quality of trying to understand the Aboriginal children in her care. She took time to talk with everyone in the community and listen to their problems. She never lost her temper with anyone, not even me when I was being a 'know-it-all', and her quality of quietness had more effect on me than any long lectures or reprimands.

One of the parents said to me one day, "You know, before Miss Olsen came the school was dead and now it is alive." Jean had caused a transformation.

Towards the end of 1959, we were told that the government was going to take over all of the Aboriginal mission schools throughout Australia because there needed to be a change in the

177

education system for Aboriginal children. As had already happened at Forrest River Mission, all schools were to be brought into the state education systems. Because of my experience at Forrest River Mission in 1954, when the two government-trained teachers had arrived, I was prepared for this change and its implications for someone like me who had no training.

The government representative, who was touring the Aboriginal missions in North Queensland advising the mission staff on the government takeover, told us that any of the missionary staff who wanted to stay on were more than welcome to do so and we would be substantially paid. However, the running of Yarrabah school would be done solely by government-trained personnel. This was a condition some of the committed Christian missionaries didn't like, including Jean Olsen, myself, and another young couple. A few of the missionary staff arranged to remain until the takeover was completed; others decided to stay on indefinitely.

I finalised my plans to join the Church Army and prepared to go to New South Wales for the two-year course. Jean and I flew together from Cairns to Sydney. During the trip I thought to myself, "While I will be missing the people at Yarrabah and all the friends I've made, I am now embarking on a new adventure and maybe it will be the most important adventure of my life." I hoped that joining the Church Army would mean that I would find what I was looking for in life – that maybe through the Church Army, I would gain acceptance. I realised that acceptance as a human being meant more to me than anything else in the world. Never before have I felt loved as I did at Yarrabah. The people of Yarrabah were very good to me and they respected me as I did them. They will always have a place in my heart.

# Twenty-two

## *"Constantly on my knees"*
### ∽ *The Church Army* ∽

When I arrived at Stockton to do my Church Army training, there was a young Aboriginal woman from Edward River Mission called Edna who had arrived before me. She filled me in on the ways of the Church Army. "Yuppun (sister)," she said to me. "Don't get down on one knee."

"You mean don't genuflect?"

"Yeah, yeah. Ngoombah (old lady) said not to."

"Why not?"

"They funny here. They don't genuflect. They don't cross themselves. They talk in church. I don't know what's wrong with them."

"True?"

"You'll find out on Sunday."

And I did find out too but I continued to genuflect and cross myself for most of the time I was at the college. Not only did Sister Bacon speak to me about my persistent genuflecting but also Captain Batley, the federal secretary of the Australian Church Army. Captain Batley was a lovely man. On one of his visits to Stockton, he asked me at breakfast if he could see me after morning tea. I had a fair idea why he wanted to see me. "Hierarchy or not," I thought to myself, "I'm not frightened of him."

"Sister McDonald," he said, "I want to speak to you about worship."

"What am I doing wrong?"

"You're not doing anything wrong. It's just that the Church Army is Low Church."

"I see, Captain Batley, but Forrest River and Yarrabah are High Church of England."

"Yes, I know, Sister McDonald," he said. "We are in the middle of the road."

"No, we're not. We're on the corner of Hereford and Clyde Streets," I said. "Well, I understand about high and low, but this middle of the road business is something new to me. What does it mean?" And I thought to myself, these gudiyars are proper walla-marrah ni barndie.

Captain Batley was unable to continue he was laughing so much. Through his laughter he said, "The Church Army would appreciate it if you could refrain from genuflecting and crossing yourself."

"Well, Captain Batley, I love the Divine Master and I shall worship him as I see fit."

"I will leave it to your discretion then," he said. No more was said about the matter and I only genuflected and crossed myself when I forgot that the Church Army was Low Church.

My time in the Church Army was a time of challenge and testing. We studied eight subjects: English, Old and New Testament, Biblical History and Geography, the Book of Common Prayer, Evangelism and Social Work. St John's Ambulance was an extra course. I thought that life on Forrest River Mission was hard but I experienced more punishments studying for the Church Army than I had on the mission.

One day, Sister Edwards and I were told by the sister-in-charge to scrub the floor and then she went away down the street. While she was gone, two gudiyar students came, took our scrubbing cloths and threw them up in the rafters. I was really wild, but we got another couple of cloths and continued washing the floor. Then one of them, a Church Army commissioned officer, who should have known better, came along and kicked me in the behind saying, "Hurry up, you black gin. Scrub the floor." This time, I got so wild, I ranted and raved and as I was saying my piece the sister came in and heard me.

"Truly," she said, "I can't leave you two sisters alone for even a little while – always making up to the brothers." I tried to tell her what had happened but she wouldn't listen. "Go to your room," she ordered. I went to my room wanting desperately to pack up and go home. I went to bed that night without saying any prayers. I was consoled by a vision of Jesus over a river that looked like the Forrest River.

The next day I was supposed to be chaplain for the day. I didn't go to the chapel. I took no service and I played the organ for nobody. I was angry, not only with Sister Bacon and the Church Army but I was also quite mad with God. I said, "God, haven't you tested me enough at Forrest River?"

When the other brothers heard about it, one of them came to me and said, "You're not going to dob him in are you?"

"Huh!" I said. "If I did dob him in, the powers-that-be wouldn't take any notice."

Six years later, I had to have a major operation on my back as a result of the damage which had been done by that kick.

I was very cranky at this first encounter with racism in the church and it really shocked me. All through my time at the college, it was "Sister McDonald do this" and "Sister McDonald do that." I was constantly on my knees – not praying, but scrubbing floors and polishing floors. I noticed that I never saw one particular wadjin (white) student in the whole of her first year scrub a floor. I noticed too that the other Aboriginal student and I were always *told* what to do, whereas the wadjin students were *asked* to do things. I often think that if I had spent as much time praying to the Divine Master as I spent scrubbing and polishing floors for the Church Army I would not be mere Constance today but Saint Constance!

As I pondered the fact that the wadjin students did not have to spend so much time on their knees, I got to thinking that maybe it was not God putting me through this trial but the fact that I was black. Even though I was from Western Australia and had received citizenship, I was still being treated as though I was not equal. The Church Army seemed to regard me as being under the New South Wales Protection Board.

Another time, we were having morning tea after our first study. One of the members of the hierarchy of the Church Army came up to visit us. I was a little late arriving at morning tea and he said, "Oh, my little dusky maiden has just come in." He came over and put his arm around me which made me really mad. As we left morning tea, I said to the sister, "The captain shouldn't have said that."

"He didn't mean anything by it," she told me.

Edna was as upset as I was, so that day we both went on strike and didn't talk to anybody for the rest of the day. Edna told me that they were trying to break my spirit, but they never did.

I used to wonder, "Why am I here? If there is racism here in the Church Army, what am I going to find when I go out to work in the community?" And then I would think that maybe this was preparing me for when I went out into the real world.

I decided that racism was not going to prevent me from completing my training. I believed that I was called by the Divine Master to be trained as a lay evangelist, and not by the Church Army. There was a lot of education that I valued in the course. I learnt how to improve the ways I dealt with people in need. I excelled in the English course and particularly enjoyed the writing of stories from the Bible. I became more familiar with Christ and his work and I developed a deeper understanding of the Australian social welfare institutions and how to work with them.

Edna and I were not quite used to these gudiyar hours, so one day when we were supposed to be doing our study, Edna put up her hand and asked if she could go to the toilet. I was beginning to wonder what had happened to her when she was in the doorway making signs at me to join her. I asked if I could go the toilet.

"Don't be too long and tell Sister Edwards to hurry up."

"Yuppun," said Edna, "I'm tired. Let's go for walkabout." We strolled off down the road from the college and along the beach.

Apparently, the sister-in-charge realised that the two Aboriginal sisters had 'flown the coop' when she got up to leave. Sister sent one of the students down to the beach to bring us home. As we walked in, fresh and invigorated from our walk, she looked exasperated, "You two sisters can't just get up and go walkabout when you feel like it."

"Well," I said, "we don't like these gudiyar hours, sitting down in chairs. We like to stretch our legs and have some exercise."

182

"You are in the city now, sisters. Next time you want to go walkabout, tell me and then you can go before you come and do your lessons. Don't make too much of a habit of it, sisters."

During my training, we all attended a Church Army mission at Harbord, NSW, where I was billeted with some parishioners named Mr and Mrs Jack and Patricia Green. Mr Green was the superintendent of the Aboriginal Welfare Board and I regarded him as one of the 'big fellas of the government'. I hated anyone who had anything to do with the government and I did not trust them. I didn't hate him as a person but I hated what he stood for. Mrs Green and I got along well right from the start as she understood why I was acting so cautiously towards Mr Green. This was the first wadjin family in New South Wales to invite me into their home.

It took a long time for me to trust the Greens and wadjin people in general because of what had happened to the Aboriginal people in the past as a result of colonisation. Sydney was a big city and I was frightened what might happen to me, especially if the police picked me up. I thought to myself, "Wadjin law is never on the Koori's side." I made up my mind that I would tread cautiously and never trust anyone until I was sure they were on the up and up and that their friendship for me was genuine and not patronising.

Mr and Mrs Green remain good friends of mine today. They did a lot for me in helping me to fit in to white society, giving me advice and helping me through good and bad times, visiting me in hospital at times of illness. They were, and still are, my wadjin family. I owe a lot to Mr and Mrs Green and their three daughters, Ann, Kathryn and Gabrielle and their husbands and children for accepting me into their families.

One day, to my surprise, my father wrote to me from Newcastle Waters telling me that he had found a young drover, George Man Fong, whom he thought would make a good husband for me. He was hard-working and earned plenty of money. I wrote back telling him that I would never marry a drover as I was not about to embark on the kind of life that Maisie had to endure. When I thought about it, I realised that my father must have gone to a lot of trouble to find out where I was, so I corresponded with George regularly while I was doing my practical training at Kelso.

Before I returned to the training college at Stockton, I wrote my last letter to George Man Fong, telling him that we should discontinue our letter writing and that I wasn't going to marry him or any man for that matter because becoming a lay evangelist was my first priority.

I will never forget the day when, at the age of twenty-nine, I was finally commissioned as a Church Army lay evangelist. Three other gudiyar students and I were the last students to complete our training at Stockton and the first officers to be commissioned in the diocese of Sydney. We were commissioned on January the twelfth, 1962, at St James' Anglican Church, Croydon, during a Church Army conference. The Greens were there at my commissioning as my good friends.

Members of the press were there and after the ceremony, a *Sydney Morning Herald* journalist came to me and said, "What was the reason you decided to join the Church Army?"

It was the first time I had ever spoken to a journalist. "I felt that God was calling me to work among my own people in the Kimberleys. I've been a missionary since I was eighteen but I've always felt inadequate working without any training. Now that I have qualifications I feel that I am able to do much more." And I added, "I owe a lot to the Church Army for two years of extensive theology and social work training."

Later, a *Sun* reporter came up to me asked me the same question. I replied, "Don't ask questions. I have already told that fella over there." I didn't want to be interviewed again. Maybe I was a little abrupt with the poor man but I had given my story and I didn't feel up to repeating it. Next day my photo was in the *Sydney Morning Herald* with a small article. I felt proud that an Aboriginal person could receive such honour.

Apart from the overwhelming control and the racist remarks that were thrown at me, I had enjoyed my Church Army training. I emerged as a much stronger person, more able to cope with being a community leader and a person of authority.

# Twenty-three

## *"Throw away the book"*
## ∽ *Holland Park* ∽

After my commissioning, I was sent to work in the Anglican parish of St Matthew's, Holland Park, Brisbane. I was seconded to the rector, whom I assisted in all the duties of the parish. I found my duties new, challenging and exhausting. Three weeks after my arrival, the rector informed me that I was to be one of the canvassers in a survey the church was conducting on a new housing estate. I was dismayed as my work load was already a heavy one. He explained the reasons for the survey, "Just as a new area is often canvassed for government records so too parish canvassing is done for church and parish records."

Though I didn't discuss it with the rector, I was dubious about doing such a task because I felt that I would be invading the privacy of the people I was visiting. And, brave as I was, I worried that being an Aboriginal person, I may not be welcomed into the homes of the white people. My experiences so far in life had taught me that there were gudiyars with very strange ideas and opinions about Aboriginal people.

All the walking meant that at the end of each day I was so tired that I often went straight to bed. Most of the people expressed surprise to see an Aboriginal person in church uniform there to canvass them about their needs.

Tom was a typical example. He had never before come face to face with an Aboriginal person. Oh yes, he assured me, he'd seen them in the distance; oh yes, he'd seen them on missions or reserves or in the media, but meeting me person to person, an Aborigine, was a new experience.

"Listen Tom, when given the chance to become educated and accepted, Aboriginal people can adapt quite well to the standards that you whites have created for us. The Church of England, in its wisdom, saw the qualities I had and helped me to become a respected member of the Australian society. You gudiyars seem to forget that my ancestors were, and will always be, the real citizens of Australia because they were here long before white people discovered this land. Racism has caused many problems and until we all look at ourselves as being equal Aborigines will always be second-class citizens."

"I agree," he said. "Not all Aborigines have had the chances that you have."

I was not popular with some gudiyars who tried to justify themselves by saying that they were more educated and civilised than the Aborigines were. There was one man who was something of a theologian. "Aborigines will never be able to attain the standard and status of whites," he told me.

I was very angry, "That is dumb. There is no superior race on earth otherwise God would have decreed it." But he was not listening.

During the canvassing, I had only four doors slammed in my face. One was by a family who did not believe in God, the second was by a family who said that they hated black people. The third family were Mormons and told me that the Anglican brethren needed saving and the fourth gave no reason at all.

Jim, one of the parishioners, thought that I was a little green in the work of dealing with people. He said to me, "Lady, how long have you been in this job as a lay evangelist?"

"I have completed two years of extensive theological training and I passed all my exams with flying colours."

"How many parishes have you worked in before coming here?"

"Well, while I was in training, we students helped in various parishes during the weekends so that we could observe how they functioned. But Holland Park is my first parish where I will be working as a full-time parish worker."

"Lady, you being young, you haven't experienced life like I have, the pain, the hardships, the ups and downs of life.'

186

I thought to myself, "Little does he know how experienced I am of pain and the ups and downs of a hard life."

However, as time went on and I became more and more involved with the people, I began to realise what Jim had been trying to tell me. I had finished my training with the naive conception that all people had the same idea of Christianity as I did. I found I was dealing with people's spiritual lives and concerns and I was standing on holy ground. Very soon I began to realise that people have different ideas of life, and especially of Christianity, and that not all people believed in the Almighty.

At this time I still believed that God actually made the world in six days. One day when I was talking to Jim, I asked if he was a scientist.

"Yes, I am."

"Do you believe God made the world and all living things?"

He replied, "My belief in God differs from yours. Being a scientist I question the validity of the creation of the world in six days."

"What an interesting fellow," I thought to myself. I came to understand that people have their own views on who and what God is and means to them, and on how to worship him.

For instance, one fellow confronted me with, "I don't have to go to church to worship God because, to me, God is everywhere."

I felt sorry for this man and I was concerned that he had not yet given his life to Christ and so I decided that from that day on I would pray for him to see the light before it was too late. But he wasn't finished with me yet. "What role does the Church play in the lives of ordinary people?"

"Well, the church is there to help with our spiritual welfare and to listen to our needs."

"Huh! I get my spiritual help by going to my local pub,"

Forgetting my Church Army training, I responded, "Yeah, I bet you get your spirits out of a bottle."

He suddenly realised that I wasn't as green as I had been sounding and with a smile, said, "Gee, lady. You're a smart one," at which, we both looked at each other and burst out laughing. This began one of the many warm friendships that I enjoyed while working at Holland Park.

187

It also marked the beginning of a new way of ministry for me. Soon after that, I was trying to solve a problem 'by the book' so to speak. A voice within me said, "The only way to solve this problem is to throw away the book (not the Bible) and be yourself." From that day, I have not worried about doing things by the accepted way. Though I have kept my Christian values and the church's teaching, I have found it much more effective to be myself and to use my own judgement in difficult situations.

I loved my job, but sometimes I felt that the rector expected too much of me, and I seemed to be always working. Being a migraine sufferer, I developed frequent headaches which were so bad that I was unable to lift my head off the pillow. Whenever I rang the rector to explain that I was too sick to work, I got the feeling that he thought I was shirking my duties.

One Sunday, I was asked by some friends in the parish if I would like to go for a picnic with them. I explained that I would be delighted to go so long as I was back in time for the evening service as I was on duty. Unfortunately for me, they did not mention that they were taking me to Surfer's Paradise. It wasn't until we headed south out of Holland Park that I realised we were not picnicking locally. I didn't know what to do as I had not even informed the rector that I was going out. "Don't worry! We'll get you back in time for the evening service," my friend assured me. At four o'clock, we packed our picnic things and got in the car.

Suddenly we heard a bang; a tyre had blown out. As we sat by the roadside watching her prepare to change the tyre, I felt like the little girl caught with her hand in the cookie jar.

Now you would have thought that changing a tyre would be easy, but no! My friend found out that she had left the spare tyre at home! She had to walk some distance before she found a phone box and rang for a towtruck. After what seemed like many hours, the towtruck turned up and took the car. Sitting by the side of the road with the rest of the family I was getting more and more depressed. I knew that it was my duty to be at the service. I knew that Monday was my day off, not Sunday.

Just as I was preparing myself for the reprimand I knew I deserved, one of the younger members of the family piped up, "Why don't we sing some choruses to help pass the time?" It was

1960: Wearing my novice uniform outside the chapel at Stockton

1960: Edna Edwards is on the right in our first week of training at Stockton, Church Army Training College

Commissioning Day, 12 January 1962 with Sister Bacon and other members of the Church Army

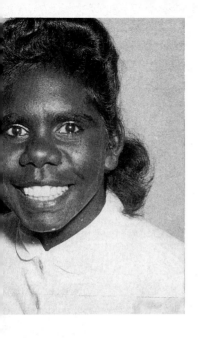

Gnowangerup 1964 With Lynette Haywood, one of the kindergarten children on the Gnowangerup Reserve

Gnowangerup reserve, the second largest in the south-west of WA

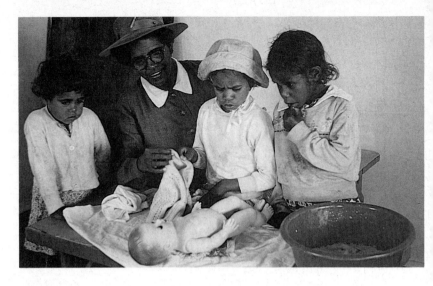

Gnowangerup children learning to look after babies

One of my favourite pastimes: playing the organ at St Margaret's church when the organist was away sick

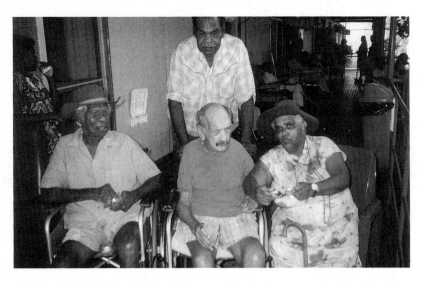

1992 Derby: Front L to R Uncle Bill Mulga, my father, Duncan McDonald and myself; Rear: Alan McDonald

With Jill Finnane at Derby

a brilliant idea. I don't know what the motorists thought of us singing and doing the actions to such an assortment of stirring songs as "Build on the Rock", "My Cup is Full and Running Over", "Waltzing Matilda" and "There's a Tavern in the Town". Some motorists slowed down; others just whizzed by. I wasn't wearing my uniform or it might have looked as though I was conducting my own little roadside mission.

Eventually my friend returned and we scrambled into the car and arrived at Holland Park ten minutes before the service. That was not time enough for me to go home, change into my uniform and be at the church on time. "Oh well," said my friend, "you may as well stay and have tea with us and relax. My parents would be glad to have you for dinner." Chatting in the lounge-room later on, her mother said to me, "If ever you need someone to talk to you ring us and we'll come and see you."

The lady of the house where I was boarding knocked on my door when I got home and said, "The rector wants you to ring him as soon as you get home. He sounded very angry." I decided to wait until the church service was over and he had had time to to get to the rectory. I tried to explain what had happened but he wouldn't listen.

I usually walked to the rectory, but next morning the rector was there at the door to pick me up. When I got into the car he said, "Please explain your absence from the service last night." I told him the story and then apologised, assuring him that it wouldn't happen again.

Three weeks later, I received a letter from the Church Army office in Sydney. It informed me that I was recalled to Sydney but no reason was given. Flabbergasted, I rang the rector and asked him if he knew that I was going back to Sydney.

"Yes," was his terse reply.

"Why didn't you tell me?"

"As the Church Army was writing to you, I didn't see the need to tell you."

I was angry so I slammed down the phone and started to sort out my things ready for packing. I knew there was nothing I could do about it. When I had calmed down, I rang my friend's father and he brought me round a couple of tea chests.

A good friend from the parish, took me into Roma Street station for the train to Sydney. I didn't see the rector or his family again. None of them said goodbye to me or came to the station to see me off. I thought it was strange but I didn't let it worry me as some of my friends were there to say goodbye.

On my arrival in Sydney, Sister Bacon, the sister in charge of the training college, which by now was located at Croydon, came to pick me up. A couple of days later, she asked if I knew why I had been recalled. "No," I said, "I haven't been told."

"Well, Sister McDonald," she said. "We feel that you have let the Church Army down."

"If that is so, Sister Bacon, then I will resign."

"No," she said. "There is no reason for you to resign, but the rector wasn't happy with your work because you were absent regularly."

"That is not quite true, Sister Bacon," I sobbed. "I worked very hard at what I had to do. I was not only a parish worker, I was also the superintendent of the Sunday School which was a very big one. The reason for my absences was the migraine headaches I was suffering because of stress and overwork. No one listened to my complaints and that made it even more stressful."

Sister Bacon explained that I would have to work in the Church Army office in Sydney, filing cards and letters and making cups of tea for the office staff. She explained to me, "Sister McDonald, if you can't take authority, you will never be in a position to give authority."

I cried more than I had cried for many years. I thought to myself, "I cannot understand these wadjin people. They recall me for falling down on the job and then they tell me I don't need to resign."

Sister Bacon then increased my confusion by saying, "You are too good an officer of the Church Army to resign." I think the tears I shed were more from total confusion than from anything else. (Years later, when I was matron at the Aboriginal girl's hostel at Burwood in Sydney, I recalled Sister Bacon's words with gratitude as I could see the importance of being able to give authority.)

For the next four months, I was under so much stress that I

190

would cry at any time for no reason. I couldn't even take my turn at being chaplain for a day without bursting into tears. I considered myself a little 'toughie' and besides, in this Christian environment, I had total confidence that the Church Army would give me every assistance to sort out the problems of my first appointment. I thought they would understand that even 'toughies' like me were vulnerable to physical and emotional hurt and could feel very much alone.

However, no one at the college, neither the sister-in-charge nor the students, would have anything to do with me. While I was waiting at the college for my next appointment, no one talked to me and I sensed that I was being punished for not living up to my Church Army training.

I recalled the times when Edna and I had to go to see the local doctor during our training at Stockton. He would say, "When you two sisters finish your training and become commissioned officers, I advise you to go back to your people." One day I asked him why? He said, "Well, if you stay in the city you will experience some things you have never experienced before."

"For instance what experiences, doc?"

"Well, Sister McDonald," he said. "I will lay it on the line. Stress, hypertension and unhappiness which causes a multitude of illnesses. At present, both of you are in good health. The only way you can maintain that is to go back and work with your own people."

"Yes doc," I said. "I am hoping that I will be sent back to Forrest River, and I think Sister Edwards is hoping to go to her people at Edward River Mission."

I think Edna took the doctor's advice literally because the first Christmas she went home, she did not return to the Church Army when the new term began and I began to question whether I should follow suit. But then I remembered that the Church Army had paid for my training and it was my duty to continue with it. Not only that, I wanted the training.

Now I knew what the doctor had meant when he told me about stress. I began to think that if I was back at Forrest River, I would be able to cope much better with this situation. If I had someone like Ruth, Aunty Louisa, Uncle Robert, Aunty Dudgulla or Aunty Mollie, they would sit down and talk to me. Maybe if Sister Bacon or the students had taken the time to talk to me, I would have felt that at least I belonged. Maybe Sister Bacon felt that I needed a quiet time to get myself together.

The only person who tried to help me and tried to understand was the cook, who was a compassionate person. I will always be grateful for her support. She went out of her way to help, not only me, but any of the students who needed a shoulder to cry on.

I found myself meditating and praying more, and so my faith and trust in my Divine Master and the kind words of a cook carried me through this distressing time. Four months after returning from Holland Park, the Church Army found an opening for me at Gnowangerup in Western Australia. I would be working for the South West Native Mission which provided country Aboriginal reserves with missionaries who lived mainly in caravans.

# Twenty-four

## "We don't deal with black people here"
### ⌒ *Gnowangerup* ⌒

I thought life had been hard at Forrest River. The houses there were livable because the walls were made of mudbricks and the roof was made of thatch, grass and timber. The only people who lived in lean-to humpies at Forrest River were the old people who lived in the camp. They wanted to live in their natural way and the missionaries did not encroach upon their privacy. It was different for the people living on the mission; they lived in the houses built to government specifications. My appointment as a church worker to Gnowangerup reserve made me realise just how lucky we had been at Forrest River.

I knew that life on a reserve was going to be different from life on a mission. I expected to be meeting new people all the time because reserves tend to be transient homes for people. I knew that from time to time there would be hardly anyone on the reserve and that at other times there wouldn't be enough room for all the visitors. I read a detailed account in a Perth newspaper of the appalling living conditions of the Aboriginal people on Gnowangerup reserve. The report was written by a young American couple who were missionaries there. The young couple were distraught at the racist attitude of the white people in the town. They said the same thing was happening in America and, as they couldn't stand the way people were being treated, they asked to be relieved of their duties so they could go back to America and try to do something for human rights at home. What I read did not surprise me, as Aborigines all over the nation were living in similar situations.

I found out that Gnowangerup contained the second largest reserve in the south-west region of Western Australia, the largest being Albany. The houses on the Gnowangerup reserve were built of iron, timber and had cement floors. Most of them had two bedrooms and a kitchen which had an open fireplace. The kitchen was also used as a dining room and lounge room. The houses were so small that if a couple had more than two children, it was too crowded. The homes became death-traps in the winter as the cement floor became very cold; many people ended up with pneumonia, bronchitis, flu and colds. The young pre-schoolers, the babies and the old were the most vulnerable.

The day Mr Jessup, my co-worker, and I arrived in Gnowangerup, the young American missionaries and some children were there to greet us. We were invited to have lunch with them in their caravan while the children were told to go home and tell people on the reserve that the new missionaries were coming up after lunch. The children were excited to see a nyoongar missionary and took off with great speed to tell everyone the news.

The news travelled faster even than the children. The whole reserve turned out to welcome us, except for the men still out working on the farms who would meet us on the weekend. The American woman announced, "This is Sister McDonald from the Church Army. She and Mr Jessup are taking over from us."

The Aboriginal people were very interested in me, asking all sorts of questions like: Where do you come from? Do you have any family? How many children do you have? How many brothers and sisters? I answered them all. Though they were sorry to see the young American missionaries leave, the people seemed to take a liking to me straight away, and I felt that I was going to get on well with them. Later, Mr Jessup drove us back to the town. He dropped the young couple off at their caravan parked behind the Methodist church and then he took me to my caravan behind St Margaret's Anglican church. His caravan was at the local showground.

As my caravan had no laundry or shower, I had to use the facilities at the rectory. When I finished washing, I cleaned out the washing machine and when I had a bath, I made sure the floor was wiped if I made any mess. One day after work I was tired and wanted a shower so I knocked on the door. The rector's wife wasn't very pleased. She said, "You've got to save water you know," and she made a few other points like that. Afterwards, she was a bit terse and I thought, "Something's wrong." Another time when I went to have a shower, they were cuddling and canoodling. I didn't take any notice but I thought to myself, "They are still a young couple and they have two children and they don't want me popping in and out."

A couple of days later, the minister said, "Oh, you know we are going to try to find somewhere for you to move where you can be flexible." It wasn't many more days when he came to me and said, "One of our parishioners has got a big backyard; she doesn't come to church but she's glad for you to put your caravan in there." I was uprooted again. I packed up all my things and Mr Jessup came and took me and the caravan to the old lady's place. When we arrived she showed me a kind of granny flat at the back. "You know it has a stove, a comfortable bed and everything. You don't have to live in the caravan, you can live in here," she assured me. I thought this was much better because the caravan would get hot in the summer. I just took out the things I needed from the caravan and settled down. The mission used to pay the rent promptly, and I kept the place very clean and tidy.

I often wondered whether the minister knew this but the old lady was very fond of the bottle and I only ever saw her sober once. When I hadn't seen her for a few days, I looked through her window and she was lying on the floor. At first, I thought she was dead. I rang her daughter and explained to her what had happened. I said,"She looks as though she hasn't eaten for days." The daughter lived some distance away but she was single so she could afford to come down. When she arrived, she said, "I'm sorry. My mother is an alcoholic."

I went to the rector, "This is no good. I am frightened the old lady might drink herself to death and I might get into trouble and be blamed and I don't even live in her part of the house." So he put an item in the paper for accommodation for me.

Not far down from where I was living there was a Catholic couple, Bill and Dorothy Dodds, who had a two bedroom place with a little room at the back. They saw the ad and offered me accommodation. I said, " I don't need to live in the house, I can live in the caravan." They looked around and saw how clean my place was.

Again, Mr Jessup came. Again I was uprooted. I put my things in the caravan and he towed it the five doors to the Dodds. Mrs Dodds said to me, "These two are rooms to rent." I said I only wanted one room. Not wanting to trouble them I said, "I can leave most of my things in the caravan." However, they put me in their room and I tried to protest, "You didn't have to do that, I'm used to dossing down anywhere."

But she smiled and said, "You are our guest and we will treat you as our guest. We know you study and prepare things for your worship," so I didn't argue any more. They slept in the little bedroom out the back. They made the other room up as a study for me. It all seemed perfect.

Everything went very well at the Dodds and I settled in contentedly. Then they bought a block of land at Albany and built a little house on it. So there I was, uprooted again. I went back to Mr Jessup. "Oh well," he said, "I think I had better take you out to the showground where my caravan is." So he went and saw the council, "Look, this lady has been pushed from one place to another. Can her caravan be parked next to mine? After all we work together." So the caravan was towed out of the yard and down to the showground.

I liked it except when the winter came; it was cold. Before I put my shoes on, I had to put my feet in a bucket of hot water to thaw them out. Because I was down at the showground, the people felt free to pop down from the reserve and have a talk with me. They hadn't been able to visit me when I was staying at the church or Mrs Dodds' place or even the old lady's place because I was in the town. My new camping spot meant I had visitors late in the afternoon or at night and the weekend.

There was no facility there for a shower. I used to get up early in the morning and warm some water up and have a shower by filling the bucket and pouring the hot water all over me. The welfare officer said, "You know, being a woman, you need somewhere to wash your clothes and somewhere to shower. You can come to our place." I used to wash my clothes, have a shower there and as usual leave everything tidy. After some time, the welfare officer's wife started getting funny and I thought to myself, "Here we go again."

I was talking to the people at the reserve and Mrs Agnes Coyne said, "Look, you bring your clothes down to the reserve and have your shower here." So I started to shower at the reserve where no one complained. I thought, "This is good. I am becoming a part of their trials and tribulations." And I felt I belonged.

Mrs Coyne and Mrs Eva Rowe washed all my clothes, and starched my uniform stiff. One day I asked Mrs Rowe, "How much starch did you put in my uniforms?" "The whole packet," she smiled proudly.

As part of my job, I had to visit two other neighbouring reserves. We used to go to a family living in a lean-to near Borden reserve. There was an old lady there called Mrs Granny Roberts who was the matriarch of the reserve. She was a Christian and she was somebody that people respected. The first time Mr Jessup took me out there, we weren't expected. When he introduced me to her, she put her arm around me and said, "I knew you was coming. God told me you was on your way so that's why I put the kettle on." She couldn't have known we were coming as we hadn't known ourselves. Anyway, one of these big old iron kettles was boiling and she said, "Sit down my dear."

It was to Granny Roberts that the people on the Borden reserve turned for help and advice. If anybody was sick, Granny Roberts would ring the welfare officer at Gnowangerup to get him to give a message to Mr Jessup and me so we could go out and bring that person in to the hospital. Most of my time in winter seemed to be spent taking people to the hospital.

The first time, a young woman in her thirties who was very ill. As soon as the welfare officer informed me, I closed the kindergarten and told the mothers that there was an emergency. Mr Jessup and I set off for Borden in the mission van. When we arrived people were gathered around Granny Roberts' house looking very worried. I asked her, "Why didn't you call the ambulance?"

197

With a shrug of her shoulders she replied, "When we tell them that someone is sick on the reserve, they sometimes keep us waiting for two or three hours." As I examined the girl, Granny told me, "When a whitefella is sick, the ambulance comes straight away, but not for us." The men put the girl into the van and we drove back to Gnowangerup. I was worried about her condition so as we got near town, I said to Mr Jessup, "We had better take her to the doctor's surgery."

He said that we couldn't do that. "The town would be in an uproar because white people don't like black people going to the white surgery. That's why the doctor has a clinic at the hospital especially for Aboriginal people."

"But she needs to see a doctor now."

"Just as you wish then," he said. "but there will be trouble."

As he pulled in at the surgery, I got out, rushed in to the waiting room and asked if the doctor could come out to see a very sick patient. The secretary looked shocked and she said, "Oh, we don't deal with black people here; you'll have to take her up to the hospital."

I said, "She needs attention now! Can't the doctor look at her? Do you really mean black people are not allowed to come here?"

"Rules are rules," she said.

With all the arguing, the white patients got up and went home and the doctor came out.

"I have a very sick woman in the car who needs your attention now." He came out to the van, examined her and then told us to drive to the hospital quickly.

"Are you coming now?" I asked.

"Yes. I'll follow you in my car."

Not really believing that he would come straight away, I kept looking back as we drove to the hospital. He was right behind us all the way and I was very much relieved. The young woman was admitted to the hospital shortly afterwards suffering from renal failure and subsequently rushed by ambulance to Royal Perth Hospital where she remained for some time.

The doctor told Mr Jessup and me that when any of the Aborigines got sick we were to take them straight to the hospital and not to his surgery, as the whites in the town didn't want the Aborigines contaminating their surgery. This made me angry, so I said to him, "Does that include me too?" He said, "No. Because the people of this town know who you are and that you are not like the people on the reserve." This made me even more angry.

A couple of weeks later I needed to see the doctor myself. I rang up and said, "This is Sister McDonald from the church; I need to come and see the doctor. Don't tell me to go to the hospital. I pay taxes, I work, and I need to see the doctor." I went to the surgery in my uniform and was again confronted by the same officious secretary. "Who is it this time?" she asked.

"Me," I replied and sat down. I was the first patient to arrive that afternoon but by the time the doctor came the surgery was full. I was ready, expecting my name to be called first. When the receptionist said, "Mrs House, will you please come in?" I rose to my feet and said, "Stay where you are, Mrs House! I was here first and I demand that I be seen by the doctor first." Mrs House sat down meekly and all the other patients looked shocked. The receptionist seemed embarrassed as she put down Mrs House's card and picked up mine, "Sister McDonald, you can go and see the doctor now." With great satisfaction I strode into his office, leaving the waiting room a-buzz.

Occasionally, when work was very busy and I needed a break, I would go to the local cafe to have lunch. I always wore my Church Army uniform and I believed I was accepted by the owners. One Saturday (my day off), I visited the cafe with three of my friends, Eva, Lois and Susan, wearing my ordinary clothes. We sat down at my usual table and I called the waitress over to give our order. She hesitated and called the owner. He immediately came over to the table, "Sister McDonald, you can have your lunch here but those others can't." He looked at my friends. "I will pack some food for them and they can have it as usual out under the trees."

Standing up, I said, "Whose policy is this? Yours? Or the townsfolk's?"

He looked at me, "I have the right to refuse service in my cafe."

Glaring at him, I said, "I will not eat in your cafe again."

He started to say, "But Sister McDonald you are..." but I

199

interrrupted him saying, "Don't say any more!" And my friends and I walked out of the cafe.

Eva said, "Oh, Sister McDonald, you bin tell'm straight."

I said, "Eva, that is the only way to do it. We have to stand up for our rights."

Lois said, "But we not strong like you." Susan, who was very young, said nothing. I tried to explain to them that if they wanted to be socially accepted, there were things that they could do about it and I offered to help them. Then I laughed and said, "What about we go and get some witchetty grubs and goanna and have a feed." We crossed the road to a shop that sold pies and chips, bought our lunch and sat laughing and joking under the trees.

After these episodes, I was quite a celebrity among the Aboriginal people. I felt sad that, although I seemed to have broken through a racism barrier, none of the other Aboriginal people could stand up for their rights in the same way. I was accepted by the whole community, both black and white, but many of the wadjillas still said, "Oh, but you're different." This always made me mad and I would say, "I am not different. These people are my people."

I decided that it was time to invite some of the people from the reserve to the family service at St Margaret's Church of England. I announced, on the Friday before, that if any one wanted to come to the service, Mr Jessup and I would pick them up at seven-thirty on Sunday. They all groaned and said, "Too early." Some of them decided to think about it and on Sunday morning two women, three little boys and a girl were waiting for us at the community hall. Mr Jessup was disappointed at the small number and said that it wasn't worth it, but I could well understand their reluctance to attend the all-white church. I reminded Mr Jessup of the comforting quote, "Where two or three are gathered in my name – I am there with them." But Mr Jessup was silent . Maybe he thought that, even with Christ there with us, we would still be heavily outnumbered.

Our little group arrived early so we stayed in the van until the warden opened up the church. After introducing the newcomers to the warden, I led them right up to the front seats. Before we sat down, the three little boys had volunteered to hand out the hymn books. The warden was pleased to let them help him and they beamed as they distributed the books as people arrived. I thought to myself, "This is wonderful. We are really fitting in."

The minister then came out and announced that the organist was sick and that we would have to sing unaccompanied. One of our little boys, in the middle of handing out a hymn book, put his hand up. "Sister McDonald can play the organ."

I went to the organ and was pleased to find that the hymns he had chosen for the day were all great favourites with the Aboriginal people, "What a friend we have in Jesus", "Rock of Ages" and "Onward Christian Soldiers".

When it came time to receive the Blessed Sacrament, I felt a bit hesitant as I was not sure how the white congregation would react. I wondered too, whether the minister would bless the little children and give communion to their mothers. Nevertheless we all walked confidently up to the communion rail, knelt down and received the Sacrament like everyone else. Looking around as I returned to my seat, I was pleased to observe that there were no outward signs of rejection by the white congregation.

However, just before the benediction, most of the white congregation stood up and walked out! "Why are they going out early for?" whispered one of the Aboriginal women to me. I had no answer, and anyway I was too choked up to speak, but I knew why they were leaving and I thought to myself, "What an insult to God!"

The following week, our same little group came to church. The children were excited but the women were reluctant. I said to them, "We have every right to be in God's house." They listened politely to me but still looked very dubious. They didn't know that I had a little plan.

Towards the end of the service, I got up quickly and told our little group to follow me. We went out and waited with the minister. As the people came out of the church and shook hands with the minister, they then had to shake hands with me and then I introduced my friends to each of them. "This is Mrs Lois Parfitt and this is Mrs Eva Rowe," I told them while making sure that they shook hands. The children in our group were far too shy to shake hands and seemed relieved when the whole procedure was over. So was I, but proud too of my courageous friends.

When I had been there about a year and had been working very hard, I needed to make another call to the doctor's for myself. I always started work at eight-thirty in the morning but my work wasn't finished at five because people used to come to my caravan in the showground at all hours. If somebody was sick, or their baby was dying, their family always came to us first. I wasn't getting enough sleep, I would come home tired, make my cup of tea and fall into bed, then get up round midnight and have something to eat. As soon as the doctor saw me, he said, "I'm going to put you into hospital. You are going to have a nervous breakdown if you don't. You're anaemic, you're tired, you work too hard and they're not worth it, those people."

Angered, I said, "They are worth it; they are my people and I have to help them."

"Well," he said, "I'm putting you into hospital anyway. You need rest so I'm putting you down in the maternity ward because there are no mothers there now." I asked him what would happen if a mother came in to have a baby. "Oh, I guess we would put you in a private room."

I thought, "An Aboriginal person in a private room. That'd be one for the books." So I spent the next two weeks in Gnowangerup hospital recovering from my nervous breakdown and hoping some mother would come in to have a baby.

I thought I was settled at Gnowangerup. The Aboriginal people were, through my efforts, beginning to have some confidence in the doctor and the hospital staff, though not so much confidence in the police. The shop owners were accepting Aboriginal people into their shops. It seemed to me that, as I had done all the work of crashing through the barriers of self-doubt and acceptance, I could now play a useful role in Gnowangerup for many years to come. I forgot that though the Church Army lets you put your roots down, it doesn't let them grow. After two-and-a-half years in Gnowangerup, the Anglican Archbishop of Perth approached the Church Army and requested that I be posted to East Perth.

I didn't know what was ahead of me. Though the powers-that-be wanted me work at East Perth, they had nowhere for me to live so they advertised. A wadjilla, Aunt Margery, who had befriended me when I first visited Perth as a young woman, saw the advertisement. She contacted Reverend King, and told him that she would be honoured to have me as a guest. I received a telegram telling me that I would be boarding at Mrs McKay's place at Carlisle. I thought, "Good old Aunty Margery, to the rescue again." It made the thought of leaving Gnowangerup much easier.

I hate wailing and sad goodbyes, so I arranged with Mr Jessup that we leave Gnowangerup early in the morning and I said my goodbyes the night before. At dawn, I heard a knock on the door and there was Eva and her husband, Lionel, and the children. "Why do you have to go?" Eva asked, weeping.

"I have to go because the Archbishop has an important job for me to do. I'll write to you. I'll keep in touch. Anyway, I must go to East Perth."

"East Perth!" exclaimed Lionel junior, her nine-year-old son.

"What's wrong with East Perth?"

"You'd be better to stay here with us."

"Why, what's the matter with East Perth?"

"You'll find out."

I thought to myself, "Here we go again. It's just like saying 'when you grow up'."

"East Perth!" said Eva's husband. "Gees, that place has a reputation. It's the slum area of Perth."

I climbed in the car and Mr Jessup started driving up the hill past the reserve and there were all the people waiting along the road. Children were waving leaves. I felt proper sad but I said to myself, "Constance, brace yourself, you've got another job to do."

To Mr Jessup I said, "What's this about East Perth? You come from Perth. Mr Jessup fill me in."

All he said was, "You'll have your work cut out for you."

203

# Twenty-five

## *"That Sister McDonald, she's the bane of my life"*
### *East Perth*

"What am I in for?" I thought to myself during the fourteen hour drive to Perth. "What is all this mystery about East Perth?" I reflected on my experiences at Gnowangerup, sorted out in my mind what I had learnt from them and realised that Gnowangerup had been a comprehensive training ground for me. By the end of the journey, I was convinced that I was prepared for whatever East Perth might bring.

When I arrived at Carlysle, Aunt Margery McKay welcomed me as one of her family. I was home once more and felt confident that this loving family would give me all the support I needed.

Next morning, I had to present myself to the Archbishop along with two English ladies, one a former teacher, the other a former nurse. They had worked in slums in England but knew nothing about Aborigines. While we waited for the Archbishop, we chatted away wondering what was ahead of us and whether we were being thrown into the lion's den. The Archbishop warned us that it would be very rough and said, "We feel you are the right people for the job." So that was that.

The Archbishop and his secretary took us down to the little place in Norbert where we were to work. The Archbishop was about to officially open a centre. The once dilapidated building had been painted and renovated. Upstairs was the entertainment area for the kids with a piano and downstairs was the Op shop, coffee shop and bathroom.

Once the official ceremony was over, the Archbishop sat down with the three of us over a cup of coffee and explained what he wanted us to do. That afternoon he took us for a walk to visit some of the Aboriginal people he knew. Everyone made us feel welcome though none of them had ever seen an Aboriginal woman in a church uniform before. I could tell that they were quite impressed. One nyoongar woman asked if I was going to live in East Perth.

"Once the parish finds me a house."

"Good," she said. "We'll be able to come and visit you."

As we returned to the centre, the Archbishop said, "East Perth is known as the slum area of the city." All of a sudden I realised what the word 'slum' meant. During our walk, poverty was obvious; there were people drinking and lying in gutters. There was so much to do I could never be late for work. The train driver said to me, "I can set my clock by you lady."

The two English ladies worked in the centre and I worked around the area wherever people needed me. Our day started with a little prayer meeting and then I would be off. I would visit the people in their homes, or go the Royal Perth Hospital and talk to all the Aboriginal patients. Children could come to the centre to do homework under our supervision. Parents would come in, have a cup of coffee and talk to us about their problems. We put people who were inebriated under the shower and gave them a meal.

The English ladies had their own accommodation. One day they said to me, "Come home to our place for lunch." I was amazed when they set up a tray for me out on the verandah. I was 'proper mad'. I left the tray where it was, rushed out, rang Aunt Margery and told her what had happened.

"Don't worry about it. They aren't fit to eat with." So I bought myself some sandwiches and ate them sitting in Wellington Park. I decided after much agonising to take Aunt Margery's advice and put the incident behind me. I meditated, which always helped me to forget such incidents and enabled me to be in a better frame of mind to cope with my work. I closed my eyes, and put myself in the hands of the Divine Master asking for strength to go forward.

A couple of weeks later, my co-workers once again asked me to visit their home. This time it was for dinner. As we sat down,

I said to them, "Why did you fellas do that to me? I suppose you don't like black people."

"We want to apologise for insulting you."

"In that case – apology accepted." We got along well after that.

I wasn't restricted to working with the Anglicans. East Perth was for everyone. At the hospital, I became great friends with all the other church workers, the Catholic sisters, the Salvation Army people and the Baptists. I used to make them all laugh. One day I said, "Why don't I see you fellas down in East Perth? You fellas should be down there too."

"Oh, Connie," one of them said, "we gave up."

"You gave up? You mustn't give up! Is that why the Archbishop brought me here? I think you fellas went and had a talk with Archbishop Appleton. Did you?" They all laughed.

One day, somebody said to me, "You'd better go see Aunty so-and-so in West Perth, she needs someone to talk to her." And so I did, though I was only supposed to work in East Perth.

Soon after my arrival, we had a chaplain's meeting at the hospital and the Catholic sister said to me, "You've done more for the people in this couple of weeks than we have been able to do in many years. What is it?"

I said, "I don't know. It's just me."

"Your reputation has spread to West Perth."

"I know. I'm visiting West Perth and that's out of my bounds. I might get into trouble."

When I got back to the centre, I rang the Archbishop's office and made an appointment. He asked me what the problem was.

"My work from East Perth is extending into West Perth and that is out of my bounds."

"Well," he said, "for protocol reasons you have to respect the other ministers. You understand protocol do you?"

"Yes," I said. "I'm beginning to understand protocol. It's all new to me."

"Well, we'll have to have a meeting."

"You must put it before the board. If you don't, I'll come and tell them myself."

"Don't worry," he said. "We'll have to see if we can extend your boundaries."

For the next two-and-a-half years, I found myself visiting people in Fremantle prison, the mental hospitals, Royal Perth Hospital, the mothers and babies hospital, the children's hospital, Charles Gardner Hospital and one or two old folk's homes. I was 'proper' greedy for work in those days. And I loved every minute of it.

I was on call six days a week with Saturday as my day off. On Saturday, I would do my housework and washing and perhaps go to the opera or ballet or just have a nice quiet day. As I lived in East Perth itself by now and the people knew I was there, it was easy for them to find me in an emergency. I decided that even though it would get me into trouble with the Archbishop, I would not only help my own people but would help anyone and everyone who sought my help and advice.

Trying to stop children absconding from school was one of my jobs. I went to all the schools and told the principals, "If Aboriginal children don't come to school, ring me. Don't ring the police or the truant officer. That'll make things worse. There'll be a big hullaballoo and you'll never get them to school." Often when I came back to the centre for lunch, there would be a message about Aboriginal children missing from school, so I would go down the street, find them and send them back.

All the pubs were on my 'hit list', especially the little corner pub that was a favourite 'watering hole' for Aboriginal patrons. If I was looking for someone, I would walk straight in and say, "I am looking for Mr so-and-so. Is he here?" If Mr so-and-so was there, I would tell him what crisis his family was going through at the time and ask him to come with me. The publican at the East Perth Hotel said one day, "That Sister McDonald, she's the bane of my life. She just walks in the pub and drags the Aboriginal patrons out."

All church workers from the different denominations got along very well. We used to meet down at Fremantle when we visited the prison. As one of the Catholic sisters said, "We are working for the same God, so we should work together." If someone came to us at the centre and they were Catholic we would say, "Have you spoken to sister or father about it? You have to see them first. If they say it is all right then I will help you." It was the same if they were Salvation Army. We would send them to the captain or the major. They would do the same for us. I would think to myself, "This is protocol."

I had never been to a city court before but as part of my job I often had to attend the local court and, just as I had in Wyndham, I kept bowing to the magistrate every time I spoke saying, "Yes, your majesty. No, your majesty." Afterwards, one of the Salvation Army workers said to me, "You don't have to bow all the time. Once is enough. And it's 'your worship', not 'your majesty'." And we laughed and laughed.

If any of the Aboriginal people were organising a funeral, they looked to me to help them through the system. When I arrived at East Perth, I knew nothing about how to arrange them. I said to the Catholic sister, "I come from the bush, so you'll have to tell me how to arrange funerals." She and the Salvation Army people were quite happy to teach me and I soon became an expert.

There were an Irish brother and sister that I used to visit. They were in their eighties and were well loved by the people of East Perth, especially the Aboriginal people. Everyone was welcome at their place in Claisebrook Road. I would often see the brother working in his garden or walking down the street chatting to people. We were all shocked one day when he was admitted to hospital with pneumonia. I was making my way back to the centre when one of the Aboriginal women, Edna, came running across to me saying, "Sister, sister! Move fast. Come quick, the old fella died."

"Died? Which old fellow?"

"That old Irish fella. His sister is up there in front of the bus telling the bus driver to drive over her. The police are there."

A couple more police cars drove up and the police rushed in and said roughly, "Come on. Come up here." I put my arm around her. Then a doctor came and wanted to give her an injection "No. She's right," I said. "I don't think your brother would want you to throw yourself in front of the bus. He'd be upset. He's up there looking down."

"Oh, Miss McDonald. We were like twins."

"I know you were. Now come with me."

"I don't want to go back to my place."

"Well then, come to the centre with me." So I took one arm and an Aboriginal woman took the other and we helped her across Wellington Park. The ten bulky police officers watched us. I turned round and said, "Officers, you have the wrong way of approaching things."

The old woman hung on to us all the way to the centre. I said to her, "You are going to have to sell your house. You are getting old."

"I'm not old."

"You're eighty-seven and your brother would want you to be taken care of."

"I don't like those nursing homes. I've heard stories about them."

Then I apologised to her. "I'm sorry. I know how you must miss your brother. You two were everything to each other. We can think about these things later on." I was amazed at my insensitivity at such a time. I was concerned about her being on her own so I said, "Would you like to come home with me tonight?"

"No," she said. "I'd rather go home. He only just died. Will you help me fix up the funeral." And I did.

One day, tired from work, I was walking slowly home from a visit in West Perth. It had been an exhausting day and I was looking forward to getting home, having a hot bath, a cup of tea and putting my feet up. While taking a short-cut across a vacant block, I heard this small voice saying, "Lady, could you come here?" I saw a wadjilla woman beckoning to me so I went over to her.

"Could you help me? What church are you from?"

"The Church of England. I'm with the Church Army."

"Oh, you're that Church Army sister? Come in."

Over a cup of tea, I asked her what the problem was.

"My husband. He is going to have a big operation for cancer. I'm worried for him because I don't want to tell him that our son is in trouble with the police."

"What's he done?"

"Have you heard on the news about some young fellows that stole a car. My son was one of them. To make it worse he ran off and took his Aboriginal sweetheart with him and her parents are upset."

I thought, "Oh boy. This is going to be difficult. Aboriginal people tell their kids, 'You leave them wadjillas alone.'"

We chatted about the two young people for a while. I said that she could leave it to me to talk to her husband.

Then she said, "Would you like to stay for dinner?"

"Yes, that would be a great help as I am really tired." Quite often, I would arrive home so tired that all I had before I went to bed was a cup of tea. Over a delicious meal, we discussed how best we could handle the situation. As I knew the girl and her parents, I offered to talk to them. After the meal she asked if I would visit her son. "Is he in the juvenile detention home?" I asked.

"No, he is in Fremantle Gaol."

"How old is he?"

"Eighteen."

I thought to myself, "Fancy putting such a young fellow in Fremantle Gaol." We discussed the problems with the way juveniles were treated by the law. I found the conversation with this concerned mother somewhat upsetting but I also found it challenging and enlightening. Usually I was kept so busy working that I had no time to analyse the causes of the problems that confronted the people I was working with.

The Church Army had not taught me to question the system nor had it taught me to do anything to change it. Yet every day I would have to handle problems that were in many ways made worse by the law. My conversation with this distraught mother was a very useful learning experience and made me realise that the kind of work I was doing was largely dealing with the symptoms of problems.

I enjoyed my work so much that I became a workaholic. I knew my health was not strong and yet I pushed myself too hard. I found out for sure that I was overdoing things when I arrived home one day, went to sit down on the chair and a pain shot through me from my lower spine to my legs. I screamed and my

210

landlady came rushing in. "What's the matter?"

"Something is wrong with my spine."

"Don't move then!"

"I can't move," I gasped.

So my landlady and her husband took me to the Royal Perth hospital. On arrival, I went to get out of the taxi but again I couldn't move.

The doctor said, "Do not go near Sister McDonald or even touch her. She's injured her back." Meanwhile I was becoming increasingly distressed by the severe pain. I knew they would not be able to give me an injection until an assessment was made of my injury so I sent up some urgent prayers. "Please, Lord, ease this pain quick." At the same time, I couldn't help but relish all the attention and excitement I was creating. Humility was still not one of my strong characteristics.

After all the tests, the nursing sister pulled back the screen and in walked a short middle-aged man who introduced himself, "I am Mister George Bedrook, the orthopaedic surgeon for Royal Perth Hospital."

I thought to myself, "First he tells me he is 'mister' and then he says he is an orthopaedic surgeon. Can I trust this fellow? Who on earth is he?"

He said, "My dear lady, you will have to have an operation."

"Is it bad?"

"It'll be no picnic," he warned me. "The pain you have experienced with breaks was nothing compared to the pain you will experience with these operations. It will probably be two years before you walk again."

"If that is the case, then I want the best orthopaedic surgeon in Perth. I don't want anyone but the best."

He looked at me and said, "You are talking to him, Miss McDonald."

I thought, "He is like me. Humility is not one of his characteristics either." Several weeks later, I had the first operation to remove bone from my hip and then when I had recovered sufficiently that bone was used in the spinal fusion operation.

It wasn't until my back had been operated on that I realised

211

I had over-taxed myself. Lying flat on my back, I pondered what had happened to me – first a nervous breakdown from working too hard at Gnowangerup, and now this. While in hospital, I was surrounded by flowers, friends and visitors, both black and white.

I started to wonder if my over-zealous dedication was a reaction to what had happened to me on the mission. I decided that the drive in me was because I had to prove my potential. At the same time, I felt that I had to help lift up the people of East Perth so that they too could see their potential. I decided that it was all my own fault. God seemed to think so too because I got no sympathy from him. Today I tell people doing that kind of work, "Just do what God gives you the strength to do. Remember that no one is invincible, infallible or indispensible. And there is always someone who can take your place and maybe even do a better job than you."

After seven months of convalescence at Shenton Park Rehabilitation Centre, I was able to walk out on crutches. I think the Shenton Park staff were glad to see me go. Being confined to a cradle bed had brought out the full strength of my rebellious spirit. When I was bored, I would pull the ropes attached to my cradle bed and sing 'rock-a-bye baby' as it swung from side to side. This upset the other patients who would ring their bells fearing that I might fall out.

At night I used to hide my sleeping tablets so I could stay awake to see one of the men on night duty whom I rather fancied. Once I had had my chat with him, I would take my tablets but found it hard to wake in the mornings.

My most serious misdemeanour occurred when it was nearly time for me to be allowed to start walking on crutches. The doctor ordered a full plaster to support my spine and my left leg. After they put on the plaster, I was wheeled out into the sun to dry. For the first two hours, I lay on my back and after that they turned me over onto my stomach. The wardsmen put the brakes on and then left me. A little voice inside me said, "I bet you can't make this trolley run down the ramp." I think it must have been Satan's voice. I thought to myself, "Right on! I bet I can!"

I put my hand under the trolley and released the brake. The trolley took off faster than I had expected. I tried to manoeuvre the trolley so I wouldn't end up in the swimming pool at the end of the ramp. I made the trolley run straight into a brick wall. Doctors, nurses, wardsmen, cooks and cleaners all came running to see what the screaming was about.

The doctor said, "You are lucky you didn't kill yourself." He said to the sister, "Put her in the plaster room and give her a sedative." After the sister gave me the injection she said, "I hope you have learnt your lesson and that when you wake up, you will have settled down."

Fortunately, x-ray tests showed no damage had been done and I vowed there and then that I would mend my ways. I tried very hard and there were no more serious incidents after that. Nevertheless, I believe that underneath all the good wishes and hearty goodbyes, the Shenton Park staff were rather relieved to see me hobble out on my last day of rehabilitation.

# Twenty-six

## *"Giving too much"*
### ∽ *The Foundation and the Hostel* ∽

After six months of light duties back at the centre in East Perth, the Church Army recalled me to Sydney. My work was limited by my health problems. For a few months I worked once more at head office addressing envelopes, licking stamps and making cups of tea for everyone. I felt bored so I was relieved when the Church Army appointed me to work at the Anglican parish of St Michael's at Surry Hills.

This was my first contact with Koori people of New South Wales. I found visiting Kooris difficult at first. Being from another state , I was not so readily accepted as I had been by my own people. I realised that I had to be cautious about how I approached these people and what I said to them. They seemed particularly suspicious of the Church Army uniform.

After a couple of months, I had problems walking and experienced much pain in my legs so I decided to see an orthopaedic surgeon at Royal Prince Alfred Hospital, referred to me by my orthopaedic surgeon from Perth. The surgeon advised me to either take long service leave or resign. So in 1967, I resigned from the Church Army.

When I left, I felt as though I had become a human being again and that a heavy load had been lifted from my shoulders. The uniform, the rules, the expectations, the institutionalisation of my work were all burdens that had held me back from being myself.

Jack and Pat Green took me into their home and I stayed there for a couple of months recuperating and helping to look after their two little girls, Ann and Kathryn. Then I lived at Bexley for a time recovering and taking care of a house that belonged to the Aboriginal Welfare Board. Aboriginal children from the country who were waiting to go to hospital would stay there with me. My brother Colin came and lived with me for a while and I got to know and care for him.

As I couldn't get around much, I took the opportunity to do some reading. Then one day, as I was sitting in the sun room reading, I heard the phone ring. It was Cora Walters (now Gilbert), a photographer with the Aboriginal Welfare Board. She said she wanted to come and talk with me.

"Have you heard about the position at the Foundation for Aboriginal Affairs?"

I had heard about the freedom rides and the Foundation for Aboriginal Affairs that Gary Foley, Charles Perkins and others like Mum Shirl had helped to set up. I had kept away from it because I thought it was too political. I thought they could have helped the Aboriginal situation in a more diplomatic way. But I knew that before the days of the Foundation, large numbers of Koori children were sent to government institutions. I thought of how the Aboriginal family structure which had existed before colonisation had become fragmented by nearly two hundred years of insensitive and inhuman government policies and I liked the idea of working for an organisation that had been set up by Aboriginal people, so I said to her, "Where do I fit in?"

"There is a position open for a social welfare worker, and seeing that you have been trained by the Church Army, I thought you might be interested in the position. The previous social worker has had to resign because of ill health."

"Oh," I said, "I'd have to think about the position?"

"Don't take too long because the Board meets next week."

"Well yes, I'll give it a go."

Cora took some photos of me and helped me to draw up a resume and collect some references from the Church Army and friends. She explained to me that my job would be different from what I was doing with the Church Army. "Instead of going out to the people, they will be coming to the office to you." A week later I got a phone call from the Foundation president to tell me that the

Board was pleased to give me the job. A couple of days later, I started work.

As I settled in to this new job, I heard the rumours, "Where this one come from?" "Where is this new lady from?...Fiji?...New Guinea?..." They had me coming from everywhere except Australia.

One day, my brother Colin came in and said, "You know those Kooris sitting in the park. Well sister, they were discussing you. They said, 'Can we trust this lady? Will she be as good as Mrs Lester? or better?' so I said to them, 'You can trust her and what's more she'll help you.' One of the Kooris looked at me and said, 'What do you know about her, brother?' 'Well, she's my sister. You can trust her and believe in her but she won't put up with any nonsense.' 'What! That little woman!' So I said, 'Well, that little woman can pack a big punch.' And we all laughed."

Work at the Foundation was very challenging. Most of my work was with women and children. When husbands were in gaol or if they were abusing their wives, then the Foundation was there to help the women find appropriate accommodation. Mothers would come to me and say, "I have five children. My husband is in gaol. He is an alcoholic. Can you please help me to go away with my children somewhere?" This sometimes meant fostering out the children for a short time rather than send them to an institution.

It was a challenge to try to find the best solution to each situation. It was up to me to first of all try to find a place for them to go where they could be together. Before putting my own views, I would say to the mother, "What do you suggest I do? Do you want the family split up or do you want them kept together?" It was hard for me to understand how a mother felt when giving up her child to the care of others, but I would always try to put myself in her position by talking with her.

Somehow, Friday afternoon invariably meant a young mother would arrive at the office with a baby or a child that she couldn't care for. When this happened, I would be unable to contact the Child Welfare Department until the following Monday. I was always afraid that if I left them with a distraught mother, they might be abandoned or abused. So I would take them home with

216

me. This way I knew that the children were properly looked after and if their mother was ill, I knew that she would get a break and the opportunity for proper medical care.

A few of my wadjin friends at Bexley got to know of my struggle. They told me, "Miss McDonald, you need a break. You can't work all the time." They often cooked meals for me so I could rest. After a while they started to meet me at the bus and if I arrived home with a baby they would take it for the weekend. I was glad of their help and their kindness and I shall never forget their consideration for my welfare and their dedication to those children.

There were rare times when, in the interests of the child, the fostering became an adoption. One Friday evening, towards the end of 1969, and just as I was about to leave the office, a young girl walked in with a toddler in her arms. She was nineteen years old. Deidre was well dressed but seemed to be very distressed. She explained that she was a severe asthmatic and had only just been discharged from a stay in hospital. She was pale, lacked energy, and looked as though she was still very ill. Like many others, this young girl was a single mother but I could see straight away that with her health, there was no way in the world she was going to cope with a youngster.

I invited her to sit down and tell me all about it. I dreaded times like these as I knew that I could not weep with her but needed to stay strong and detached. All the while we were talking things over, I was sending up little prayers asking for divine help.

After talking about her problems at length, she decided to have Mark fostered out. So I made all the necessary arrangements and Annie, a wadjin woman, and her husband and family came and took Mark away to care for him.

Annie's home was always open to Deidre and she visited Mark until he was three or four. Then, one day I got a worried phone call from Annie asking me to find Deidre as they had not heard from her for a while. I was unable to find her. I came up against a blank wall with all my questions. It puzzled me and reminded me of the times when I had questioned people about my own mother.

217

Annie rang me from time to time until Mark started school and then I didn't hear from the family until I received a phone call from Mark. He was sixteen years old and he was ringing to see if I knew where his biological mother was. I promised him that I would try to find her. This time I rang all sorts of places including the New South Wales north coast and Victoria but nobody seemed to know anything about her.

Then in 1991, I was holidaying with my friends, the Mansfields, when I suddenly decided that I would ring Annie. As we talked, Annie told me that one day she had said to Mark, "I want you to meet the lady who arranged for you to be with us." "Is she black or white?" he asked her. "What has that got to do with it?" she asked him. "Anyway she is an Aboriginal lady and you should be grateful to her."

"Well, I don't want to see her," was his answer.

I knew it was going to be difficult but we arranged to meet the next day. I was excited to see them when Annie, her husband and Mark arrived. Mark wouldn't get out of the car so I went over to speak to him. When I said hello, he put his head down and said nothing. "Don't push him," I said to Annie and we set off for a drive chatting about my life after the Foundation while Mark sat in silence.

On 26th of January 1993, Rowena Finnane and some of her young friends took me to the Invasion Day Celebrations at La Perouse. For Aboriginal people it has always been a sad time because for us this day was the beginning of the invasion that killed our people and destroyed our land and our way of life. Since 1988, Aboriginal people have gathered on this day to celebrate our survival despite so much tragedy. I was proud to be a part of it.

As I was sitting watching the dancing, there was a tap on my shoulder and a handsome young man in an akubra hat said, "Hello."

"Who are you?"

"Mark."

I nearly fell off the chair with shock. He rang me later and asked if he could come and talk to me. The first thing he did was apologise for his rudeness two years before and then we had a cup of tea and talked about his studies.

218

"Let's go for a drive, to Redfern" I said.

"What do we want to go to Redfern for?"

"This might be the day we find your mother."

We stopped a couple of times to introduce ourselves to Kooris in the street. Then we went to the Aboriginal Medical Centre to see if we could trace his mother there. The woman who looked after the records was not available until later so we decided to have lunch at the new Aboriginal restaurant across the road from Redfern Station.

Before we got out of the car I said to Mark, "There will be a lot of Koori people in here and, if you want to know where Deidre is, you will have to ask them yourself." We put in our order and sat down to wait for our food. After a while the manager came over to talk to us. When he went away, I said to Mark, "Now is the time. When he comes back, ask him if he knows Deidre." It wasn't long before the manager returned. Mark looked up at him and said, "Do you know Deidre Jones?"

"Deidre! I used to live next door to her." Mark and I became excited. "Hang on," he said, "I'll check that she is still there."

He ducked into his office and returned shortly to give us her address. We thanked him, finished our lunch and then hopped in the car. I said to Mark, "Don't build up your hopes. Deidre might welcome you with open arms. On the other hand she may not want to see you. What ever happens we have to accept her decision."

"I'm feeling dubious about meeting her," he said, as we looked for her street. Finally we found the address, knocked on the door and a young man answered the door. We inquired if Deidre lived there.

"Yes," said Jimmy. "Aunty Deidre lives here."

"Can I speak to her?"

"No. She is at TAFE."

"What time does she get home?"

"About four-thirty."

"Can we come back at six? This handsome fellow standing behind me is Aunty Deidre's eldest son," I told him.

Jimmy looked surprised and said, "No. Aunty Deidre's eldest son's name is Bill."

"No," I said. "This is her eldest son."

"No," he said. "There is only Bill and Tommy."

"All right," I said. "We'll be here at six."

Mark and I drove out to a prayer meeting at La Perouse that was part of the continuing Survival celebrations. We prayed for Mark and his biological mother and returned to the house at six. I was about to knock on the door when it opened and Deidre was standing there.

"Do you remember me?" I asked.

"Yes," she said.

"Do you know this handsome young man?"

"Yes. It's my son, Mark," she said looking overwhelmed. She took us into her kitchen and we sat down and talked about the long separation.

Mark spoke first, "Deidre, who is my father and what is his nationality?"

Deidre told him that his father was Portuguese, but didn't tell Mark his name. She warned Mark against seeing his biological father. Then Mark asked Deidre why she hadn't come to visit him. "The people who were caring for you didn't want me to visit you," she said.

"But Deidre," I said, "their home was always open to you. You could have visited him anytime." Deidre then started to cry and I said, "Well, he is here now." Deidre put her arms around him. I thought to myself, "My work is now over concerning this child. He has both his families." I was pleased that Mark's long search had ended.

Later, after visiting Mark's younger brother in hospital, Mark and Deidre drove me back home to Revesby. On the way we pulled in at a petrol station and while Mark was filling up the petrol tank I said to Deidre, "Did you ever think you would see your son again?"

"Yes," she replied. Deidre then turned around, looked at me and said, "Miss McDonald, I may not be a Christian like you but I knew in my heart that one day God would bring my son to me and that the person who would bring him back would be you, because you are the person who I came to for help. Thank you for bringing him back to me." And she started to weep. I thought to myself about how we often belittle young unmarried mothers who find themselves in a difficult situation.

Very few of the children fostered through the Foundation for Aboriginal Affairs were legally adopted like Mark and most were returned to their families after a fairly short stay in the foster family. It was always heartbreaking for the white families to hand back the children but they knew that it was inevitable they would be returned. I enjoyed the work, especially when I saw children who had been cared for with patience, understanding and love by white foster parents, being returned after a crisis was over to their own families where they belonged.

Working for the Foundation meant that I met a wide range of Aboriginal people, many of them talented and generous leaders of the community and I became good friends with a lot of them. Though it was difficult and often heartbreaking work, I received support and encouragement from a large number of wonderful Koori elders. Mrs Shirley Smith was always calling in to the Foundation to help. Another Koori, Mrs Polly Smith often helped me and later on became my relieving matron when I was running Grantham Hostel at Burwood. She became a very good friend, telling all her children and grandchildren to call me Miss McDonald or Aunty – and to never call me by my Christian name. In tribal Law, this is a mark of respect.

Mr Stan Roach and his wife became my Koori friends while I was working at the Foundation. He would often call in just to make sure everything was going smoothly with my job. I could not have done my work without their generous help.

It was while I was working at the Foundation that a young wadjin woman called Helen Anderson (later Mansfield) answered an advertisement for a secretary and auditor for the Foundation. There was a bit of a disagreement over Helen's appointment because she wasn't a Koori. A meeting was called and it was resolved that Helen was the best person for the job and afterwards I said to Helen, "If you have any more problems, just let me know." From that day on we became good friends Helen and her husband, David and their children, Jenny, Stephen and Kimberley always make me welcome at their home.

After two-and-a-half years of working at the Foundation for Aboriginal Affairs, I had a stroke and a heart attack and to my disappointment the doctor advised me to resign. When I left I received a beautiful letter from the late Mr Tom Williams, President of the Foundation – a letter I still keep to this day.

Helen Anderson arranged for me to go to the Salvation Army home in Stanmore to recuperate. I was walking down Enmore Road when a car pulled up. It was a child welfare officer. She said to me, "I've caught up with you at last. Do you live here or are you visiting."

Next day, the same officer called at the Salvation Army home. "What can we do for you?" Brigadier Entwhistle asked.

The welfare officer said, "I want to speak to Miss Connie McDonald."

"You know she has been ill, don't you? The doctor advises complete rest so I would appreciate it if you didn't worry her at this time." So she left but returned again the next day.

"What is it now?" the brigadier asked.

"Can I speak to Miss McDonald? It is very important."

"Unless there has been a death in the family, I will not have her upset." She called me in but insisted on being present while the woman from Welfare spoke to me.

"What is so important that you have to see me?"

"Are you aware that there is a hostel for Aboriginal girls at Burwood?" she asked.

"Yes, I have heard of it."

"They are in a quandary. The house parents have had to give it up because the house mother had a nervous breakdown."

"What do you want me to do about it?"

"We wondered if you could take over – just temporary until we find someone."

The brigadier looked angrily at the welfare officer and said, "You can't expect Miss McDonald to take over. I won't allow it."

"When can she take it over?"

"When she is well. If the hostel has to close, it has to close. She is under our care. Miss McDonald was put here by a friend and we want her to get well before she leaves." At this the welfare officer stormed out.

The brigadier looked me straight in the face and said, "I don't care if the hostel burns down, falls down or whatever. You are not taking over tomorrow." I felt humbled that someone should care about me with such dedication. It meant a lot.

Two weeks later, the manager of the Kirinari Hostel at Sylvania, Mr Eric Frater came to the home and asked if he could see me. Again Brigadier Entwhistle stayed in the room with us.

"What do you want to see me about?" I asked.

"About the hostel at Burwood."

"Have you got someone there?"

"Yes, temporary, but we would still like you to come when you are able."

Several weeks later I said to the brigadier, "I think I am much better when I am doing something. I'd rather be working than twiddling my fingers." So the next week an Aboriginal friend, Connie Stack, took me, my belongings and my dog to Grantham Street, Burwood.

I thought to myself, "I have never had children of my own. How am I going to cope with this lot?" And indeed my work at the hostel was more challenging than any of my previous jobs. I was glad they were young adults and that they could do a lot for themselves. Nevertheless, I was never in bed before midnight and I had to be up again at five o'clock each weekday morning. I was always glad when Monday came round as it was my day off.

My life at the hostel would fill a book on its own. As in all families, there were some who would not conform to anybody's rules no matter what. (They sound just like someone else I know!) All these I called my Ned Kelly group. They broke curfew, arriving home at all hours of the night and early in the morning, then expected to stay in bed all the next day.

The first year was particularly hard as I was expected to be cook, cleaner, confidante, mother, father and gardener all in one. My health broke down again so I sent a letter to Kirinari and they arranged for a cook and a house cleaner to help out.

At one stage I caught the Ned Kelly gang trying to smuggle a young fellow upstairs so that he could spend some time with his girlfriend. At the precise moment they were climbing up the stairs I came out of my room and saw what was happening. I invited the young members of the Kelly gang into my office.

"Please explain," I said.

Bold as brass, one young girl looked at me and said, "We only wanted him to spend some time with his girlfriend."

"Well," I said, "he could have gone to the front lawn with her. There are seats out there."

"They weren't going to do anything, matron."

"I don't care whether they were going to do anything but you know the rules. Upstairs is out of bounds to visitors."

The girls were not always difficult. There were times when they showed their appreciation by taking me out to dinner. I enjoyed looking after them, but in 1975, exhausted once more, I decided to hand in my resignation. There was no letter of thanks from Kirinari, nor was there one from the Child Welfare. I did receive a reference from the late Arnold Seitz, a specialist field officer with Child Welfare, which included the comment, "Connie is a good woman whose health has suffered by giving too much of herself..."

And Child Welfare did come out to Burwood to tell me that they had just opened a new home for boys from the courts at North Sydney. They thought that if they could be given a family atmosphere they would fit in better to society. "Oh well," I thought, "I'll give it a go." I lasted in the job at North Sydney for six months. I left for my own safety. This challenge was too much for me altogether and I decided to retire – terrified for my own life. Once more I rang Helen Mansfield. She picked me up with Lulu the dog and took us home to her place. That was the end of my working for the Welfare Department.

I spent a few quiet months as a nanny to the Morris family in Springwood whose grandparents are close friends of mine and in 1977, suffering from severe arthritis and scarcely able to walk, I went to live in a little cottage in Hazlebrook owned by the Department of Main Roads. I was at my lowest ebb. I know what people mean when they say they have hit rock bottom. Poverty overtook me. I had extremely poor health and I suffered from severe depression. I couldn't cook, I couldn't shop, I was lonely, and I wanted desperately for someone to visit me. My neighbour,

Meals-on-Wheels and the home-care lady were my only contacts. Eventually the home-care lady got in touch with the St Vincent de Paul Society of the local Catholic church. She told them that I was in desperate need of everything but warned them that I was very proud.

St Vinnies came to my rescue. First they visited, saying, "Miss McDonald, never let pride get in the way of your asking for help." Then they arrived with two loads of wood for my stove. Another man turned up with a small truck full of groceries, blankets, a heater and also food for my dog and cats. Each week they sent someone just to see how I was. If it wasn't for them, I believe I would have died of depression, stress, a stroke or starvation.

The missionaries had taught me the Word of God and told me that God loves us all. The people in the St Vincent de Paul Society showed me that this was really so by their practical, non-patronising and non-judgemental approach. As the months went by I made some very good friends in the St Vincent de Paul. Previously, when I had heard about Catholics, I would think, "I hope they don't want to change me." I found that fear to be unfounded as none of them ever did try to convert me. They were people who were genuinely concerned about the poor, the lonely and the sick.

During this time no Anglican people came near me except for the minister. They may have prayed for me, but nobody came and I almost felt like giving up religion altogether. I came through because I knew that St Vinnies were there. I have never forgotten them and I thank them for helping me through this low point of my life.

# Twenty-seven

## *"You should give up your Aboriginality"*
### ↬ *The Anglican Church* ↫

When I arrived at Padstow in 1981, I was frequently in and out of hospital. Crippled with arthritis, suffering from headaches and depression and unable to get out, I depended on my friends Helen and David Mansfield for support. No longer at the low point I had been at Hazelbrook, I felt different. I felt as though I was a palm tree standing alone in the desert – with plenty of water around me but roots that could not reach out to that water.

All through my life, I have had good Anglican friends. Being an Anglican, I expected the church communities to welcome me and give me support when I was in need. This rarely happened. Although the minister of St John's Anglican Church at Padstow, Reverend Don Wilson, often visited me and although some members of the parish became close friends of mine, I didn't ever feel as though I belonged to the church community. I couldn't understand it. I wondered, "What do I have to do? Maybe trying to attain gudiyar standards all these years, I have been acting under a delusion." I was not hurt by this experience but it did puzzle me. Looking back now I think that because of what had happened to me in the past, I found it hard to trust people. Maybe the people in the Anglican community could sense this lack of trust.

One day the Divine Master sent help. Again it was the St Vincent de Paul Society. Someone gave me their phone number and they came immediately to my support. They made me feel that I was not entirely alone. My roots were able to reach out to the water and my spirit flourished again.

The Izzards, my Catholic neighbours, were also caring people who were always concerned for my welfare. Of an afternoon, the

Izzard children would pop over, saying, "Mum sent me over to see how you are, Miss McDonald." I deeply appreciated their care. As I recovered my health and started to get around, I found that the wider community in Padstow was also good to me – the shopkeepers, the people in the street, the local children, all showed me care and respect. I was surprised that the help came from people outside my own denomination.

Padstow was not the only Anglican Church where I had difficulties in fitting in. There were other times when I felt as though church people were turning their backs on me. I would think, "How can they all go to church, say 'Our Father' and then come out and turn away when I try to make conversation with them?" It always astounded me.

Sometimes church people can say things without thinking. Many years ago, I was speaking after church with an Anglican friend. We were conducting a 'post mortem' of the sermon on Christianity. I said to my friend, "Why you gudiyar's religion is so over the top? We Kooris. Our religion is simple."

She said, "You are an intelligent and educated woman and a good Christian."

"What has that got to do with it?"

"You should be able to cotton on to white man's religion. Now that you're a Christian, you should give up your Aboriginality."

I looked at her and said, "You're not serious are you? I am an Aboriginal and I'll always be one. I can no more change my Aboriginality than you can change your whiteness. Aboriginal people had their own spirituality long before colonisation."

She did not like what I said and I was aghast at her attitude – end of conversation. Fortunately, some months later, she told me that she realised that her comments had been wrong and to this day we are still good friends.

From time to time, I have been to St James Anglican Church, King Street Sydney, with my friend Jean Olsen, from Yarrabah days. My experiences there have been vastly different from other Anglican churches. Every time I go there I feel as though I belong. After the service people are very friendly, there is always a cup of tea in the crypt, people talk to each other and there is always concern for my health.

I've trained as a lay evangelist. I've attended church regularly. I've played the organ in Anglican churches. I've preached in Anglican churches. I've taught religious instruction in schools and at Sunday School. I've visited white as well as black people in their homes, hospitals, prisons and children's institutions. I've always dressed well and I've lived a morally upright life. All these things I was taught to do by the Anglican church. I was told by white people, when I began to travel, that unless I attained all these conditions I would never make it in white society. All this while I've been thinking that by doing these things the Anglican church and society as a whole would accept me.

I am past being hurt but I still wonder: Why does it happen? Is it because I don't fit their expectation of the way I should behave? Is it because I won't let anyone patronise me? Do I challenge their stereotypes? Is it because I am no longer in a church uniform? Why do I feel so comfortable in St James?

Or is it that the Anglican church is too conservative for me? Do I expect too much of the church? Is the church too pre-occupied with being respectable? Is this why I have so rarely seen Koori people in Anglican churches?

I realise that I would not be who I am if it were not for the Anglican Church. My life may have taken a different direction. The Anglican church gave me training and spiritual guidance and set me on my life's path – have I failed that I do not feel fully accepted in the church?

In spite of my experiences, I will continue to live the way I was brought up. We are all born spiritual people. It was through the Anglican Church that I developed my Christian spirituality and relationship with the Divine Master. From when I was a child, I knew that there was a Supreme Being that cared. The magnitude of this caring was explained to me by the Anglican Church. For this, I will always be grateful.

God created me and loved me from the beginning so I will never forget my Aboriginal spirituality. I have combined both spiritualities and beliefs. Though I love and accept the Anglican Church, it will never take me away from who and what I am.

# PART THREE

## GOING HOME

# Twenty-eight

## *"We're glad you're still the same, Aunty"*
## ∽ *Wyndham and Oombulgurri* ∽

For nearly twenty years, I did not see or hear from my father. I stopped sending him letters and gradually cut myself off from thinking about him. Occasionally I wondered whether he was still droving or whether he had passed beyond the vale. I was still very hurt.

On the morning of Christmas Eve in 1974, while still matron at Burwood, I received a phone call from a sister in Darwin hospital telling me that my father was a patient there and had asked her to contact me. "He is going blind and he wants to see you," she said. As far as I knew, he was still droving cattle so it came as a shock to me to think of someone like him, who had worked all his life, not being able to see.

"How is his health?" I asked.

"He's all right, but you should come and see him."

I was surprised to hear that he wanted to see me. After my words to him on the Wyndham wharf, I thought he would never want to see me again. I had no relatives to ask what I should do, except the Divine Master and he had nothing to say. After much consideration I decided to go and see my father.

It was hard to get a ticket at such short notice but, due to a cancellation, I was able to book one for Christmas morning so I packed my bags. I rose early, had a shower, and was about to ring the taxi when I turned on the radio. I heard a news flash, "Cyclone Tracey has all but destroyed Darwin and people are being evacuated." I didn't know what to do. Then Ansett rang to tell me that all flights to Darwin were cancelled.

Thinking he had been evacuated to Melbourne, I decided that I would go there for my Christmas holiday. Not finding him in Melbourne, I was worried that something might have happened to him. I rang the police in Wyndham. Several weeks later, they contacted me to say that my father was living at Doon Doon Station in the Kimberleys with John and Nancy Martin (Talbot). Nancy is a relative of my father, and as soon as she and John heard about the cyclone, they had driven to Darwin and collected him from the hospital.

By this time, the girls were returning to the hostel and I could see no way of leaving my responsibilities. If we had been very close, girls or no girls, I would have dropped everything to go and see him. As it was, I agonised, "Who needs me most – the girls or my father?" "Does he want to see me because he at last recognises me as his daughter or is it because he is going blind?" Eventually I decided to stay with my job at the hostel and look after the girls.

Cyclone Tracey and the deaths it caused set me thinking. I wondered whether I should go back and live in the Kimberleys so I could be close to my father. I thought, "That person is my father; I am not going to dump him."

I was beginning to feel a strange feeling towards him that I hadn't felt before. I wanted to understand why he had abandoned me and I wanted to get information about my mother. Something was drawing me to him. And yet I kept thinking that if I made the trip, the same thing might happen as when he rejected me at Alice Springs. I did not want to be traumatised again so I put the idea on hold.

My work as matron of the girls' hostel, then as house mother to the boys at North Sydney, and my recurring illnesses left me no time to correspond with my father or my friends. Then when I arrived exhausted and in poor health at Padstow, I was only able to think of myself. Recovering my health became my main aim. I wanted to return to being able to be of some use to the people around me.

By 1984, my health was a little better and I decided I would make contact with my father so I started to phone him at Doon Doon. I learned that he was now totally blind and was dependent on Nancy and John. I would say to Nancy, "What is my father doing at the moment?" She would say, "Grandfather is out sitting under the gum tree listening to nature." When he came to the phone, although he didn't say it, I could detect that he was pleased to hear my voice once again. I was starting to think about this reconciliation business. I was even beginning to realise that the onus was on me to break this enmity between father and daughter.

News of my brother Colin's death in Adelaide in 1987 shattered every part of my being. His mother, Maisie, had died many years before. He and I had always been very close. I had known Colin from when he was born, I had cared for him in many ways as he grew up and we had kept in touch by phone. I rang the police at Wyndham to ask them to contact my father and tell him the news. Colin's death jolted me out of the long period of introspection that had been associated with my ill health. It brought home to me my need to look more deeply at myself in relation to my father.

It wasn't long after this that Jill and I started to write this book. I often spoke to Jill about my desire to return to the Kimberleys and see my father. "I'd love to see him and hold his hand," I would say. "I want to touch him and see what kind of response I get from him," and Jill would say, "Something will turn up."

The more we worked on the book the greater the urgency to see him became. One morning during my customary meditation with the Divine Master, I heard him say to me, "Constance, you must go to visit your father." "How can I go Lord, and visit this man that I don't even know? How can you ask me to love someone that has abandoned me? I don't have the means."

Then in June 1992, a couple of months after her mother died, Jill rang me and told me that she would like to use some of the money she had inherited for a trip to the Kimberleys. We would spend a week or so in Wyndham where we would try to organise to fly across to Oombulgurri, which was the old Forrest River Mission. Then we would go to Derby to see my father where I would stay on for a few more weeks and get to know my father while Jill returned home from her first holiday away from her husband and children.

232

Thinking about my father, and what I should say to him when I saw him, I heard a voice say, "What your father did in his younger days is his own business. It was his life. You should forgive him for not being there when you needed him. If you can't forget, you can't forgive. If you can't forgive you can't love."

On the 21st of August 1992 (a week later than originally planned, because I had an emergency stay in hospital), our plane taxied along the tarmac. I was homeward bound. As we sat in the plane I started to worry. I kept saying, "Jill, will my people welcome me? I'm not sure whether they'll think I'm too flash." Jill reassured me that everything would be all right, then she put the earphones in and listened to music – talk about subtle!

When we changed planes at Darwin, we spent a couple of emotional hours with Marie Burke, who had been cook and assistant matron at St Mary's Hostel in Alice Springs, and her daughter, Wendy, who had been ten years old when I left there. Marie kept sobbing, "I didn't ever think that I would see you again. It must have been God's wish." And we laughed and cried, swapping stories and remembering together. When I said to Marie, "I was a good girl wasn't I?" she replied, looking at Jill, "Yes – as far as we know," and gave us all a half-smile. Seeing Marie brought back for me happy memories of life at Alice Springs – memories of how Marie Burke had helped Sister Eileen to lovingly sort out our problems. As Wendy drove us back to the airport through the hot Darwin suburbs, I prepared myself for the next stage of our journey, the return to Wyndham. I could feel myself shaking inside so I sent my prayers up through the aeroplane to the Divine Master.

On our first day at Wyndham Port, I took Jill around to show her what had been a thriving town. We saw the former courthouse where I had received my citizenship, the old gaol that is now the new courthouse, the old post office which is now a museum and the new Wyndham gaol which had been the gudiyar hospital. We looked straight up from the town to Mt Albany and Mt Bastion. For me this was a spiritual experience as I thought back to the old people's stories about the tribes that lived at the base of these sacred landforms. I remembered thinking as a child that the two mountains looked as though they were huge rocks that had rolled across

233

the plains and come to a stop just before the Cambridge Gulf and in my childish imaginings, I thought the Great Spirit had changed the rest of the rocks into mud flats. Between the mountains we saw the Chumulli Range through which the drovers used to bring the cattle to the abattoirs.

As yet, none of the Aboriginal people knew I was in town and I was still very nervous about what my arrival might mean. We sat down for lunch beside a couple of jungerrie trees at the cafe where Mrs Flinder's Dress Shop used to be. It brought back memories of the time my step-mother, Maisie and I bought my first shop dress. Jill and I looked at the menu up on the board and giggled when we saw "bungle burgers" there. As we finished eating, two Aboriginal girls came to the shop. One of them looked over in our direction and said, "Are you Connie McDonald?" I was amazed that such a young girl would know who I was. "How do you know me?" I asked her.

"My mother used to tell me about you. You used to be a teacher." Her aunt Dora Grant arrived, gave me a big hug and kiss, saying in the midst of our tears, "Remember – you used to teach me in kindergarten." Dora was a relative of Judy Taylor, who had come to me with leprosy when we were on walkabout. As I talked with Dora, I settled down. The embrace I received from her was the first one I had ever received from someone from Forrest River Mission. I was surprised by the ease with which it happened. It meant more to me than Dora could ever imagine. For someone from that community to show such love and regard for me was overwhelming. It made me realise how much things had changed now that there were no government policies to stop us from relating naturally to each other. On the mission embracing wasn't allowed. The missionaries were always separating us children from our people, trying to make black whitefellas out of us. When Dora reached out to embrace me, I didn't know what to do but I let my defences down and accepted the love she was showing and I thought, "I am glad I have come." The whole cafe witnessed the emotional welcome and I'm sure everyone was touched by the joy that was radiating out from us. Even gudiyar tourists who were visiting the cafe were moved to tears.

234

This was beginning of my realisation that the burden that I had carried through my life – the belief that I belonged to no one – was unfounded and it was the beginning of a reunion with my people which was to last all the time I spent in the Kimberleys. During the days that followed, many of my fears disintegrated.

As we chatted, Dora's husband, Willie Grant, a friend of my cousin Alan, arrived. "I'll go and ring Alan now," he said. Later, they took us for a walk to meet people like Ruth's father, Dick Macale and Clara Mitchell (Leray), who had been one of the younger girls when I was a senior dormitory girl. I remembered Clara as a happy and beautiful young girl, whose mother used to sneak to the back fence of the compound in order to talk to her and bring her some bush food. It used to tear me up inside to see the way her mother was treated because she was a camp narlie.

Then we walked past the gaol. Before colonisation there had been only one law, tribal Law. In tribal Law there had never been any prisons. Offences had been dealt with straight away. Colonisation brought with it the government law and church law. That meant Aboriginal people had to live under three laws. It was laws, laws, laws and you daren't break any of them. It is no wonder that there has always been and still is even today an over-representation of Aborigines in gaol compared to the rest of society. When I was growing up on the mission, anybody taken to Wyndham to the gaol was rarely allowed to have visitors, not even their parents. Only if someone was ill would their relatives on the mission be allowed to go to Wyndham to see them. This instilled in us youngsters an overpowering fear of being locked up.

As Jill and I walked with Dora, I could see that this was different from the old prison. We were astounded to see the prison gates open and family reunions taking place all over the gaol yard. Inmates were tending the prison garden, playing the guitar and singing. It was so different from the Wyndham I knew thirty-five and more years ago.

Next day, I felt ready to find some more of my people. This was easier said than done, because there was only one taxi and the day before we had waited in vain for it to pick us up. After trying once again to get the taxi, we decided to contact a member of one of the Chinese families I had known.

Whenever I used to visit Wyndham from Forrest River, the Lee Tongs, like the other Chinese families in Wyndham, were always friendly to me. Young Billy Lee Tong was the outgoing member of his family. As a young woman I would often see him climbing a grape vine, swinging from the trees or poking his tongue out at people as they walked past. Whenever his mother caught him giving cheek to me, she would send him to his room and then invite me in for a cup of tea. "He naughty one, that boy," his mother would say and I would smile like a cheshire cat saying, "No, Mrs Lee Tong. He's just a young boy – full of fun."

That cheeky little chap is now a respected friend of mine. As soon we made contact with him, he, his wife Dorothy, and his youngest son Lindsay put themselves completely at our disposal, taking us to visit people who would remember me and calling out to introduce me to others who were walking past. All the while driving us around, Billy came out with funny yarns and historical stories of life in Wyndham. Billy and I spent much of the time trying to outdo each other with our storytelling. Dorothy decided that we were both on a par.

At Warriu Old Folks home, named after the late King Peter Warriu, I sat down with my people who had been adults at Forrest River when I was growing up. When Evelyn Carroll, though blind, realised it was me holding her hand, she grabbed it even more tightly. To see her and Mummy Nora's daughter Eileen Mitchell and my older cousin Rosie Gerard (nee Gregory, now deceased) was something I thought would never happen again. Here was I saying hello to my elders and they were accepting me as I was. As I met my people, communication came easily because I found myself speaking the way I used to speak and using my language wherever I could.

One night, Billy took us to see Ruth Macale (now Oxenridge). To Jill's delight, Ruth started to tell some funny stories of scrapes I had been in as a youngster. "Remember when we used to get you to do things because your bones meant you couldn't be punished."

While we were at Ruth's place a slight, alert looking woman walked in and I asked who she was?

"Ivy Carter," she said and we embraced as memories flooded back of the times I had spent while a young woman as a welcome member of her family.

As a child I had often dreamed of going up to the top of Mt Bastion to look out at the Five Rivers. I wanted to look for myself at the rivers as they flowed into the Cambridge Gulf. With my bone condition, I was never allowed up the rough, bush track because someone would have had to carry me. Now fifty-nine years old, able to get about with the aid of a calliper and walking stick, my dream came true. One evening at dusk, the Lee Tongs drove us up to the top of Mt Bastion to watch the sun set over the Five Rivers.

While there Billy introduced me to a gudiyar man whose grandparents were the founders of Wyndham town. When Billy said, "This is Connie McDonald," the man said, "You're Duncan's daughter aren't you?" and shook my hand. Thirty-five years ago, I would not have even dared to speak to this man. Looking out over the Five Rivers, I thought, "Are these rivers a symbol of black and white coming together at last?"

The welcome I had received in Wyndham had not only been from my own generation but also from the second and third generations of people I used to go to school with. The hospitality of Wyndham helped to allay my fears about how I would be received when I went to Oombulgurri. Nevertheless, I was extremely nervous about making the trip. I kept making excuses, not wanting to go. My self-doubt and my fears of rejection took hold of me. I chastised Jill for booking the plane and then I got stuck into Billy Lee Tong, telling him, "If we don't go right now, we'll be too late." Jill and Billy put up with my ranting and raving and when we were on our way to the airport I kept thinking to myself, "Why am I going? Perhaps the plane will break down and we won't be able to go."

When Billy introduced us to the pilot and we started to climb into the tiny three-seater store plane, I let go of my fears for a time as I had to look after Jill because she was scared of the little plane. "Just close your eyes and when you open them you'll be there," I told her. But there was no way Jill was going to close her eyes. She wasn't going to miss out on anything. But I think that quietly she was saying her prayers.

As we flew over the Five Rivers, it must have been an overwhelming experience for Jill as she saw there below her the winding snake-like Forrest River, just as I had explained it to her. As the plane flew over the mouth of the river, I was transported right back to my childhood. Then, as Oombulgurri came into view, my heart overflowed with a feeling of belonging. I thought, "This place grew me up. This is my home. Oombulgurri is my mother."

As the manager drove us up to the store, I became excited again. Once more I was able to walk on the sand where I had taken my first steps and where I had played as a child. I remembered sitting on the ground letting the sand run through my fingers. I wished I could sit down there and then and once again feel mother earth. I thought, "Now I am here as a ngumbahblah (old woman) and the earth is holding out her arms to welcome me."

As Jill and I stood there wondering whether we were welcome, we decided to wander off towards the school (a vastly different one from the little one-room school I had attended and taught in). No one knew we were coming but word started to go around that I had arrived, so we had a long talk with the principal and some of the elders and then shook hands with some beautiful pre-school children on their way home for lunch.

As I shook hands with the little ones and told them to tell their parents that Connie McDonald was here they looked at me as if to say, "Where this one come from?"

A young fellow named Michael Martin was an assistant school teacher just as I had been so many years ago. He showed us all around the school and talked about life at Oombulgurri. The school gave us a lovely lunch and by this time people, including Margaret Smith, were beginning to gather outside the community office waiting to meet us. Margaret Smith was a committee member of the Oombulgurri Community and one of Rosie Gerard's daughters. Michael said, "Do you want to go for a ride?"

I climbed in the front and Jill and Margaret Smith got in the back of the ute and we bumped off on a dusty tour of many of the places that had been important in my childhood. While this was not a Sunday picnic for Jill, I think she thought every mouthful of dust was worth it, though I am sure she also thought, "Sydney is not like this."

Michael took us to O'Donnell's Crossing where we used to catch barramundi and to Dadaway where we would dive for gardjah (lily roots) and ducks. I remembered how we'd pull the ducks down under the water by their legs, then twist their necks, swim to shore, pluck the duck and then throw it on the fire. I remembered how we'd take our pandanus baskets, swim out to the water lilies, pluck the purple pods full of uloogoo (seeds) put them in the basket and then dive down, hanging on to the galong-ang-arrah (stalks) until we reached the gardjah. Then we'd dig up the root and make for the surface.

Back on land we'd peel the pod and put the uloogoo in another pandanus basket to dry, we'd wash the gardjah, scrape a hole in the fire and then cover them with hot embers and sand. The galong-ang-arrah we ate raw. They tasted like a sweet celery and we'd sit on the rocks chewing them while we waited for the lily roots to cook. By the time the roots were cooked the seeds would be dry and we would then grind them between two stones to make flour, all the time putting a bit of water with it to make a sweet batter that we then shaped into little cakes or a damper and cooked them in the hot sand.

As Michael took us around, I reflected on the times we had sat on the banks of the river eating these delicious foods. Later on as I chatted to some of the men I had taught at school, I reminded them of some of the wonderful bush foods we used to eat and I asked them to tell their children about them and show them how to collect them. I reminded them of glay, a little green fruit which we ate straight from the tree or mashed between stones, goondee, a blackberry-like fruit and I talked about the market gardens that the mission used to grow.

Margaret Smith told me, "Yes, Aunty. We are starting now to tell our children all about their culture and we are starting to make decisions. We are having meetings." I thought about the meetings that we had while I was on the mission. They were not our meetings. I was thrilled to know that at last these meetings were being conducted by Aboriginal people.

As we chatted Margaret said to me, "You're not flash. You're still the same – still cracking jokes."

"Why should I be flash?"

"We're glad you're still the same, Aunty," and she added, "Nobody really wanted you when you were a child but now we all respect you because you picked yourself up."

The time at Oombulgurri was all too short, especially the fun and laughter I had with the children and young people. As we were leaving to go to the aerodrome, a sad feeling came over me. I thought, "Maybe I will never see this place again." Our goodbyes were said with a mixture of laughter and tears and as the plane flew over Oombulgurri, I asked the pilot to dip the wings to say farewell. My heart bled as I looked down on Oombi. "Connie," I said to myself, "Don't you bawl now!" I thought about the words of one of my relatives, "You are the same as us, Aunty. You belong to us."

And later, while in Derby, I composed a song to express my feelings.

### Oombulgurri

*It was good to see you once again, Oombulgurri*
*The place that nurtured my very soul*
*For it was you I turned to for peace and solace*
*When all the world seemed to come tumbling down*

*(chorus)*

*O Oombulgurri, O Oombulgurri*
*The place that nurtured my very soul*
*For it was you who taught me right from wrong*
*Teaching me to love and respect all mankind.*

*In 1933 my mother and I*
*Landed safely on your friendly shore*
*Not knowing for us what was in store*
*As we made our way to the mission station*

*In 1934 my dear mother died*
*The mother I was never to know*

240

But you O Oombi came to my rescue
You became my mother and my best friend

At times when I was in such great pain
Suffering from all my broken bones
The trees around me would rustle their leaves
And the birds would sing in sweet harmony.

For it was you Oh Oombulgurri
Who asked the birds, trees and children to sing to me
To ease the pain I so often went through
And it was you Oh Oombi who taught me to smile

35 years ago I left you Oh Oombi
To spread my wings for some distant shores
As we sailed down the Cambridge Gulf bound for Darwin
I waved my last farewell to you Oh Oombi

35 years on I have come back for a visit
A visit made possible by God and a friend
I have come back to see my dear father
Who has reached the ripe old age of 82

The first time I saw you Oh Oombi, after 35 years
I wept and wept tears of great sadness and joy
Thinking how I had missed this most wonderful place
The place that nurtured my very soul

Thank you God for sending me back to the Kimberleys
To visit my dear father, relatives and friends
And also that I may see you once again Oh Oombi
For maybe I shall not pass this way again.

When we started to work on this book, we wrote down "Every person needs to belong." Maybe I had to leave the Kimberleys to find out who I was, but my return showed me that I did belong to my people. When I left I was, I realise now, an angry young woman, but when I returned the anger was no longer there and I was able to see the love that was there for me. As I reflected on all these experiences, I came to regret those angry words that I had spoken to my father on the Wyndham wharf all those years ago and I began to think more and more about what I would say to him when we met.

During the next couple of days, Billy Lee Tong took us to meet with other wonderful friends and relatives. Each time we met we would talk, as dictated by tribal custom, about their families and extended families, then we would talk about growing up, old times and other stories. I was invited to the high school where I spoke to students who included the grandchildren and great grandchildren of the people I went to school with and of those I had taught.

I reflected with Jill on changes in the town that thirty-five years had made. I remembered one time in the 1950s when Leita Turner (now Bell), one of the teachers at the mission, and I were returning after the Christmas holidays. We were booked in to the Wyndham Hotel but when the manager saw me he said, "You can't stay here. No blacks stay in this hotel. You go and stay with your relatives."

As I went down the steps I said, "You know I've got my citizenship rights, don't you?"

"Oh, that puts a different light on it," he said.

"Goodbye," I said.

"Come back," said Leita. I was tired. I wanted to sleep. I didn't want to face the people in the hotel and I wasn't in an argumentative mood. Besides, I knew that I'd be much happier at Ruth's place anyway. Leita was upset but I wasn't, because, Wyndham being what it was at the time, I expected nothing more. I got back in the taxi and asked him to take me to the Macales where Ruth welcomed me with open arms.

In 1992, the care, courtesy and warmth I received while staying at the Wyndham Port Motel was a clear contrast to that experience. I was pleased to see the ease with which black and white were now interacting, "At last we are being recognised as people," I said. "Thirty-five years ago, Jill, I would not have been able to book into this hotel with you and thirty-five years ago, blacks would not have opened their mouths to utter a word to whites."

True to his word, Willie Grant contacted Alan McDonald and let him know that I was in town, so among the many phone calls that I received while at the motel was a call from Alan. The relationship between Alan and I as we were growing up was more like that between brother and sister than cousins. He would tell me his girl problems and I would tell him my boy problems.

"Hello, Sis," he said.

"Where are you?"

"I'm here at Mistake Creek for a meeting."

"How is my father?"

"He's all right! You're not coming back to argue with him again, are you?"

"No, I'm just coming back to Derby to see him. I hope that he will accept me as his daughter."

Alan then told me, "I'm coming down with Margie and the girls to see you." I could hear from his voice that he was pleased at the prospect. The fact that Alan was prepared to travel from Mistake Creek, Northern Territory back to Billiluna to pick up Margie and the girls, then get a lift to Hall's Creek to catch a bus to Derby made me look at myself differently. That long exhausting journey meant more travelling for Alan than it had taken for us to get to Wyndham from Sydney and he was going to do it so he could see me. I knew we would get along well.

On our last evening in Wyndham, cousin Freda Chuling's son, Frankie, took us on a drive. It was a profound moment when we arrived at a spot, a few kilometres out from Wyndham, where he told us, Sing's garden used to be. As we walked around Frankie said, "Under one of these trees is where you were born, Aunty." His mother had heard about my birth and had told him all she knew. He explained to me that government records, that stated that I had been born at Four Mile, were wrong. They were, like many government records about Aborigines, simply a guess.

At that moment this abandoned plantation became sacred to me. As I stood there I thought, "This was where my little mother gave birth to me. This was where mother earth embraced my mother and me and while giving care and easing the pain of childbirth for my mother, welcomed me as she embraced my little naked body. Not only mother earth but the whole world welcomed me."

Frankie also took us to visit some relatives of my father, the children and grandchildren of Mona and Sandy Talbot. The Talbots were not mission people so I had only known them when I spent holidays with Uncle Sandy, Aunty Mollie and Alan. The family were sitting around a fire, all ages, happily chatting and laughing. As Frankie drove into their yard, I called out, "Connie McDonald here, I've come to visit you." On hearing my name they rushed over to tell me who they were. I felt immediately at ease with Jill Cigobia and Geraldine Lippit (both nee Talbot). They sat at my feet and talked about their family, and I thought, "I wish I had had a family like this."

All the time I had been in Wyndham I had enjoyed telling people funny stories. This night, it was my turn to listen, as Geraldine popped up and said she could tell funny stories about Duncan, my father. Later that night, my friend Jill told me that she had thought, "Here is another storyteller like Connie. I could sit and listen to her all night."

I didn't want the time of departure to arrive because I could feel my emotions starting to overwhelm me. In our short time together, we had bonded as a real family.

Later, as I pondered these things and listened to Jill and Frankie talking about politics I thought to myself, "Here goes my father again," and listened, fascinated to think that this younger relative of mine was well into politics. My father would have been delighted to have talked to Frankie.

Back at the motel that night I said to Jill, "Maybe all my years of thinking that no one cared, maybe I was mistaken." Then we chatted about what it would be like when I went to Numbala Nunga nursing home at Derby to see my father.

I couldn't sleep. I wondered, "What will my father think when they tell him I am there? What will he say? I am fifty-nine – will he accept me as his daughter now? How will I be able to communicate with him now that he is blind and partly deaf?"

244

On our way to Derby next day, we spent an afternoon with cousin Freda Chulung in Kununurra. While she was glad to see us, I perceived that we had come at the wrong time. She was watching her favourite serial, *Days of our Lives*. I gather from her daughters that it was 'criminal' to even talk while this program was on. My half brothers Jock and Jacko and Jacko's wife Elizabeth soon arrived. As soon as I saw Jacko I said to him, "You look like your mother."

It was hard for me to embrace them. I guess it was probably hard for them to at last see their older sister. Though I had seen Jock twice when he was three years old, we didn't know each other at all. We didn't seem to know what to say to each other. It was difficult for me to readily accept them as my family members because this feeling welled up inside me, "They'll abandon me like my father did." I shouldn't have felt like that but thoughts kept coming into my mind. "They grew up with our parents and I didn't."

After a while we went out on the verandah while Jill took some family photos and we began to chat more easily. One conversation led to another and I started to exercise my rights as the older sister. I growled at Jock because of his drinking and at Jacko for other things. They just listened.

I was excited about the coming birth of Elizabeth and Jacko's first baby. I kept patting Elizabeth's very pregnant malla, saying, "Hullo, niece or nephew. This is your Aunty Connie."

# Twenty-nine

## "I am his daughter"
### ◈ My father ◈

From when Jill and I first landed in Derby, I was anxious over what would happen when I went to visit my father at Numbala Nunga nursing home. At the back of my mind was the incident at Alice Springs when I had asked if I could come and live with my father, Maisie and Colin as a family.

I went first to the office of the nursing home and then wandered along a hallway that seemed to go for miles. I thought to myself, "Now I am really on my own." I stopped a few times. Each time a voice said to me, "Keep walking." I went on until the verandah came into view where my father was sitting asleep in his wheelchair.

Suddenly, I felt as though I was being taken into another dimension. The hallway was still there but there seemed to be no building. My father was sitting on a canopy of clouds instead of his wheelchair. I thought, "Maybe father and I have passed beyond the vale! Maybe we finished!"

Standing next to him was a young girl I had seen before. When I was thirteen, my father had shown me a photo of my mother and the vision standing there was exactly like that photo. As I drew nearer, I heard my mother say, "I loved him and I still love him. You must love him too."

Being on the defensive, I thought, "Why should I?"

"Because he's your father."

At that moment I heard another voice, a voice that I have heard often in my lifetime, "Forgive him. Forget everything and love him. Do not abandon him – he is your father."

When I reached my father, one of the sisters said, "Wake up Duncan. Your daughter is here." Then she said to me, "Take hold of his hand."

I had never held my father's hand except when we shook hands when I first met him. As I took his hand in mine, I thought, "This person is my father, my own flesh and blood." I didn't think that my heart would open to my father or that the hardness in my heart towards him would turn into love but it had.

"Would you like something to calm you down?" said the sister.

"No, thanks. I'll be all right."

"Speak to him," said the sister.

"Hello father," I said loudly. "It's me."

"Who's me?" he asked.

"Connie, your daughter, and Biddy's."

He clasped my hand and he said, "Where did you come from?"

"Sydney," I shouted.

"You came all the way from Sydney to see me?"

"Yes, father." The moment I held his hand and told him I loved him, I felt as if a charge of electricity was passing through us both. My father said, "What's that?"

I knew what he was talking about and I said, "It's the Holy Spirit – God."

Still holding my hand he said, "I feel as if there has been a load lifted off my shoulders." I felt the end of the enmity between us and that I could now rightfully say, "He is my father. I am his daughter." Though he was blind, he could tell that I was crying and he also shed tears.

That first day in Derby is still special to me for another reason. On that day, I was also reunited with my cousin, Alan McDonald. Growing up in Wyndham, Alan was known to all as the Big Fella. As tribal Law dictates, I greeted Margie, Alan's wife, first then welcomed Alan and their grandchildren, Marietta, Kay and Jenny. Then Alan and I started talking about old times and about family and friends. If I went on too much he still told me off – and coming

247

from, Alan, I took it. Alan, as always, was prepared to listen to me, even when I got on his nerves. That's family.

As we sat in the garden at the Kimberley Lodge, I asked, " Alan, what did my mother die from? Was it from natural causes."

"Aunty Biddy just died naturally."

"Are you sure?"

"Yes, my parents would have told me if they suspected anything. That's it."

I had to accept what he told me. If he had known any different he would have said so. I thought to myself, "Maybe the uneasiness will pass now that I have heard it from Alan." And I decided that I would concentrate on getting to know my father better.

"Tell me about my father," I said, "because you had more dealings with my father than I had, Alan. What manner of man is my father?"

"Speak English, sister."

We looked at each other and laughed.

"You are just like your father. He is full of fun. In spite of what you have heard about him, he is a good man, and would never let anyone go without food or shelter or clothes. He has suffered too during his life." For hours during the next weeks, I listened to Alan as he told me about my father and his family.

There was also a lot of soul searching for my father and me. One day he said to me, "I wish I could see you." Most of the time we would just sit there and hold hands with not a word spoken. Together, during the next three weeks, we shed tears of healing, tears of joy and tears of acceptance, and maybe we both matured as people. We told each other things that we could never tell anyone else; he confided in me and I in him.

One day, as we were sitting out in the grounds, he took my hands and turning his face to me said, "Connie, I loved you from the first day your grandmother put you in my arms ten hours after you were born. I felt this strong emotion as I realised I was holding my first born child, and as I looked at you, I knew you were something very special. I loved you that first day, I've loved you all my life, I love you now and I will love you till the end and I feel proud that you are my daughter."

All my life I was waiting to hear those words. I said, "Father, I've always loved you too." From that day, my father became the most important person in my life.

Leaving him behind was something I dreaded. When it came time to return to Sydney I went to see him for the last time. When the visit was over my father wanted me to take him to his room but I was at breaking point and so I was glad Alan and Margie were there. "Say goodbye to him," said Alan.

"Goodbye father," I said.

He said nothing. He was crying as Alan took him back to his room and Margie comforted me.

"Sister-in-law, he'll be all right. Alan and I will look after him."

We all embraced and cried. That's family.

In June 1995, a young relative rang me and told me to come to Derby as my father was dying. I was in the middle of the worst bout of flu, but against my doctor's advice, I knew I had to go. One of the sisters at Numbala Nunga said to me, "Connie, your father is hanging on to life because he wants to see you."

When I took his hand, he held on to it so tight it hurt me. I knew that he was dying; I sat beside him, tears streaming down my face. He turned to me and said, "Connie, I knew you would come."

I said, "Father, if you were in another country, and you needed me I would have found a way to be with you." Then I said, "Relax father, I'm here with you now."

The second day I was with him, all he wanted to do was hold my hand. I put my arms around him as best I could and held him to me, kissed him and said to him, "Goodbye father!" and told him I loved him. He turned his face to me and God opened his eyes and my father said to me, "Connie, I'm glad you came, and I'm happy to be able to see you as you are now." Then he became blind again. He had said to me in 1992 that he wished he could see me. God had performed a miracle for my father. The bond between us may have been severed by death, but as love is forever, so too is the bond between father and daughter. Vale, father. Vale.

# Thirty

## *"Look after my little girl"*
## ∽ *My mother* ∾

I believe that children of any age are very perceptive. When I was a little child growing up, I knew that there was something missing when I found myself going from one family to another. I can remember times when I was in hospital crying my eyes out and wondering why no one was with me. When I saw the other children, with their parents I could sense that it was different for me.

The dormitory children used to tease me and say, "You've got no mother. Your mother dead." I did not take much notice until the day Mummy Nora told me that she wasn't my mother. I wasn't angry. I just couldn't comprehend that my mother was not with me. I said, "Tell me what you mean about my mother dead?" When Mummy Nora explained to me, I suddenly felt alone. "Why did my mother have to go away?" I asked her.

Puberty was when I most needed my mother. Growing from a little girl to a woman is an experience that every girl goes through and I thought most often about her at that time. Every now and then throughout my life I have thought that my mother was with me. Every time I broke my bones I felt that she was there holding my hand or my leg and the pain was eased.

My mother's one worry as she was dying was that her little girl would be taken care of. Not long ago a woman, who was a senior girl at the time of my mother's death, told me, "The day your mother died, she called one of the senior girls to her. You were lying by her side and your mother said, 'When I am gone, please look after my little girl.' It wasn't an order; it was a plea from your mother and after she said it she closed her eyes." After they buried my mother she took me from the hospital to the dormitory where she cared for me until the mission decided what was to happen to me.

I told this woman that I recalled some of the senior girls telling me that, a couple of days after my mother died, I gave up all nourishment and wasn't sleeping. She said, "Maybe you were willing yourself, even at that age, to go with your mother or maybe she wanted to take you with her. The missionaries were worried and you were growing weak. After a while you were taken into Wyndham to the white hospital. People were saying, 'This little ngumballa is going to die because she misses her mother. Biddy's dead and her little girl is going to die too.' The Forrest River people were worried. It was a hard struggle for the gudiyar staff at the Wyndham hospital to get you to take nourishment but it wasn't long before you were thriving again."

Even today my mother is important to me. Although I cannot remember her, I love her. On my return to Revesby after my visit to the Kimberleys, my mother became more important to me than she had ever been before. I did not understand the love of my parents until the spiritual experience of my mother's presence on my first visit to my father in Derby. Although it was late in life, I am glad that I found that my parents do love me.

And after all these years, I found out how my mother died. There were no suspicious circumstances, no need for me to feel anxiety. My father was away droving and my mother hadn't seen or heard from him for a long time. There had been extensive flooding and there was news of people drowning. She feared that he had drowned and that she would never see him again and she was pining so much for him that she fell ill and died.

*Dear mother, I know that all my life you have been looking down on your little girl, worrying about me. You need not have worried about me, mother, because along life's way the Divine Master has provided care, help and strength through many wonderful people.*

251

# *Epilogue*

I would like to pay a tribute to who all took care of me during my childhood: my family, the people of Forrest River Mission, now Oombulgurri, and the missionaries. Also I want to thank all my family, my relatives and friends throughout Australia who have been a part of my life.

While I may have gone on about missionaries in this book, I would also like to pay a tribute to the Australian Board of Missions for sending the missionaries to us. I would not be the person I am today were it not for them. Having an ethical base for my life, and the values that came with the Christian message, have given meaning to my life. My daily meditation, in company with the Divine Master, seeking his help and strength just for that day, has strengthened me to face life with courage, strength and dignity.

The past is the past. We must not forget where we come from. Without ancestors there would be no society. I have decided that though I will not forget the atrocities of colonisation, I must not dwell on the past but look to the future and what it might bring.

When I started to write this book it was my mother and a knowledge of her that I was seeking. What I found was my father and the opportunity to develop a deeper relationship with him. I thank my people for saying to me so often, "When you grow up, you'll know about things."

It was hard for me to want to grow up. My ever-present physical pain made it hard for me to think about my future . As a child I felt set apart from other people but as I developed and lived through not only my own struggles but the struggles of my race, I realised that we all have our humanity in common and that together we can shape our future.

Though people may see me as immature because of my disability and my rebellious nature, I can see that it has been by accepting my weaknesses and turning them into strengths, in learning to accept myself just as I am, that I can now say, "I believe

God set me apart just to be who I am today. No one can change me; I am me and I shall remain me. I can say now to my people I have finally grown up."


FOOTNOTE: The skipper returned to Australia in 1993, and we picked up where we left off, and we are now one!

This book is also dedicated to God.

*Thank you, God the Creator, for creating me.*

*Thank you, Father of all mankind, for being my father.*

*Thank you, my Divine Master, for taking over my life when I became bereft of my mother.*

*Thank you, dear Lord, for providing me all my wants and needs.*

*Thank you, dear Saviour, for the wonderful missionaries and people of Forrest River Mission (now Oombulgurri) for taking good care of me.*

*Thank you, Holy Father, for sending missionaries to teach us your Holy Word.*

*Thank you for easing the pain of broken bones, insecurity and loneliness.*

*Thank you, dear Lord, for your guidance, forgiveness, patience, care love and all the good things you have given to me all my life, family, relatives, friends, and loved ones, happiness in adversity, joy in loving and serving you.*

*Thank you, Divine Lord, for bringing my parents and myself together in that spiritual vision and experience I had on the first time I met my father after thirty-five years. To forgive is divine.*

*Thank you, loving Father, for showing me what and how to love.*

*Thank you, loving Father, for reconciliation which took place between my father and me, and, on behalf of my father and myself, we thank you dear Lord.*

*Thank you, dear Lord, for my life which I re-dedicate to you every day. Amen.*

Constance McDonald

254

# Background

Running into the Cambridge Gulf of far North-western Australia are five mangrove-flanked rivers. One of these is the Forrest River, named after John Forrest, government surveyor and explorer. Its Aboriginal name is Munon-gu. It is a saltwater river, infested with crocodiles, sharks, sea snakes and stingrays. The river twists its way through a picturesque part of the Kimberleys. About five kilometres from the Gulf, the mud banks and mangroves give way to steep, ancient gorges, rugged and mysterious and sacred to the tribes of the meandering lower reaches of the region.

The Cambridge Gulf is a wide expanse with a deep channel and always contains water, invariably muddied, as the tide is never at rest. The Gulf and the five rivers which run into it have an enormous tide fall. The rush of the incoming tide as it pushes its way up the Forrest River can be heard long before it is seen. This 'tidal murmur' is unlike any other sound on earth. It reverberates like a huge wave breaking continuously on the shore. Twice a day, it has been music to tribal ears ever since the dreaming. Except for a narrow channel, the Forrest River is empty when the tide is out and with care anyone can walk across from one side of the river to the other.

South-east of the Forrest River and on the other side of the Cambridge Gulf is the township of Wyndham. Towering over this remote little township are Mt Albany and Mt Bastion and stretching away into the distance are endless salt and mud flats. Reportedly the hottest town in Australia, Wyndham was until recently a busy port town for shipping beef from Australia to all parts of the world. Navigation in and out of the Cambridge Gulf was both difficult and treacherous. Then, as now, it was dictated entirely by the tides. Wyndham was a point of contact for many people on the move: Afghan camel drivers, Chinese traders, Aborigines, sailors of all nationalities and stockmen who during the early part of this century drove cattle from Queensland and all parts of the Northern Territory and Western Australia to the Wyndham meatworks.

The Wyndham region had been an important trading centre long before it was called Wyndham and long before Captain Cook sailed into Botany Bay. The Macassans from Indonesia came for fish and trepang, a sea slug they regarded as a delicacy. They brought with them tobacco, sugar, tea and cloth to trade with the local Aboriginal tribes. Women were included on these trips and marriages were arranged between the Macassans and the Aborigines.

The Gulf and its rivers divided the region in such a way that the local tribes were small in size and only met together for special tribal celebrations. At these celebrations marriages were arranged, new corroborees were taught and stories were told. Munon-gu, the Forrest River, was often a meeting place for these gatherings.

By the 1930s, the Aboriginal people had been dispossessed of most of their land in Wyndham except for several small 'selections' reserved by the government for their exclusive use. The settlement at Four Mile was one of these. The selections enabled the government to have control over the lives of the Aboriginal people.

The Reverend Ernest Gribble started the Forrest River Mission for the Anglican Church in 1913. In 1926, the Reverend James Noble, an Aboriginal deacon, helped lead trackers who found evidence of the massacres by police of tribal men, women and children in the Forrest River region. Noble found evidence that people were shot and their bodies destroyed by fire. Gribble informed the Aborigines Department. Several sites were examined by Mr Mitchell, an inspector of Aborigines, who confirmed that an unknown number of Aborigines had been shot and their bodies burned. Gribble's demand for a full inquiry stirred local opposition to himself and the mission. He even felt his life was in danger when he went into Wyndham, and Robert Unjamurra insisted on being his bodyguard.

Throughout July, no action was taken to investigate Gribble's allegations and he wrote to the Archbishop of Perth. Police Inspector Douglas examined the site in August and September and agreed with Gribble. Gribble's charges received wide publicity and in 1927 the government ordered a Royal Commission to investigate the alllegations. Unfortunately, the rain and floods of the wet season had removed most of the evidence. Despite this, Commissioner Woods concluded that at least twelve people were shot by the police party.

Arriving in 1942, the Reverend John Best described the Forrest River Mission in the following way:

> *We arrived at the mission landing place at 8.30 am. The landing place is marked with a large concrete cross.... A few native people, mostly the dormitory girls and boys had come down to meet the launch, but never a word was spoken........*
>
> *The mission compound is several minutes walk from the landing place. After walking for a short while through cane grass about eight feet high, we arrived at a cyclone gate covered by a whitewashed archway of logs. This is the entrance to the mission compound, which looked beautifully green and is well shaded by ornamental trees, amongst which bottle-trees with their odd bulbous trunks play a predominant part.*
>
> *The compound is several acres in extent, and includes a quite large number of buildings. The paths are laid out and bordered with stones and ornamental trees. Entering from the south and proceeding down the main central path, the buildings on the right are: The laundryman's house, the boys' dormitory, the boys' clothes room, the boys' eating-house, the tool and saddle room, the Church, the Mission House (mine) and Matron's house, the meat house, and the people's kitchen. Other buildings to the east of the main path are the girls' dormitory (to the rear of Matron's house); the girls' eating-house, the teacher's house and nearby the school.*
>
> *On the left hand side of the main path as you enter you come first of all to the store (just above the Church), then Mr Thompson's house (just opposite the Mission House), the staff kitchen, the staff shower room, the dispensary and the hospital.*

> *Down the western and eastern sides of the compound are the*
> *married people's cottages. These are mostly built of mud brick,*
> *painted red and lined with white. These houses are one-roomed,*
> *with a galvanised iron bungalow type of roof which provides a*
> *verandah all round.*
>
> *At the northern end is the blacksmith's shop... Within the main*
> *compound are the vegetable gardens at present sadly in need of*
> *rain. Nearby are the mule and horse paddocks, the cowyard for*
> *milking, the slaughter yard, the goat pen and the cow paddock At*
> *present as a result of the floods earlier in the year, everything looks*
> *green, but later in the year I believe the countryside becomes very*
> *scorched and barren. (Australian Board of Missions Review, 1*
> *July, 1942, page 100)*

The old, and not-so-old tribal people who did not want to live in the mission compound, lived in what was known as the camp. The camp was situated about half a mile from the mission and consisted of about twenty acres of land owned by the tribe. In fact, the tribe also owned the land the mission was built on. The camp brengens and narlies chose to live on their own land, coming to the mission compound only if they needed medical assistance, and to draw their daily meals which were prepared for them in the communal kitchen. It was the policy of both the government and the mission to discourage the Aboriginal people from eating bush food as it was not considered very nourishing.

In 1933, there were approximately 150 people resident on Forrest River mission and the number in the camp ranged from 20 to 150, depending on how many people were wandering through the rest of their tribal territory.

# List of words from Aboriginal languages

## Oombulgurri language

| | |
|---|---|
| Bungle | urine or to urinate |
| Brengen | Kimberley tribal man |
| Bremlah | eternal springs |
| Bungaree | leprosy |
| Bungarun | leprosarium |
| Darar-bru | die |
| Dudgulla | kind-hearted |
| Gaga | Aboriginal mother |
| Galong-ang-arrah | stalks |
| Gudiyar | white person |
| Gardjahs | lily roots |
| Glays | green stone fruits which grow on trees not a bush and taste like gooseberry |
| Gnarnie | orphan |
| Goolie | blood |
| Goondee | blackberry-like fruit |
| Gudiya | white person |
| Gunyah | traditional Aboriginal shelter |
| Jaja | Aboriginal father |
| Judja | God and white father |
| Jungerries | Boab trees (sometimes called Boa-bab trees) |
| Lalla | white sister and Aboriginal sister |
| Malla | stomach |
| Marna | white mother |
| Mindigmurra | flowing stream |
| Minmint Garlu | policeman |
| Munaburra | beautiful |
| Narlie | Aboriginal tribal woman or woman |
| Ngabaloos | breasts |
| Ngumballa | child - girl child |
| Ngoowahlee | teenage girl or young woman |
| Ngumbahblah | old woman |
| Nulla Nulla | fighting stick |
| Ubla | white brother and black brother |
| Ubergarge | halfcaste |
| Uloogoos | lily seeds |
| Umba | kangaroo |
| Walla walla | crying |
| Walla-marrah-ni-barndie | mad in the head |
| Warie | faeces |
| Warra | walk |
| Wearie | emu |
| Wongalongs | children |
| Woora | foot or walk |
| Woorgoo | pubic hair |

259

| Yallala | baby |
| Yirrbarra | shame |
| Yallyallgee | teenage boy or young man |

## Perth and SouthWestern Districts Western Australia language

| Wadjilla | white person |
| Nyoongar | Aboriginal person |

## NSW language

| Gubba | white person (a derivative of the word government) |
| Koori | Aboriginal person |
| Wadjin | white person |

## Yarrabah Nth Queensland language

| Dadda | title of respect for elderly man |
| Migloo | white person |
| Murri | Aboriginal person |

## Edward River language

| Ngoombah | old lady |
| Yuppun | sister |